Romantic
Potency

Romantic Potency

Cornell University Press · Ithaca and London

THE PARADOX
OF DESIRE

Laura Claridge

First published 1992 by Cornell University Press.

International Standard Book Number 0-8014-2696-0 (cloth)
International Standard Book Number 0-8014-8016-7 (paper)
Library of Congress Catalog Card Number 91-55556

Printed in the United States of America

Librarians: Library of Congress cataloging information appears on the last page of the book.

♾ The paper in this book meets the minimum requirements of the American National Standard for Information Sciences—Permanence of Paper for Printed Library Materials, ANSI Z39.48-1984.

for Jon

> Some of us come on earth *seeing,*
> Some of us come on earth seeing colors.
>
> —LOUISE NEVELSON

Contents

PART III   *Byron: Art of the Perpetual Tease*

Acknowledgments

To borrow from another text about desire, I have often depended upon the kindness of strangers; but more important to this book is my tending at the hands of many friends and colleagues. Donald Ault read sections of the manuscript and responded with an enthusiasm that motivated me to shape it in the directions of his thoughtful suggestions; Stuart Curran, in the mode for which he is famous among American Romanticists, took the time to comment with great specificity on my first draft of the Shelley chapters. His pivotal role in reshaping the conventional male Romantic canon vis-à-vis those hundreds of lost female voices continues to contour the directions of my present studies. Marjorie Levinson, Donald H. Reiman, and the late Michael G. Cooke deserve special thanks for their willingness to respond helpfully to work they were not necessarily sympathetic toward; in each case, conversation proved generative for my own thinking. America's premiere Lacanian, Ellie Ragland-Sullivan, was kind enough to read a portion of the manuscript in order to reassure me of my "right" to speak the Lacan that I do. And the Washington Area Romantics group (WARG), under the direction of Neil Fraistat and Patrick Storey, has proved a warm and cozy home in which to try out new ideas, in the process allowing me to draw upon a wealth of information and intelligence.

I thank especially my colleagues John Hill and Charles Nolan—

ix

with particular appreciation due Bruce Fleming—for always being available (and on short notice) to read and comment helpfully upon passages that often went directly against the grain of their discontent with poststructuralist playfulness. Laurence Mazzeno negotiated as many breaks as he could for a then-new faculty member; Allyson Booth, a recent new colleague herself, has given selflessly of her computer-ease. I also thank the Naval Academy Research Council for several summer grants, the Department of English for its willingness to fund travel whenever and wherever, and Katherine Dickson, Ludmilla Kucher, and Georgia Liakos for library and secretarial support. Debora Rindge spent much time helping me locate artwork for the cover. The two readers at Cornell University Press provided excellent and insightful feedback. And, as many acknowledgments attest, Bernhard Kendler embodies the encouraging and tactful editor we all want to find.

As important as are the above, however, two people stand out as incurring my deepest gratitude: Elizabeth Langland and Joseph Wittreich. Elizabeth has been the best friend possible, somehow finding a way to be both my professional consultant and my personal confidante for many years. Her self-possession and sweet steadfastness continue to inspire me. Joe, through his expansive vision, generous spirit, and rigorous standards of competence, is the scholar-teacher whose example always underwrites my own strivings.

Finally, I indulge in that greatest pleasure of all, thanking those nearest and dearest to me. My children, Ian and Devon, enact between them a gracefulness and a good-willed patience that shames me into trying to emulate my young offspring: not quite the way I thought it would be. I deeply appreciate their uncanny, knowing allowances for people—even mothers and fathers—to chart their own courses. But still, it is to their father, Jon Palmer Claridge, that the most profound debt is owed. His tending speaks to a belief in nurturing others that makes his own artistic vision so generative of new spaces.

Segments of the following chapters have appeared in altered form as cited: Chapter 2, in "Liminal Gender: Wordsworth's Silent Women Reconsidered," in *Romantic Continuities,* ed. Michael Gassenmeier (Essen: Verlag Die Blaue Eule, 1991); and Chapters 5 and 6, in *Out of*

Bounds: Male Writers and Gender(ed) Criticism, ed. Laura Claridge and Elizabeth Langland (Amherst: University of Massachusetts Press, 1990).

LAURA CLARIDGE

Annapolis, Maryland

Romantic
Potency

Introduction

For far from ceding to a logicizing reduction where it is a question of desire, I find in its irreducibility to demand the very source of that which also prevents it from being reduced to need. To put it elliptically: it is precisely because desire is articulated that it is not articulable, I mean in the discourse best suited to it, an ethical, not a psychological discourse.

—JACQUES LACAN

If thought is not measured by the extremity that eludes the concept, it is from the outset in the nature of the musical accompaniment with which the SS liked to drown out the screams of its victim.

—THEODOR ADORNO

If they'd known what I was saying, they'd never have let me say it.

—JACQUES LACAN

This is a study of desire voiced in poetry. It sets forth the premise that the extraordinary power of what has come to be regarded as the Romantic imagination stems in large part from the paradox of poets grounding their desire resolutely and often self-consciously in the vicissitudes of language, the very medium guaranteed to thwart their ends. Romantic potency begets itself through writers exploiting an inherently delicate position: the apparatus that best sustains desire—textuality, or language—frustrates its consummation. But such an obstruction keeps the tale from being told, and in so doing, justifies a

I

poetic voice—as well as the next poem. To the extent that we have long recognized both the thematic and the formal insistence of desire in Romantic poetry, it is an old story. On the other hand, we have shortchanged—or lacked the tools to explore—a certain textual excess that scores this literary body of work in such an internally consistent yet locally emphatic way as to produce a *jouissance* that explains our precritical intuition of the truth of periodizing Romanticism.[1] Obviously, then, I do not claim for such a study as this one the power of demystification; but as one recent astute deconstructor of Romanticism has reminded us, "demystification might not be the only form of enlightenment" (T. Rajan, Introduction, 3).

We gain insight into the dynamics of Romantic poetry and into the validity of asserting a certain homogeneity for a particular Romantic canon by exploring Romantic longing anew as Jacques Lacan's "manque-à-être," or "want-to-be," as Lacan prefers in translation, in part through assenting (if only fictionally, for the purposes of this project) to Lacan's radical highlighting of the a priori instability of the ego itself, a position often either occluded or denied in other psychologically inspired studies of the Romantics. "Want-to-be" (akin to Friedrich von Schlegel's "becoming"), the key to desire: the radical and the humanly unsatisfiable yearning of the infant for the lost Eden of a unified self—before the advent of symbolic organization. The Romantics attempt the impossible: to transcend the medium of words and reach that original paradise of silence—but with their voices intact. The poets desire more than they can speak, but their "impotence," their inability to escape language, ensures the life and infinity—the potency—of their art. And it is here that Lacan can revivify what is, after all, an otherwise rather tired perception. For he insists upon taking the late Freud of "The Splitting of the Ego" very seriously and reorients the trajectory of psychoanalytic thought by emphasizing how the subject is always and everywhere alienated and fissured as a feature of its very "foundation." Impotence, in other words, subtends all subject/object dialectic, creating the very lack that urges movement toward (an always illusory) synthesis.

Language, at least the metaphysical traditions of the Western lan-

---

1. See chap. 1, "On Interpretation," in Fredric Jameson, *The Political Unconscious,* for a provocative reading of desire as a heuristic system, especially as it intersects with other hermeneutical models.

guage in which we have spoken since Plato, insists upon housing itself within the oedipal signifier, a place where desire is always predicated upon that which someone else had first. Hence the peculiar problem for a generation of poets deeply engaged in questions of originality: the genealogy of language hardly encourages serious claims of self-creation. The deepest recesses of the self—in what feels like a most private psychological economy—turn out to be social after all; for, as Shelley confronted most dramatically, the self's construction depends upon a theft, an illegal, or at least unoriginal, borrowing of another's tongue. Absolute freedom from this borrowed self, however, demands a poet's vocation and voice as its price. Samuel Beckett's "Breath" takes the dilemma of original voice about as far as it can go: the mise-en-scène consists of thirty-five seconds that record one breath of birth and one of expiration, with the play set on a dim stage dressed with garbage and nude, impassive actors. Even as Beckett's play foregrounds the abyss that threatens the would-be original poet, it also points to the most "original" element of Romantic poetics. The conventional (male) Romantic canon depends upon the great paradox of language: that we become human, language-producing, and thus mediators of the real—potential possessors of the vatic voice—at the selfsame moment that we become alienated forever from that which seems, at least, most authentically "self." Language confers meaning at the price of imposing silence as the only locus of authenticity. Desire as the subject's divisiveness from its own being, its birth into meaning: this is the recurrent leitmotif of Wordsworth's poetry, a dilemma that establishes itself as the Romantic sensibility reworked in radically different ways—one recuperative, one adversarial—by both Shelley and Byron.[2]

A retrospective of Romantic criticism suggests that the scholarship of the 1970s and early 1980s sought to isolate a major Romantic impulse: the quest of transcendence, the anxiety of self-consciousness, the search for origins, a preoccupation with the fragment, a concern with memory and absence—all tendencies powerfully explored, at least in the past decade, through unsentimental poststructuralist vocabularies. More recently, there has been a reaction to such "textual," seemingly intrinsic emphasis by way of a renewed value assigned the

2. The philosophical traditions of desire that usefully complicate our reading of Wordsworth's poetry are well traced by David Simpson, *Wordsworth and the Figurings*, 87–107.

historical, contextual, and material conditions of the poetry. My own goal is quite different: I mean to supplement the received readings of Wordsworth, Shelley, and Byron, to fill in with Lacanian insights the gaps that other critical traditions, particularly those of psychological provenance, have left unremarked. Lacan is controversial; even Lacanian specialists argue fiercely among themselves as to the "correctness" of any particular psychoanalytic rendering. I take my lead in justifying the use of such a potentially discursive methodology from, oddly enough, an analysis constructed on behalf of the historicist John Barrell, wherein Morris Eaves concisely defines the parameters of any critical commentary: "A discourse can be recognized as such by the collocation of numerous factors that in effect select certain subjects for certain treatments and exclude others. For most purposes, I believe, it is sufficient to describe a discourse as a coherent cluster of metaphors" (429). My subsequent use in this book of the Romantics-and-Lacan is clearly predicated upon such a collocation that will tend to emphasize particular features and produce certain results: any methodology must admit to such limitations. At the same time, the slipperiness that marks the substance as well as the stylistic contortions of Lacan allows readers a certain freedom in letting the literary text speak of its own plurality to us; Lacan's elusiveness argues against the totalizing, fixed textual readings so enervating to critical exegesis.[3]

I recognize in advance the particular dangers of such an enterprise: one runs the risk with Lacan of either dishonoring—via an agonized attempt to clarify through heavy-handed schematization—his opaque, philosophical/psychological figurings of the world, therein losing exactly the errant brilliance of his "free style"; or one writes through Lacan—reinacting, reinventing, his ideological spirit of willful idiosyncratic play at the possible expense of ensuring an audience to whom one speaks. I try to negotiate diplomatically between these two extremes, without sacrificing the virtues of either. By using Lacan with Wordsworth, Shelley, and Byron in order to illuminate through both the ontogenetic and phylogenetic histories the different responses of

3. For interesting (and not uncontroversial) commentary on ways Lacan as a new Freud can be put to use in poststructuralist historical textual enterprise, see, for example, Jameson, "Imaginary and Symbolic in Lacan," and Althusser, "Freud and Lacan." Furthermore, a useful overview of the difference between Lacan and Althusser on sexual subject formation appears in Teresa Brennan, "Impasse in Psychoanalysis and Feminism."

three major Romantic poets to a linguistic and psychological emphasis of their literary times, I have sought to elicit a "coherent cluster of metaphors" that defines in new ways the old Romantic linchpin of desire. At the same time, I hope to avoid what appears to me the most deadening fallout from methodological explication, the monumentalizing of literature that should instead be speaking to us of libidinal motility, of the excess of art that extends beyond any ratiocinative modes and that keeps us coming back, year after year, critical season after season.[4]

I want to pause now in order to offer, as self-consciously as I can, some of the critical precepts that guide my project. I hope most of all to imbricate the Romantic poets with the rhetorical suggestiveness of Lacan, in such a way that who came first does not matter—and that Lacan's negativity, his hollowing out of ego into a treacherously anxious location of identity, helps objectify the subject—to imply, at least, the contingency of the subject upon all it inhabits, its aleatory organization, along with the sense that in this contingency the subject invariably becomes an object for someone and something else. I am quite aware that in a reflexive critical act, I have brought into being the optatives I often articulate as being of the text. I reach back, through Lacan, to activate an individualist—versus social—economy of literary expression, using (as all heuristics are) a tendentious probe—Lacanian language. Such paradigmatic desire was not a self-conscious poetic predication, an authorially intended commodity; but this truth does not invalidate its historical presence as underwriting the libidinal grammar of an epochal, literary canon. As I have made clear above, I take Lacan as an intellectually motivating paradigm through which I can read artists who seem to configure poetically some of Lacan's own academic and therapeutic puzzles: the artifact, or the aesthetic, exploring through its medium problems that felt essential to the poetic begetting of the male Romantic poets. To the charge that pairing those who speak the same language is mutual aggrandizement, I would add that this coupling pressures out of its union some moment of difference

4. See, for a sensitive and self-conscious discussion of the issue of reading against monumentalization, de Man's "Shelley Disfigured," in *Rhetoric*, 93. In addition, I would argue that poetry can work as a mythical, autotelic discourse that yields to the reader a kind of pleasure specifically related to its onanistic tonality, akin, psychologically, to the seductiveness Freud locates in others' narcissism, in that the poem enacts the subjective self-centeredness that most of us cannot allow ourselves.

that gives us, at our own distance, a chance to gain anew from both discourses.

It is apposite here that I set out which of Lacan's features I wish to appropriate—and inevitably that is what I do—as descriptive of the tension through which these British Romantic male poets thought. It will be clear, I hope, from this statement that my project is different in nature from those whose intent has been to mine the fissures in subjectivity constituted in and reflected by Romantic poetry, the fractures between surface and depth: this has been done, and done so thoughtfully and thoroughly vis-à-vis different methodologies that we may have come round to the terminus ad quem of deconstruction: the depth has become surface, or rather, there is no distinction anymore—with the whispered danger that we have merely "discovered" what the poets left oddly ill-hidden anyway.[5] Thus, while clearly indebted to the different critical pressures that have vitalized the field of Romantic studies, I mean in this book to suggest ways that libidinal energies pluralize texts as they underwrite the always-lacking subject/author of the poem, necessitating the need for another poem, another reader, because the artifact can no more stabilize the discourse of subject formation than can language ensure a noncontingent communication. Desire (investigated herein through a Lacanian perspective, invested in the poetry by the authors) complicates the whole from a foundational level in such a way as to justify our own sustained generational inquiry.

In recovering the importance of the paradoxical nature of language both to confer and defer desire, I intervene in order to assert writing as an endlessly reproductive plot of life against death. One could, of course, immediately argue that, both for me as author as well as for those poets I study, there appears a suspiciously consolatory emphasis on the impossibility of psychic satisfaction, therein rendering nugatory any political urgencies toward action elsewhere: if you believe, systemically, in a Lacanian sort of way, that you "can't get no satisfaction," where is the moral imperative to do other than invest in the consolations of structurally inevitable "inauthenticity"? I would respond that it is not necessarily ethically superior to cast poetry as explicitly (or implicitly) calibrated acknowledgments of the political grimness of the

---

5. And, of course, my concern here reflects Jerome McGann's critical inquiries into Romanticism: our engagements with the texts have resulted in a recuperation of exactly what the writers intended to be understood as their theme; they have mastered us, all the while we thought we were discovering them.

"real" context subsidizing that poem. Certainly this is one proper agenda, both for the writing and the reading of poems. But we also know that poems tell more than a single story, and if at this time in our critical histories we have become alert to the historical displacements enacted in the "inward" quest of British Romanticism, we can also afford to reexamine what textual, structural psychologies compel the movement of these engagements.

It may well be that the Romantic poets I discuss gain mental space from their investments in a symbolic structure that guarantees their sense of belatedness. In an epoch whose rapid transformations prompted questions about the efficacy of poetry as a social conduit of visionary change, the poets, exhausted by the promise and the effacements rendered through political, cultural, and economic revolutions, wrote out/of a matrix of unsatisfiable desire that, paradoxically, refigures itself as consolation in a world whose flux might otherwise threaten, implicitly, poetic annihilation. To the extent that my own readings lack circumstantiality, I replicate this consolatory linguistic movement: time and space displaced into form. Such a strategy (both poetic and critical) of unsituated, systemic desire encourages two opposing energies: it allows for the experience of excess, the license of what Alan Liu calls the "Disturbed Array" ("Power of Formalism," 730), while containing, structurally, the potential (lawless) licentiousness that assigns no end, no point to subversion. Thus Romantic desire is a conservative containment but within libidinal economies that insist upon a self/social construct as the only grammar with which to write. If, as Liu posits, "the hidden telos of any analysis of ideological struggle, after all, is that at the end of struggle lies new, free, or true Man (in a relativistic idiom: the salient class or type of man at the time)" (732), Romantic desire complicates this utopian assumption, exemplified most clearly perhaps in the (non)concluding semantics of Shelley's *Prometheus Unbound*: the "new" man at the end of struggle can only repeat both the labor and the liberty; the telos of achievement slips through the compositions of (timeless/placeless) desire. This pattern does not deny cultural history: it simply works at a different task, specifying instead a linguistic, textual psychology; and to that extent it is an avowed formalism.[6]

6. But again, as the recent reconstruction of Joseph Goebbels's 1937 "Entartete Kunst" exhibition reminds us, formalism contains its own anticonservative impulse: even the Suprematist exactness of a Kandinsky or a Mondrian was indicted by National Socialism as

Furthermore, as Terry Eagleton has noted, "there are texts which establish a less 'fraught' relation to ideology, without thereby merely 'reproducing' it" (*Criticism,* 93). While he applies this point to purposes different from my own, it serves nonetheless as a useful reminder that illuminating the textual contradictions that subtend life and art is only one of the many stories that (an inevitably overdetermined) poem can tell. To read (and to participate in the writing of) the incommensurability of desire and language is to remind ourselves of the limitations of human potency. Lacanian structures of thought allow, indeed demand, a consciousness of the lack on the part of the thinker, a sense of a "science" that cannot conclude in a truth, therein (claims to Lacan's phallocratism notwithstanding) encouraging, at least in theory, an unwillingness to perpetuate the illusion of demarcated boundaries, a knowledge of inclusion versus exclusion.[7]

The Romantics (perhaps all poets) privilege what Lacan calls the "imaginary" over the "real." For Lacan, the imaginary represents the realm of that illusory fullness of the primal union with the mother. This order compensates for the "real" world of the human being born fractured because premature, in a state of psychic and physical incompletion—the real world of facts, unmediated by the desire born in some space between the imaginary and the symbolic (linguistic) realms of experience. Lacan posits that the self models its ego upon what it perceives as the ideal unified gestalt of its mirror image, whether that image be literally the self or, typically, the mother. Thus, while in truth the ego is an alienated identity from the outset, predicated on an other, it allows for the illusion of a harmonized subject. Throughout Wordsworth's and Shelley's canons, we can trace the movement of desire back to the poet's "remembered" (but in truth, re-membered) fullness in his primal union with his mother, a drive almost written in to any poet's attempt to create himself. This drive toward an imaginary

---

dangerously escapist. The potential subversion, of course, resides in eluding the ideological moment, a lam that implies an alternative construction (as yet unrecuperated by the state) being scaffolded elsewhere.

7. As Shoshana Felman reminds us about the psychoanalytic structure in general: it is "essentially, constitutively dialogic," though, and most important, "[it] is not a dialogue between two egos, it is not reducible to a dual relationship between *two* terms, but is constituted by a third term that is the meeting point in language . . . a linguistic, signifying meeting place that is the locus of . . . insight" (*Jacques Lacan,* 56). Thus it is that such a discourse is peculiarly well suited to intervening in the Romantic dualistic epistemology.

origin strives to get behind language, to circumvent the father's imprimateur, to reduce to zero the tension always holding meaning in abeyance. The return to an early, unmediated Eden holds out the promise of undoing the fractured "diasparactive" nature of the human being-in-language; but as Lacan insists, this paradisal fullness is always an illusion in its own right. Dehiscence lies at the heart of the human condition; we are born premature, in a state of muscular and neural inadequacy, marked as "separate" from the moment we emerge from the symbiosis of the womb. But because the onset of language defines the world in terms radically "other," the mythic tendency is to recast all prelinguistic stages as "pure" and whole.

Thus, desire seeks its consummation in a backward movement toward the mother. Yet, as the result of language, marked culturally by the phallic Name-of-the-Father, entering and determining the existence of the subject, that subject must spend its life seeking satisfaction "according to a paternal formula, and in time" (Davis, *Fictional Father*, 187). As Robert Con Davis has noted, "the great alternative [to binding desire to the father's Law] is the spectre of the unchecked death wish," which is, he reminds us, "the great theme of romantic poetry" (*Fictional Father*, 188). But what all three of the poets under study here discover (with Byron alone plotting escape through *alliance* with the patrilineal) is an even more somber truth, because now there is no question of alternatives: their poetry instantiates the contemporary psychoanalytic position that "to become a father is to fall under the mark of death" (Brenkman, 424).[8] The father, if against his will, becomes implicated in the succession of generations; even when dead, as Freud speculated wisely, his grave will lay claim to those he has propagated. The poet—the brave poet—faces twin horrors: he is indebted to the father, and he, in turn, will inevitably enslave others to himself. There is no originary word that escapes determination from the paternal system in which it is inscribed: "In the beginning was the Word; the Word was in God's presence, and the Word was God." The son's presence to his father coexists with the incorporation of son into father. Thus, to become situated in language is to align oneself with the force one wishes most to fight against: a predestined speech. "Death.

8. At the very least, it is of psychological interest that in his own life Shelley fell ill upon the birth of each of his children.

Death is the opposite of desire," Blanche Dubois cries out. But her insight is only partial: death is the inevitable outcome of a desire doomed to unfulfillment and born, in part, by the very mark of the death it would escape.

Still, the Romantics are acutely aware of death as the end of their search for primordial union. For the Romantics as for Lacan, death resides in the rupture that both initiates the child into language and creates desire; as Heidegger describes it, death is that moment when one encounters the ultimate limit that defines existence. In articulating an essentially Romantic problem, Lacan emphasizes that the infant's assumption of the inescapable symbolic Law of the father first coincides with the human experience as Being-unto-Death. Consequently, inherent in the Romantic search for origins is an encounter with death at the very moment language asserts itself. In "The Economic Problem in Masochism," Freud asserts that the impulse to destroy (to reduce tensions to zero) is almost always accompanied by libidinal satisfaction, placing the pleasure principle totally in the service of the death instinct, whose aim is to conduct the restlessness of life into the stability of the inorganic state. There is thus, for both Freud and Lacan as well as for the Romantics, an inseparability of desire from death. The first knowledge of death, of limit, occurs the instant "desire becomes human," as Lacan explains: children are born into the symbolic order of language when they accept absence by deferring and retrieving the "thing" through words (Freud's *fort/da*). From this point on the child is a Being-unto-Death who will push language to its limits.

When Ernest Jones discovered the "sexual inequity in symbolism"—that phallic symbols dominate all others—he worriedly turned aside to other concerns (Gallop, *Daughter's Seduction*, 16–17). Lacan, however, exploits this finding and recasts Freud's classic castration scene into linguistic terms. The maternal phallus, versus the male penis, becomes the cornerstone of castration theory. The phallus, as a mark of *jouissance*, is lacking to male and female; it is that which the subject always wants to be for the mother, while at the presymbolic, prepaternal stage the subject also assumes it is that which the mother possesses. But upon the subject's birth into the symbolic order it learns, from the authority of paternal Law, that it can never be the phallus for the mother, and that the mother cannot offer it hers. The mediation of language castrates the subject in exposing the impossibility of its ever possessing the phallus/fullness for its mother. The father owns, in the child's eyes, the prior phallus, a priority that determines the child's intersubjective place in the kinship structures of its society. Thus, the Name-of-the-Father, inscribing the subject into patriarchy, becomes Lacan's linguistic equivalent of Freud's "real" oedipal father.[9] Still, the father who supposedly possesses the phallus knows too the experience of castration from his own early inscription into the system. The phallus becomes the symbol of omnipotent power, a power the subject would like to steal for itself. It is thus the privileged Lacanian signifier, "the attribute of the powerful (the presumedly omnipotent and omniscient) phallic mother, the symbolic father, the King, the Other."[10] What the bold poet must do is to attempt a foreclosure of that phallus—to write at the spot before its mark appears. Since, however, the phallus as signifier assumes position precisely at the onset of the child's assumption of language, it is an impossible task to preempt it in writing—except in paranoid discourse. In his symbol-typing, Lacan pretends to no absolute barring of penis from phallus, writing as he does unabashedly from his own male-inscribed discourse. The erect penis is the most obvious sign of desire and thus a further justification for its "universality" as privileged signifier (Brenkman, 441). In the signifying phallus are conflated elements of desire, and so this symbol becomes the perfect mark of both desire as loss (due to the alienating entrance of the Name-of-the-Father) and the primal object that is lost—the mother. In obedience to the Law, the child renounces the claim to be the phallus for the mother, and thus the juncture of male and female phallus "completes in both sexes the questioning of the sex by the castration complex" (Lacan, *Ecrits,* 198).

"The desire to foreclose the father's name and to establish a name for one's self" developed, with the Romantics, "into a burning, all-consuming obsession," claims Davis (*Fictional Father,* 145). Other critics of Romanticism, including Harold Bloom and Leslie Brisman, have

9. Although Jacques Derrida attacks Lacan's situation of the phallus as constructed upon a notion of indivisibility that finally renders it as a first (transcendental) moment in signification, Barbara Johnson argues—I think, correctly—that Derrida should instead acknowledge a conception congenial to his own: "What Lacan means by saying that the letter cannot be divided is thus not that the phallus must remain intact, but that the phallus, the letter, and the signifier are not substances. The letter cannot be divided because it only functions as a division" (166).

10. I am indebted throughout my description of the phallus as signifier to Jane Gallop, *Daughter's Seduction,* 95–96.

developed this theme, but they have relied primarily on the contest between poets or on a desire to recapture the first word. The darkest element in the obsession of self-creation, however, is the moment of revelation when the poet recognizes that in writing his first word he dispossesses himself of authenticity. He records the trace of a Law that has determined him irrevocably; and while Wordsworth often wrote his strongest poetry from his ambivalence toward the father, Shelley's personality demanded that he instead struggle to break that Law, rather than pretend to a subversion of it, while Byron, in a myth that explains better than anything else our consistent sense that he stands apart, inhabited it until he managed to make it look as if it were his own.

Lacan and the Romantics have much to say to each other, I have suggested, regarding the desire that is salient to both their discourses. If most of us find Lacan's deliberate evasiveness irritating at times, his poetic ambiguity serves a student of literature well. Such refusal on Lacan's part to make total sense works against what I see as the greatest danger of applying any psychologically or philosophically bound heuristic (and what other kind could there be?) to a text—the inevitable "discovery" of depth covered over by surface, of fragmentations that really contribute to organic wholes if we only know where to look. Such explorations have been vastly important; they set the stage for any thinking outside their conclusions, but it is precisely that outside, that location of excess, that outruns any attempted containment of a text to which it would otherwise function synthetically—by which Lacan's refusal to bring it all together at the level of style allows us a way to speak of desire through an undomesticated Freud. One could ask, of course, whether the choice of any psychoanalytic methodology to explicate Romantic poetry is not, in fact, too neat a fit; a preoccupation with subjectivity and language forms the core of both poetics. Still, I would respond with my belief (under heavy attack in various quarters) that there is no historical period in Western culture that would not be illuminated by extending and applying Freud's late and troubled insights in *Beyond the Pleasure Principle*. And in the end, Lacan's redactions of his Viennese teacher formulate linguistically this controversial hypothesis of the odd imbrication of life and death, and, at least as significantly, the split nature of the very ego that twentieth-century intellectual life has tended to naturalize instead into a safe taxonomy upon which to regulate both social and self-control. Because the Romantic poets foregrounded desire as the expression of their life instincts, it is this emphasis that I pursue; if I were writing on the Augustan poets, for instance, with their textual energies deriving so much from the pressure of paternal lineage, I would probably model my inquiry upon the Oedipus complex in a way reminiscent of William Kerrigan's study of Milton, *The Sacred Complex,* though I would think it through too in Lacanian vocabulary.

I maintain, therefore, that Lacan is peculiarly appropriate for the poets I study at the same time that his theoretical insights hold explanatory power for any literary period. In 1979 Paul Fry suggested that the heavy emphasis on language as the ultimate arbiter of identity in Percy Shelley, at least, pointed to the value of applying Lacanian theory to the best literary poetic exemplars of desire. In fact, the obviousness of wedding the infamous contemporary purveyor and explicator of desire with those poets most famous for situating it in the literary text makes the relative paucity of responses to his call suspect: why has so little been done with Lacan and the Romantics?[11] In addition to the almost insulting opacity that one confronts when dealing with the psychoanalyst—and a certain readerly resistance to the specter of such a match, after working one's way through a similar dazzling obscurity in, say, Shelley himself—it may well be that students of Romanticism prefer to entertain cleaner ideological lines of inquiry than a Lacanian one can allow. For instance, deconstructive methodologies stake a certain intellectual integrity upon being indeterminate; it is clear at least that there is meant to be no first premise situated in a self. To Lacan, however—and at just those points where Lacan intersects deconstructive paradigms—a desiring self asserts a presence-in-absence as the desire created out of language. On the other side of this methodologi-

---

11. But there has been some response: see, for example, Paul Privateer's "Romantic Voices," forthcoming from the University of Georgia Press; and of course, Fry himself invokes Lacanian schema for his rich commentary on Shelley in *The Poet's Calling in the English Ode.* Furthermore, Robert Young has read *The Prelude* from a specifically Lacanian perspective. In addition, Alan Liu, in a kind of study whose emphasis upon the real of lived experience might, at first glance, seem resistant to Lacan, instead perceptively alludes to Lacan's "enormous potential for extending psychoanalytic study of Wordsworth beyond the elementary Freud" (*Wordsworth,* 516n). The terms Liu sets out, however, remind us how easily Lacan is allegorized and then merely stretched over the poets; I have tried to intertextualize them instead, though at points I too allow for the illumination that such allegorizing procedure can effect.

cal disagreement is the energy expended over the last five years on assessing what is, precisely, outside the text. Historical contexts are themselves seen as fodder for psychological repressions and displacements.[12]

In many ways the recent cultural materialist interrogations of Romanticism have provided the richest examples of psychological "displacement" discourse. It is all to our good that this new cast to critical thinking on the Romantics has claimed center stage—indeed, one could argue that now a necessary generational upheaval has occurred as a result of these paradigms, thus reopening our thinking on the canon in crucial ways. But, as with any emphasis, the newly entrenched illuminations tend to squeeze out other ways of seeing. It might seem awkward at this stage to plead for the re-vision enabled by a perspective more explicitly indebted to psychoanalytic ontologies: after all, the critical playing out of oedipal dramas and agons, especially with Wordsworth, recalls that very scene whose time had come and gone a decade ago, a type of inquiry that needed to make way so that other kinds of questions could be asked, ones that depended less on an implicitly held autotelic nature of literary texts. But it is exactly at this point that I would stake my claim for re-visioning the Romantic poetic world of longing. It is true that Freud is Lacan's fodder; but the ways in which he complicates his philosophical father allow us a new path back into the issues of power, sexuality, and expression. Such a critical analysis in no way competes against other kinds of study for supremacy; it seeks instead to complicate explanations of the writing subject as it is constituted by and expresses itself in a personal historical time. To some extent, my governing heuristic gestures toward an essential humanness that to a particular audience will disenfranchise me from the start; but we also do well to acknowledge the subtlety of such "human essence" writ in by Freud from the beginning—and foregrounded by Lacan. Subject formation depends upon the society into which the subject is delivered: any absolute claims to the authority of origin are thoroughly contested by the theorists—and the theories—themselves. One has to confront desire in these terms: the psychological tradition claims for it the status of a categorical essence, perhaps a

12. For almost "mainstreamed" examples of the particular riches that such an approach can yield, see Marjorie Levinson, *Wordsworth's Great Period Poems,* and John Barrell, esp. chap. 5, "The Uses of Dorothy: 'The Language of the Sense' in 'Tintern Abbey.'"

cleavage between the Kantian noumenal and phenomenal taxonomy. On the one hand, it would appear open to the charges leveled against any claim to a transcendental status.

What confounds an otherwise just criticism, however, is that which makes desire into a tool of integrity: the variousness of its cultural configurations. That is, from Freud we learn that desire is, from its inception, indiscriminate in both its aims and its objects; this position, of course, means that the "essence" as it is figured through the manifold historical aims and objects defines different realities.[13] Thus epochal definition merely recognizes temporal configuring of literary productions that enact a period's humanizing desire. But I also hold as a particular recompense of this book its theoretical position that although desire is both created by and reflected in the social, at the same time it functions as a retrograde moment, an arrest in the flurry of activity that emphasizes the historical, lived quality of time—as an aloneness in its experience of lack as its "foundation," exhibiting in its double nature the excess always present to any moment of our attempts to create meaning. Desire is, one could do worse than claim, the signature of any ontology.

I pause here to illustrate my project of Romantic desire with a semantic brief that points to just this twinning of definitions through which we configure our world. The word "quiddity" exists on two oppositional levels: definition 1 offers "a trifling point: quibble"; definition 2, "whatever makes something to be of the type that it is: essence" (*Webster's Ninth New Collegiate Dictionary*). Desire, in the ways it underwrites the human subject, would seem to be a quiddity: on the one hand, that which is too inevitable, trivial, too much a part of the irritating and insistent quotidian, to merit attention; but, in what only appears therein to be a contradiction, too profound, too definitional, for us to deny its claims to being of the very essence. I intend that my renderings of Romantic desire unsettle what are otherwise quotidian moments in such a way as to allow us to make of them strange acts. As the power of art that moves us beyond any explanation we can muster, desire—at the same time both *besoin* and excess—speaks in and through material, relational encounters with the world, allowing us to glimpse the peculiar potency of an aesthetics that can

13. See, particularly, *Three Essays on the Theory of Sexuality*.

figure the rifts in the real of existence, which seem, however paradoxically, to constitute what it means to be human.

A very different historical approach involves the use of avowedly feminist critique, where the gendered material conditions of production provide the scholarly field to mine. Certainly there is an exciting, fruitful new direction in British Romantic studies introduced by recent gender inquiry, a trajectory important, clearly, to any project such as my own that scaffolds itself upon gendered desire. Anne Mellor's recent collection of essays, *Romanticism and Feminism,* for example, attests to the compelling feminist critiques currently being conducted on the subject of Romantic appropriation of "femaleness" for the aggrandizement of male literary consciousness. My own exploration of the sexual dynamics constitutive of a male poet's literary desire that would voice a boundary-free language obviously intersects at points with such criticism as dominates Mellor's volume, though in many cases I swerve from the conclusions therein. In addition, I do find worrisome the recent wholesale assumption that the male Romantic poetic imagination depends upon an appropriation of "the female" for the strongest rendition of self-consciousness.[14] Mellor, for example, maintains that

14. Some of those whose work on this issue I most admire (such as Alan Richardson, "Romanticism and the Colonization of the Feminine," and Marlon Ross, esp. Ross's book, *The Contours of Masculine Desire*) stress the male tendency to tap into the "female" as a selfishly empowering act, always a co-option. Although I agree that such gestures abound, I would argue against the starkness of this position in three ways. (1) It cuts in both directions. Examine "female" texts for use of gender and you will note that there is an inevitable play to circumscribe male potency, a ploy enacted by the vagaries of language that would empower its author. (2) Language by its nature as a field for competing desires will always be fodder for power negotiations, and sexuality complicated by gender will be one of them. (3) There exists in the poetry a textuality that invokes gender in a subtler and more complicated manner—finally, in a less offensive manner—than any treatment has yet allowed. Forgotten in recent feminist models that almost assume, a priori, the appropriation of the female by the male canonical figure is the possibility of the male's legitimate belief in the chance for self-enlargement through inhabiting, at moments, a female space or voice. See, for example, Joan deJean's study of the Sapphic tradition in which the more typical hostile male reaction gives way to its opposite: "[There exists a] small number of exceptional cases in which a male writer forges a bond with Sappho so powerful and so personal that it is possible to speak of a case of poetic doubling, of impersonation or ventriloquism rather than mere transvestism. These instances are closer to Cixous's coming to writing (even though the man of letters is not necessarily a novice), an individual empowerment through a blending of a personal fiction of female desire and Sappho's expression of that desire. In these cases—I think most notably of Ovid, Catullus, Racine, and Baudelaire—the male writer's motivations are far more complex than that behind the simple act of appropriation that empowers the young writers who are coming of age. In fact, in the history of representations of Sappho, it is almost always writers of lesser talent who forge the kind of predictable relation to Sappho that is founded on an attempt to contain her voice of female desire" (7).

the male Romantic poets have been "heralded because they endorsed a concept of the self as a power that gains control over and gives significance to . . . a nature troped in their writings as female" (8). While recognizing the need for such suspicion, I'd like to suggest instead a different paradigm with, I believe, equally powerful explanatory value. It is at least possible that our canonized male Romantic poets have been regarded as achieving certain extraordinary unsustainable "highs" in poetry because, though they at times pursued self-definition through the gendered opposition that constituted identity in their worlds, the economies energizing the majority of their poems aimed at recuperating the special potency that accrues to marginalized forces, in this case, woman as that which is not already written. Saying this is not the same as accusing the poets of appropriating such female voices.

Maleness is implicated in my text primarily through familial and sexual tensions, wherein the three poets I'm considering in this study—Wordsworth, Shelley, and Byron—act out their psychological needs in language, inevitably failing to satisfy themselves, of course, and thereby justifying yet another attempt to write the truth. It is this position that sustains my interrogation of desire, silence, and sexuality in the male Romantic poets.[15] Thus I treat the poetry as texts of desire, presupposing that a desiring subject constructed that text, at the same time recognizing that the desire we interpret breeds itself out of the very language in which the poet would speak his (very specifically gendered) need—as well as his interpreter, who inevitably is speaking (of) her own.

15. I want to note here the tendency that at times threatens to undermine feminist inquiry: a particular vulnerability toward "idealiz[ing] the oppressed," to use Jessica Benjamin's phrase. Her clear-sighted articulation, at once a commonplace and a reminder of the need for vigilance, is worth citing at length: "Every binary split creates a temptation to merely reverse its terms, to elevate what has been devalued and denigrate what has been overvalued. To avoid the tendency toward reversal is not easy—especially given the existing division in which the female is culturally defined as that which is not male. In order to challenge the sexual split which permeates our psychic, cultural, and social life, it is necessary to criticize not only the idealization of the masculine side, but also the reactive valorization of femininity" (9). As a feminist myself, I nonetheless worry that the dynamics of identity are more complicated than the current prevalent feminist position on the "typical" male Romantic ego would allow; in one sense, we are all Lévi-Strauss's *bricoleurs,* constructing (out of necessarily stolen goods, Lacan would add) ourselves out of whatever we have at hand. This is not to blink at the potential for real abuse of the vulnerable position in which women have been situated; it is just to say that the whole story of poetic identity in language is more complicated than the necessary Realpolitik of feminism sometimes allows.

It is well, perhaps, to call attention at this point to the speed with which *Romantic Potency* proceeds: I move quickly over a wide range of poetry, in an attempt to construct a grid whose coordinates readers can, at more leisure, invoke to fine-tune poems of their choice. Though at times I find it necessary to engage in formal, close readings of the texts, generally I find exhaustive and detailed explication not to my purposes herein, but a practice instead that weighs down the movement of what I am trying to capture. Thus I proceed rapidly— meaning to map out the textual movement of the search for a grammar that will speak of an author's self-sustaining desire as it founds (and funds) itself in language that *confounds* itself in the dilemma of consummation, the threat of resolution that stays the need for repetition. I depend not on a theme but on a reading of conflict that, rather than constituting the "depth" or "real meaning" of a text, energizes all those themes and historical and ethical engagements (or displacements) that are part of the heritage and material of the Romantic literary tradition.

In selecting Wordsworth, Shelley, and Byron for my poetic texts, I have been concerned to represent fairly, though not exhaustively, the major impulses of the traditionally defined Romantic canon. The particular usefulness of this triumvirate occurs, for me, in the opposition of Byron to a linguistic conception in Wordsworth, and in the positioning of Shelley as a middleman between the two. For as much as Wordsworth laments the potential corruption of language predicated upon random correspondence, Byron locates his freedom in just such linguistic instability. The theme of Romantic desire, of longing for that which is absent, becomes a structuring trope for Blake, Coleridge, and Keats as well. But Blake's enormous myth-making genius threatens to swallow any abbreviated study of his intersection with the French mythographer: he yields better to a full-length study that confronts his particularly effective illusion of a separate signifying system, a study that would be sensitive to where Lacan would enlighten rather than enslave Blake's revolutionary desire. Coleridge and Keats run the opposite risk for this kind of study: they may well be the easiest to focus through my lens, not because their poetry is less complex than that of their peers, but because Coleridge was forthright so early with his despair over locating a paradisal desire, with a kind of poetic foreclosure on desire the result; and Keats's theme was so overtly the contest between the competing desire of the "real" that poetry could yield versus the "imaginary" or dream world. Both poets rather openly exhibit what I call Lacanian desire, and it is my intention that the reader, after reflecting upon my text, respond more fully to this trope as it peaks early in both Coleridge and Keats.[16]

Not surprisingly at this point in our critical histories, then, Wordsworth establishes the vocabulary for a discussion of desire as the motor of Romantic poetry, in many ways a local rather than strictly literary decision on my part, inspired because of the suspiciously congenial home he has found in recent cultural materialist studies. In a complicated way, this is to say that our current normal reading of the "real" Wordsworth depends upon our assumption that he either consciously or unconsciously translated political anxieties into a poetics of transcendence.[17] In attempting to foreground Wordsworth's sexual dynamics that play the claims of the law against those of the would-be self-authenticator, I aim at establishing a middle ground between those older literary psychoanalytic models of drives and defenses and the recent relocation of those economies in historical grids instead. As Martha Nussbaum reminds us: "The categories in which a society articulates [its sexual experiences] shape the way its members see the world, and themselves as desiring subjects" (571). I mean, then, for my readings of Wordsworth's textual desire to open up a theoretical space for future complications of history and sexuality.

My hunch (which has led me to begin a study tangential to but separate from this present one) is that Wordsworth sought, defensively, to write a masculine poetry that would transgress the ornamental neo-classical age that preceded him, an age, as Terry Eagleton and Naomi

16. And, in the aftermath of a combined reading of those two very different works that both nonetheless develop full psychologies of the poet (Levinson, *Keats's Life*, and Waldoff, *Keats*), it is hard for me to imagine a study possible for some years that could justify Keatsian desire as its subject.

17. Conversely, it would appear that Byron and Shelley lay out their politics—their explicitly historical engagement with their worlds—as part of their poetic mandates to write. See, for example, James Chandler, Marjorie Levinson, Alan Liu, and David Simpson on Wordsworth; Michael Foot, Malcolm Kelsall, and Daniel P. Watkins for recent repoliticization of Byron, and Michael Henry Scrivener and P. M. Dawson on Shelley. I note too the interesting question in the implicit psychologizing of several of the most impressive of these books on Wordsworth, the problem of the criterion of judgment. For once one founds a study on displacement, then the implications of surface and depth, of intention vs. repression, must be addressed: who or what grounds such a call on truth?

Schor both remind us in very different ways, that intoned "feminine" values in poetry.[18] The preface to the second edition of *Lyrical Ballads* was, after all, in many respects a call to reinvigorate poetry—to make it masculine vis-à-vis the vernacular (traditionally, the only voice available to women) against the genteel, feminine association that even the strong heroic of the Augustan Age elicited. One can compare Robert Frost's twentieth-century struggle to "harden" the lyric into a rugged, realistic form, a movement that inevitably suggests a deep fear of female engulfment, of being defined too thoroughly by that which one is not: an incredibly strong desire for the female on the part of the resistant male poet.[19] That desire may well express itself stylistically— and, paradoxically, given Wordsworth's self-mandate to be a (gendered) man speaking to other (not necessarily gendered) men, as a continuity with the eighteenth-century emphasis on the "feminine" detail, inasmuch as Coleridge himself complained of a fastidiousness in description as well as the poet's preoccupation with fortuitous circumstances.[20] Wordsworth's sensitivity to linguistic theories translates into a peculiarly bifocal perspective: on the one hand, corruption is paternal, as we might expect, the material of repetition and tradition and necessity versus originality. And Wordsworth reluctantly accedes to this legend, if fighting it all the way. Yet the particular relief one senses in the poet when he comes down on the side of the father also stems from his tension over identifying the female (among several enabling positions that stake out a claim for a phallic woman) first and foremost with the blissful semiotic world of image versus speech; he worries deeply over the contradiction of locating the authentic poetic (precorruption) voice in the very space where articulation is impossible. Poetry as silence is a formula the poet flirts with, provocatively, in those most historically minded texts *The Borderers* and *The White Doe of Rylstone*. In the "Vaudracour and Julia" section in book 9 of *The Prelude*, the price of Vaudracour's becoming a "mother" to his son is his

18. I do not mean to deny Hans Aarsleff's well-taken point that while "Wordsworth rejected the poetic practice and the dominant poetic theory of the last century, [he nonetheless] built his own critical theory on the philosophy of the same century that had given language a central role in our understanding of the ways of knowing, communication, and the potentialities of expression" (373).

19. See Frank Lentricchia's essay in Claridge and Langland, *Out of Bounds*.

20. David Simpson suggests that Wordsworthian insight depends upon "*denaturing*" the object through his figurative modes (*Wordsworth and the Figurings of the Real*, xviii).

reduction to silence at the end: the cost of authenticity is voice. Thus, even as he deplores the "fluctuations" of language, we can imagine Wordsworth's gratitude that flux guaranteed voice at the same time that it bore the mark of the mythical preoedipal space of confused maternal, semiotic babble—a hint of the prototype infusing its futures.

We also see Wordsworth at work fixing the processes of signification in such texts as "Poems on the Naming of Places," where he attempts to phallocratize, to masculinize, the process of making meaning: in the "Poems" he defensively kills women with the word, barely vigorous enough, the poetry implies, to stay the engulfment. Particularly since Shelley rewrites Wordsworth, and Byron depends upon his poetry as an important ideological intertext, Wordsworth's negotiations with the pressure that gender exerts upon language assume great importance for my study of Romantic desire.

For the complications enumerated above, I therefore afford Wordsworth the most space. Because the emphasis of my study is heuristic rather than historical, I have articulated Wordsworth's desire through a self-interested rather than strictly chronological ordering of his poems. In particular, in ways not felt as urgently in my treatment of Shelley and Byron, I have sought to revivify and resituate the received tradition of his reliance upon (mother) nature that any student of Wordsworth must confront. This I have done through gendering the desire, the diasparactive character of Romantic poetry that Thomas McFarland cites in a quite different context. My first chapter develops some dynamics of desire heavily indebted to Lacan and Freud, and I then apply such economies to several brief readings of poems that locate most complexly Wordsworth's struggles with the space he encodes as female in his poetic myths. I seek throughout to maintain an openness to the literary works that allows them to illuminate Lacan (and Freud) as well as the other way around.

Since my interest lies in emphasizing Wordsworth's early drift in the "lawful," less fearsome direction of a mythic male even as he worries that its opposite en-genders authentic voice, I devote the next chapter to elaborating the poet's translation of linguistic and psychological anxieties into two of his extended, major works, poetry that basically frames the rich years 1796–1807—*The Borderers,* 1796, and *The White Doe of Rylstone,* 1807—texts that thus become crucial for any claims my study makes for the overall importance of what I explicate as Wordsworthian desire. If our newly domesticated reading of Wordsworth accuses him of having written a kind of displacement poetry that comes perilously close to appearing to be an act of bad faith, one way to enlarge such critical response is to examine the pressure he exerts on relationships ostensibly governed by gender polarizations. In both *The Borderers* and *The White Doe,* we confront a strategic confusion of binary voice: the textual female functions as both full and empty, inside and outside, a negotiation that, in my reading of British Romantic poetry, I see increasingly as a foundational enterprise.[21] Poems such as "Tintern Abbey" or the "Intimations Ode," which overtly "turn on loss particularized in one way or another" (Weiskel, 139–40), I have passed over in favor of texts less auspiciously open to my approach. In addition, these "poems of absence" that are friendly to my thesis have been usefully deconstructed of late, as in Frances Ferguson's exploration of Wordsworthian language in the Lucy poems and *The Excursion (Wordsworth)*, and, from a different and equally exciting perspective, in Marjorie Levinson's treatment of the most famous period pieces (*Wordsworth's Great Period Poems*). And, after much consideration, I have decided to use *The Prelude* only episodically as an intertext for arguments whose worth I want to develop elsewhere. Although a full-fledged Lacanian exegesis of *The Prelude* would be an eminently worth-while project, it is not, in the end, appropriate for the textual spread I mean to achieve here. Certainly with the help of the very fine Freudian renderings of this poem by Herbert Lindenberger, Richard Onorato, and Thomas Weiskel, among others; the feminist/psychoanalytic reading by Mary Jacobus; and the abbreviated Lacanian explication by Robert Young, the groundwork for such a large-scale project is in place, further facilitated, I hope, by the paths my study pursues.

Finally, in my last chapter in part I, I offer what I take to be a new

---

21. As Michele Le Doeuff points out, a certain systemic rendering of gender produces the operational grounds for Western philosophical discourse: "The man/woman difference is recruited as a way to signify the general opposition of the definite and the indefinite, or of the valid and the excluded, an opposition one of whose figures is the couplet *logos/mythos*, since *mythos* is the old wives' tale, or at best the inspired narration of a Diotima" (7). We might also calibrate Wordsworth's use of gender through a Foucauldian-inspired concept of silence as a playing field in which we could assign a certain kind of carefully strategized female as opening up the field to otherwise occluded possibilities. See, for instance, Foucault's by now widely worked-over definition of power (93).

way of reading *Peter Bell,* one that sees this poem as undergirded by Wordsworth's anxiety toward the social mediation of language and culture that he had feared from his poetic beginnings would prove the only safe situation of voice, even though he recognized the cost to vatic claims such a location would exact.[22] I mean for my study of Wordsworth to build a case for reading *Peter Bell* as far more important to canonical understanding of its author than has so far been avowed.[23] I reconceive the terms of prior criticism of this poem by locating the following complex question as its real motivation: how can one maintain poetic strength while at the same time acceding to the phallic legacy of the father's pen, an inherited common language that alone ensures an audience for the poet? Peter Bell is yet another satanic figure who would be an outlaw; he must, in Wordsworth's perhaps crippling wisdom, be brought back within the law or risk self-annihilation. It is not irrelevant, I think, that the concordance to Wordsworth reflects a roughly equal number of references to father and mother, especially since critics have tended far more to the latter term. My study of Wordsworth depends upon a dialectic between these terms that is present, I maintain, from the outset of his canon, and which is skewed even at the beginning—and herein lies the shift in emphasis I would like to see take place in our critical tradition—in the direction of the paternal Law, the properly inherited word, as enabler of poetic voice.[24] It is, of course, a position exactly at odds with Shelley's, as well as in

22. Bill Jensen's comment on a tradition of art that does not base itself upon the conceptual but instead upon "a flat-footed, groping way of letting the content be born into the paint" (Smith, "Bill Jensen" [35]) oddly replicates to my mind the way that *Peter Bell* reads. Yes, the narrative line is almost childishly clear, on the one hand; yet at the same time, one feels the meaning being formally exacted in spite of itself.

23. Mary Jacobus in fact does read *Peter Bell* as far more important to an understanding of Wordsworth's poetics than generally acknowledged, especially as the poem was begun in 1798 and intended originally for inclusion in *Lyrical Ballads.* To Jacobus, *Peter Bell* is "an attempt to define Wordsworth's personal vision—the way of seeing things which had made collaboration on *The Ancient Mariner* impossible" (*Tradition,* 262).

24. For previous work on the father and mother figures in Wordsworth, see Michael H. Friedman and, of course, Geoffrey Hartman. Specifically psychoanalytic studies incorporating the parent figure are numerous; for example, see Richard Onorato, Barbara Shapiro, and Herbert Lindenberger. Gayatri Spivak has done the kind of textual/sexual analysis I'm interested in; cf. her essay on book 6 of *The Prelude.* Though his book appeared after my chapters on Wordsworth were written, William H. Galperin's recent study of the shape of the poet's career serves as a helpful companion to my efforts to foreground important textual examples in the traditionally held "rich" period that instantiate the entire canonical motivation. See particularly his first chapter, with its survey of the disparate critical traditions, each of which produces a differently historicized subject as Wordsworth the poet.

contradistinction to the alignment with the maternal, the position to which critics interested in this subject have long subscribed.[25]

Wordsworth flirts with the idea of undoing those binary divisions that create meaning, but since he finds himself unable to collapse the dualism of gender, he resorts to a severely categorical mythic determination of his voice. The word or the wordless clasp of nature that precedes it? The male or the female? Yet at the same time, most challenging in and to Wordsworth is his intuition that such easy gender oppositions fail to capture the true complexity of voice—that the (after all, phallic) mother does not blissfully escape her construction through the phallic scaffolds of meaning, even as her lack of a privileged legal stature grants her precedence to "the prison-house" of the "Intimations Ode"; and that the father is hardly voiced by a degenerative phallic genealogy of language alone: in a repeated metaphor for Wordsworth, he was nursed at his mother's breast. Critics have, for some years, evoked parental figures as motivating tropes for Wordsworth, but the desire coded through gender in the text has rarely been deployed as a heuristic.[26] My first chapter, "Woman and the Threat of Consummation," situates Wordsworth's deep mistrust of the female as that hallowed but castrating place of silence that therefore propels him more surely toward his integration with society and away from the claim to an iconoclastic voice.

If silence threatens Wordsworth, it beckons Shelley as the consummation of desire. More than any other Romantic writer—with the possible exception of Blake—Shelley exhibits a "modern" distrust of language as a system that creates the poet rather than a system that is

---

25. I should note here the impossibility of conducting any such investigation without a sense of profound debt, felt by others engaged in totally different types of critical enterprise, to Geoffrey Hartman, whose own suggestions that all was not well in Wordsworth's imaginative encounters with a maternal nature at least play a part in motivating my re-vision through gender and poststructuralist ways of looking at the same field.

26. One of the first studies to engage issues of gender and the Romantics, Michael G. Cooke's insightful chapter "The Feminine as Crux of Value" embraces a thesis I shall subsequently reshape to my own purpose: women receive strong attention in Romantic texts, Cooke believes, because Romantic literature is one "of power, with the emphasis on human value and meaning, rather than a literature of power politics, with the emphasis on formal social relations" (120). Cooke argues persuasively that the Romantic poets push toward "a new economy of gender relations" (159). Paradoxically, in light of the commonplaces of Wordsworth criticism, I would hold that for Shelley, perhaps, the woman signifies a possible mode of power and human value, but that for Wordsworth particularly, a woman functions precisely in the poetry as a sign of the "power politics" of language and life.

created by him.[27] Shelley presents a special case in that he is both the most skeptical of the Romantic poets in terms of what language can reveal of truth and the most (implicitly) insistent that somewhere there is a truth the other side of language. As one critic avers: "The problem is not, in his view, that language is incommensurate with the world of ordinary, sensible experience; the problem is rather that it is commensurate with nothing else, that by the very nature of its structure and the function of its parts it falsifies not the phenomenal world of things and activities, persons and places, temporal and spatial relations, but the transcendent world of the One" (Bruns, 159).

A Lacanian foray into Shelley's canon unveils the despair Shelley experiences at language's *ensuring* the absence of an originary and grounding premise, and his anxiety as he confronts the possibility that there is no cantilever of meaning outside of language. Jerrold E. Hogle and William Keach, two of the most recent and insightful readers of Shelley's language, would ameliorate this despair, denying it a constant presence in the canon. Hogle emphasize Shelley's celebratory recognition of language as always already metaphoric, as that which, if remembered, would undercut the worship of rigidified systems of signs ("Shelley's Poetics," 184). My study tends, on the whole, to be less optimistic in that I underscore the poet's relentless frustration at being unable to escape this same rigidity as his poetry becomes a fixed sign itself. It is this frustration, for instance, that compels *Alastor* and *Adonais*. And where Hogle allows Shelley to escape confronting, through metaphoric displacements, the inevitable occlusion of any original moment (165), I would describe instead the Lacanian imaginary order as the source of Shelley's power-engendering metaphors, the scene of traumatic loss that will be repeated as it is displaced ad infinitum. Still, Hogle's "subliminal activity" resembles, at least, what I locate as peculiar to Shelleyan desire. Hogle maintains that "the ideas, emotions, and faculties that lead to great poetry and all its progeny

27. The careful and impressive case that William Keach has made for Shelley's ambivalence toward and distrust of language has exerted a definitive influence upon subsequent readers of the poet's linguistic attitudes, if the 1989 issue of the *Keats-Shelley Journal* can be taken as a standard. Fully three of the articles invoke a saving optimism in their explications of the poet's worry that language corrupts, and with poetic subjects as disparate as "Mont Blanc," *Prometheus Unbound, Julian and Maddalo,* and *The Cenci.* Since I treat these same poems in my study, this particular issue of the journal works as a provocative (if, to my mind, finally too optimistic) counter to my argument.

emerge from a process of transfer and substitution rather than a first Unity or a grounding Presence" (159). I, however, would extend Shelley's interest in "the before unapprehended relation of things" (*Poetry and Prose*, 278) into an ideal moment located in the collision of metaphor and metonymy, a collapse into a moment of truth available only at the expense of language consuming itself. This is the direction in which Shelley's desire moves, this fast, relentless accretion of meaning as if the poet would dare to outrun, outstrip, meaning itself.

My study of Shelley's poetry also departs from Keach's impressive analysis, as I lack his confidence in Shelley's engendering ambivalence, the position, as he puts it, that the "antithetical impulses in Shelley's disposition towards language pressure and energize each other" (xvi). Keach believes that such critics of Shelley's language as Susan Hawk Brisman and Gerald L. Bruns insist too firmly on Shelley's modern stance toward the constitutive role of language (35), but I find their positions worrisome only to the extent that they underestimate the pain Shelley's insights cost him. That Shelley wants to locate thought anterior to language is, in fact, the desire that I find motivating his poetry. The pleasure he occasionally takes in exposing logocentrism results from the boon to poetry if an originary truth cannot be unveiled: desire can then never be fully articulated, and thus "all high poetry" (*Poetry and Prose*, 291) will be ensured infinite life.[28] Ultimately, although my own reading of Shelley gains in richness when informed by Keach's context, my conclusion is different: I believe Shelley's frustration with language the cause of a brilliant linguistic dance of desire whose effect eventually would have been an early poetic demise to the kind of poetry definitive of the poet up to his death, the Dies Irae sung in his (albeit fortuitously) last major poem.

To some extent, then, I mean my Shelleyan discourse to counterweigh the renewal Brisman sees as enabling Shelley's poetry, a renewal she wishes, in 1977, to see investigated: "Some study that sees how conviction shapes poetic structure, or that otherwise explores the passage from apparent collapse to renewed assertion, may add evidence to our intuition that the metaphor of the fading coal in some way defends Shelley against the fear that there may be no 'original' moment of

28. For a useful if brief discussion of Shelley's location in the prevailing sign theories of the time—Drummond, Berkeley, as well as redactions of the ancients—see Hoagwood, 61–66.

'purity and force' for the poet to recover" (86). The important exploration of a kind of poetic enabling illusion that Brisman called for has been wonderfully supplied by recent critics I have noted; my own reading suggests a darker linguistic valence. My intention is to explore Shelley through Lacanian pathways in an effort to extend, not negate, the rich dialogue recently spoken on Shelley and language. In my selection of texts for this section, I have tried to represent fairly both the span of Shelley's short career and the breadth of his great achievements, so that, for example, I use *Alastor* as an early seminal key to the desire that inspires the poet, while I juxtapose it to the greater aesthetic culmination, *Adonais,* which nonetheless is a late recasting of the same conclusions. "Mont Blanc" and "Hymn to Intellectual Beauty" neatly contain in their brief lyrics the major familial dynamics that constitute Shelley's quest, the positive economy of which results in *Prometheus Unbound,* which I include in this chapter as companion to the twinned earlier poems.[29] *Epipsychidion,* invoked here for its major engagement with the issue of linguistic bondage, crenellates in interesting ways the epistemological dimensions of that conversation poem, *Julian and Maddalo,* which, I feel, deserves a larger thematic context than has typically been afforded it. Except for *Prometheus Unbound,* I have omitted long works such as *The Revolt of Islam* in the belief that my book is better served by a larger survey suggestive of the typically canonized works than such inclusions would allow.

Predictably, the last poem I treat is *The Triumph of Life,* which presents a special challenge. Critics who insist on its nihilism are accused of translating a coincidence—a dark, unfinished poem as the adventitious last gesture of a prematurely dead writer—into an illicit tool for retrospectively shaping the poet's entire career, as well as predicting its future. Yet as my own discussion makes clear, I do believe that this poem centers upon an important fatalism toward language, so that a reading of its confrontational discourse of desire becomes necessary for my project. Let me approach the problem thus: it is not

29. Even here, though, in spite of the scope of such a poetic text, I maintain my methodology of moving rapidly and tendentiously. In addition, I have felt for some time that if any of Shelley's texts actually suffer from overexplication, from too many close readings and too many renderings of the philosophies subtending them, the poems in this chapter do. In any event, it is not my intention to add to this particular, exegetical tradition; for two of the most recent fine, detailed readings of *Prometheus Unbound,* see Sperry, *Shelley's Major Verse,* 65–125, and Hogle, *Shelley's Process,* 167–211.

without relevance here that Shelley's last lyrics sing of Jane and her guitar. As George Steiner reminds us, "only music can achieve that total fusion of form and content, of means and meaning, which all art strives for" (2). We can observe Shelley's poetry seeking to "dissociate itself from the exactions of clear meaning and from the common usages of syntax," not necessarily tending therein to the "ideal of musical form" that marks French symbolist poetry, but certainly striving for an authenticity Steiner locates as the task of the modern "poetic" novel such as *The Death of Virgil* (28–29). Steiner believes that here "language gathers to a dim, sensuous rush as remembrance, present awareness, and prophetic intimation joint in a single great chord" (29), a goal that would be at home in Shelley's *Defence*. As the novel pushes harder and harder against language, it finally yields the specter, in its last sentence, of the poet Virgil crossing "into death," as he realizes that "that which is wholly outside language is outside life" (29). It is Shelley as this retranslated Virgil that pervades *The Triumph of Life*, and that, I believe, stalks his entire canon.

The silence that underlies Shelley's passion is one side of the dilemma of language as prison house: the obverse is unending noise, cacophony as celebration, as flouting of language, the inescapable medium. Byron glories in repetition as the alternative to despair.[30] While this "answer" clearly informs *Don Juan*, it is more surprising to locate a philosophical consistency running throughout his canon, as he explores from the first cantos of *Childe Harold's Pilgrimage* the contest between authenticity and language. "One of the great and persisting problems of Romantic criticism [is] where to fit the Byron of *Don Juan*" proclaimed George Ridenour some years ago ("*Don Juan* and the Romantics," 563). *Don Juan* continues to be heralded as the poem to which Byron's previous work finally (appropriately) gives way, as

30. Peter J. Manning's study (*Byron and His Fictions*) of the parental configurations that in turn motivate the stories Byron would tell, serves as a touchstone of any psychological criticism of this poet, especially since Manning handles what could devolve into an old-fashioned Freudian allegory with delicacy and literary appreciation for his subject. My own study, however, will appear quite different in nature to his, even though at times I will be speaking of similar representational strategies on Byron's part, especially, for instance, the poet's realization of theme at the level of form in the governing rhetoric of repetition in *Don Juan*. I rely upon a heavy investment in the textuality that is sexualized, a matter of a poststructuralist emphasis clearly undergirded by Lacan himself, one which leads me to different kinds of insights from those available to Manning's own important inquiry.

the culmination of the writer's struggles to define his "real" poetic talent. If, however, we explore Byron's career through the encodings of desire, we arrive at a stronger appreciation of an emotional texture translated into a linguistic sinew that unifies his corpus, a textual enunciation of philosophic sensibility informing poems only seemingly at odds with his acknowledged masterpiece. It is probably false to impute an unfolding teleology to a canon, as if a theme progresses, necessarily, from inception to its fulfillment. Rather, poetic desire weaves its way throughout a poet's career, somewhat sequentially to the extent that a poet works out—repeats and works through—the demons that in part motivate the production of art. But there are regressions and displacements, until a clear-cut chronological argument oversimplifies the truth. Thus it serves my purpose well that Byron's first and last great works, *Childe Harold's Pilgrimage* and *Don Juan,* were long-term poetic investments that in one's end (1817) and the other's beginning (1818) almost overlap.

It is the full-fledged if ill-focused desire haunting *Childe Harold* that demands its inclusion in this study. I mean it to serve with *Don Juan* as a book end to imply the similar key to Byronic textuality that these two large works yield. *Childe Harold* and *Don Juan,* marked by their historical production and by critics' interpretations as disparate company, could profitably be studied as companion pieces, though I have elected to use them as a frame, wherein the end points back to the beginning. The drive to locate proper authority—the Popean stake in it—clashes in *Childe Harold* with Byron's always growing belief that such authority must lie elsewhere, the elsewhere of a limitless desire enabled by the symbolic, both in its attention to language and to the patrilineal debt it incurs. At the same time, Byron's other impulse toward locating that authority within—and defining the circumscribing Law of the Other for himself as he locates it in one he loves as himself—threatens him with self-annihilation. In Louis Crompton's comprehensive study of Byron's sexuality, we observe this impulse working in Byron's personal life as his love relationships with men and with Augusta Leigh, his half-sister, provide the intense experience that comes closest to slaking his enormous desire. As Crompton's study suggests, however, Byron was aware of the intolerable price society would exact for its exclusion if the poet dared locate his desire outside the law, through same-sex or incest relations. Indeed, this very knowledge may have steered Byron away from a Shelleyan discourse, as dependent as it was upon the consummation of desire.

The "problem" of Byron, of course, extends beyond the internal unity of his body of work. For Byron's canon is still too often distinguished from the more serious intent of his fellow writers, when instead it clearly contains an economy of desire akin to that of his Romantic compeers, though working through the Romantic conundrum of subject-object delineation to strikingly different conclusions. My study of Byron emphasizes two points: that yearning as it becomes desire in language is still the salient feature of Byron's poetry— including *Don Juan*; and that Byron's earlier poems, which appear superficially most opposed to the themes of *Don Juan,* instead play out the same anxieties, leading as they do to their psychological and poetically enabling resolution in the epic masterpiece. *Manfred* and *Cain,* for example, when read in tandem, reveal the degree to which Byron wrestles with defining the Other through a self-reflection in love, either through incest or through a severance of bonds with those others who would insist upon community as grounds for the poetic voice. *Manfred* renounces the epipsychidion union as that which destroys as it would grant authenticity, while *Cain* points somberly to what will become the joyous resolution in *Don Juan*.

One can, in linguistic generation, locate authority as one speaks oneself into being. It is no mere coincidence that this concern is cast out of the context of the Fall from paradise. We recognize Lacan's Imaginary Eden, where identity was based on an illusion of wholeness dependent upon the absence of language for its success. As George Ridenour has demonstrated, a running intertext of Eden infuses Byron's canon (*Style*). Robert Gleckner builds upon Ridenour's observations when he posits this motif as the structure for *Don Juan*: "a poem of endless cycles, . . . endless repetitions of the Fall, which form the skeletal framework for the myriad variations Byron plays upon the nature of the fallen" (330). And more than a decade ago, Peter Manning pointed to Byron's situating of the "origin of language in the Edenic harmony of mother and child" in *Don Juan* 2.163–64 ("*Don Juan,*" 218). Where Manning asserts the sexualization of words in this scene, we can append a Lacanian paradigm of Eden and language: the sexuality at the heart of Eden, of the mother, of language, all in the end come to stand for death to Byron, to a self either made by others (language), or annihilated by the intensity of the self present to itself in the mother. Thus simultaneously Eden must be left behind, and a means must be discovered of appropriating language while expropriating the female vestiges always clinging to the father's word. Byron's attitude toward language as bisexually inflected—as attaching to the female as well as the male—may have allowed him to discover in it the *jouissance,* Barthes's slippery pleasure of the text, in place of the oppression that both Wordsworth and Shelley confronted. And while the implications of Byron's own well-documented bisexuality for his poetry lie outside the scope of this study, it seems inevitable that the particular textual liberation he achieves relates in some way to his personal sexual/textual-ity.

I have also felt it important to include one of Byron's historical plays in order to mine his dramatic presentation, in an Augustan direction, of a nonetheless Romantic conundrum: can there be a legitimate Law? While the other poetry of all three writers in this study covertly engages this question, Byron's open admiration of a neoclassical order and form permits him its most overt expression. Too, it is necessary that we perceive Byron's honesty in wrestling with the problem of language and authentic voice, for in this context, his celebration in *Don Juan* acquires more weight. If, as Jerome McGann claims, *Don Juan* "is both a critique and an apotheosis of High Romanticism" (*"Don Juan" in Context,* ix), we feel it is an earned duality if we read such vexed alternatives as *Marino Faliero* first. *Don Juan* better assumes proportion in Byron's canon as we recognize its use of the law against itself: of a self-created language wrought from an explosion of the old into a new archaeology—the order that the social being writes after discovering the tricks that paternal language would play on it. Edward Said speaks of the affiliative function of institutions as a "compensatory order" (19) for the failure of the filiative. That is, a new order of generation, deliberately built upon the tools of one's community—the new order Freud forged by bricolage out of late-Victorian society—can preempt and substitute for the old paternal generation wherein hierarchy is bequeathed to the younger sons and daughters. *Don Juan* works in just this way: it posits that if filiation, as biological repetition, is an "unreasonable alternative" at best, or an "unattainable one" at most (Said, 17), continuity may then be served by affiliation, by institutional and social repetitions, by the repetitions, Byron might say, of language as it outlives the original Law, a new language that eludes burial by its sons. The project of *Childe Harold,* to insert the poet into the social order as a proper biological father, comes full circle in *Don Juan,* as language takes the place of the filiative, having thwarted those dangers the father generates, threats that Wordsworth and Shelley confront and Freud confirms. Thus Byron makes of the problem of language an ennobling myth out of which he can name himself his own father.

By now it is clear that this book assigns to an updated post-Freudian marriage of language and psychology a particular explanatory value: a psychology of desire whose local manifestations in male British Romantic poets engendered structural and thematic tools for writing (out) of both consummation and deferral—a poetics of having it both ways. We know that we can never totally divorce our own ideology from the system generating us, and so did the Romantics. Yet individually each poet seemed to understand how necessary the illusion was that his was a mandate to write outside of ideology. To write a poetry of desire, one must pretend, at some level, to the possibility of escaping what others see as immutable limitations. One caveat: my construction of three different myths by which desire underwrites Romantic poetry is meant to be descriptive, not evaluative. Byron's "answer" may be more congruent with our contemporary efforts to assault an inevitable logocentrism and to use or abuse the word from within its system, thus allowing us the illusion that we, at least, can face the truth. The congenial feel of Byron's myth comes from its closeness to the constructions of our own time rather than from any certified advance in epistemological method. I believe strongly that nothing inherent in the individual Romantic myths elevates one above another, aesthetically or philosophically; each merely creates the necessary context out of which the poet can most fully articulate the paradox underwriting his voice—sustaining his potency as a purveyor of desire.

PART I

Wordsworth: Flirtations

Our steps are so easy and familiar to us that they never have the
honor to be considered in themselves, and as strange acts.
—PAUL VALÉRY, *Dance and the Soul*

Chapter 1

Woman and the Threat of Consummation

If to be male—in filiation with the father who names—is to write, then the line of cohabitation with Mother Nature, who preempts the need for the pen, must invoke fear in the poet. More than in any other Romantic poet, the typical familial paradigm of power relationships as defined through gender is problematic for William Wordsworth; and, by imposing literary form upon his inquiry into the gendered dimensions of being-in-the-world, he engenders a poetry of peculiarly communal power.[1] From the beginning of his career, Wordsworth writes a poetry grounded as deeply in the lawful space culturally occupied by the paternal as in the mythic, maternal preoedipal sublime, where most of his critics have placed him.[2] Freud's insistence that repression is never successful is borne out in the return of the suppressed male whom Wordsworth covertly holds to engender true voice; nonetheless, readers have been powerfully persuaded that Wordsworth founds his

1. What Gayatri Spivak suggests for Wordsworth, for example, is actually far more consistent a strain in Shelley's poetry: the father equals history and hence subverts the poet's claim to origin; the mother fails to carry on the name, and hence vis-à-vis nature as mother, Wordsworth can project himself as "son *and* lover, father *and* mother of poems, male *and* female at once" (47). In its concise elegance, Spivak's insight implies at least the collapse of gender that yields the peculiar sense of "universal" versus sexualized poetic discourse in Wordsworth; yet we must recognize at the same time that, ultimately, the poet sustains the projection only as bravado that quickly fails.

2. F. W. Bateson's reminder that Wordsworth cites his father only twice in his poetry points to a repression that energized and troubled the poet's canon, even as he spent his overt desire on poetic possession of the mother (50–55).

poetry upon the claims of the maternal first and foremost. Always complicating any identity with a "female principle," however, is Wordsworth's anxiety over his position in a patrilineal model of linguistic authority.[3]

I pause here to offer a synopsis of recent critical engagements with the category of the sublime, in hopes that a new synthesis of such insights will allow us a point of entry for Wordsworth's imbrications of gender, desire, and language. Regarding maternal and paternal alignments in language, Margaret Homans complicates in provocative ways Thomas Weiskel's speculations as she reminds us that the onset of language marks for Wordsworth the mother's death.[4] She extends Weiskel's assertion that Wordsworth's staged encounters with the sublime function to stave off the killing nature of language (since in moments of visionary power the image, not the signifier, seems operant) into a position that Wordsworth's "resistance to reading" is "based on a wish to recover, or not to reenact the death of, the mother" (45). Thus, on the one hand, one could gender the sublime as female, the place where language is absent. Naomi Schor, however, posits the sublime as a "masculine aesthetic," which is "designed to check the rise of a detailism which threatens to hasten the slide of art into femininity" (22).[5]

3. As Dorothy's comments illuminate the very real professional anxiety William felt over Mary Robinson's volume of *Lyrical Ballads* competing with his own, the question of female authorship provided further complication for this male writer struggling to situate himself in and against the antinomy of nature vs. culture. Even the supposedly generic terms of disapprobation for the contemporary writing scene—the condemnation in the preface to *Lyrical Ballads* of "gaudy, inane phraseology," for instance (suggested to me by Stuart Curran in private conversation)—looks suspiciously aimed at the Della Cruscan school heavily in vogue during the 1790s (though critiqued in parodies by William Gifford, which hastened the demise of the literary influence) and largely represented by women well known to London literary circles: Hannah Cowley, Mary Robinson herself, Hester Thrale Piozzi. Thus Wordsworth fought the engendering of his writerly myths of self-creation on a female-encoded space of both nature and culture, where he had to confront the possibility of a phallic woman who indeed had it all.

4. Though, for what still seems to me the most acute analysis of the more generalized pressure of death-in-language, see Ferguson, *Wordsworth*.

5. Marjorie Levinson's reminder of the oddity of Wordsworth's style—the impression it gives of an "extreme artlessness, an apparent absence of style"—aids our gendering of his poetics as well, especially as it converges with this particular implication of gender in the sublime (*Wordsworth's Great Period Poems*, 4). In a study that, in spite of its very different methodology from my own and, perhaps, its necessary impatience with my kind of return to a personal psychology, nonetheless shares an emphasis upon articulating a silence too often left uninterrogated by Wordsworthian critics, Levinson urges today's readers to find a use for Romantic transcendence through "refus[ing] the transcendence until such time as we can trace its source and explain its character" (57). Such a pursuit motivates the following analysis, both as it invokes other critics' lines of reasoning and as it sets out my own understanding of the desire underwriting a specific poetic project, a desire that is, in various displaced forms, repeated throughout Wordsworth's canon.

I would like to suggest that the very mobility of Wordsworth's mythology of the sublime marks the representational strategy Wordsworth tried to work out, one that would allow him full rein of visionary imagination without its occlusion. He tried—but failed—to bifurcate the sublime into an extraordinarily potent conduit of desire, a place liminal always to the other location so that in its presence one could, so to speak, have it both ways. Wordsworth allows the sublime to be female in its silence, yet not as a deferral of linguistic fatality, but, paradoxically, as the presence of all signification overwhelmed by feminine power—language, a male *eidos,* translated into silence through an apparently ontological maternal bonding. The sublime is the collapse of gender—of male and female moments in linguistic engenderment—but with a dialectical sequence of female (prelinguistic speechless unity), male (linguistic indebtedness), and female again (the priority of silence over voice). I emphatically do not hold that Wordsworth believed there was a language capable of capturing, under any conditions, a "time before signification's depredations" (Homans, 64), but that he was instead self-conscious of the need to construct a myth that could pretend to such a status. The suggestion of the tripartite movement that I present above allows us a glimpse, at least, of a model Wordsworth uses to found his desire as a poet.

Wordsworth waffles over the location of voice, and, in terms that extend previous critical nostrums about his reliance upon nature as female, we can add that he flinches at nature's strength precisely because he has encoded there the myth of a phallic mother who threatens to consume him even as she also offers the preoedipal silence of the sublime as well as the speech of the Law.[6] Wordsworth's verse as a

6. Margaret Homans persuasively associates the "acquisition of representational language" with a sense of loss on Wordsworth's part (42), but her assertion that the sadness stems from the boy's renunciation of the mother must be qualified with a less categorical suspicion on the poet's part: Wordsworth's woman has it all, far too much; it is she who must be domesticated. Jessica Benjamin, extending the French analyst Janine Chasseguet-Smirgel's theory of the child's need to "beat back the maternal power," provocatively argues that this very role of the all-too-potent mother determines a child's later alignment with paternal powers, in that the phallus becomes powerful precisely because of its "ability to stand for separation from the [extremely powerful] mother" (94–95).

Discussing the role of motherhood in Mary Wollstonecraft's writings, Laurie Langbauer alludes to a linguistic and philosophical reality that resists reducing gender roles to categorical functions: the mother as the ostensibly fixed category of the "maternal chora" is constantly undercut by her construction in and of language; she is "half-man, partially constituted as a subject, within mastery and language"; the maternal system is already realized within a system of representation and cannot stand alone in a pure opposition to the paternal (215). Wordsworth's poetry records his repeated discoveries that gender resists the poetically

whole ultimately claims the social phallic voice of the paternal line—a movement undergirding his poetry from its inception—although his visionary moments most often seek to appropriate the space he assigns to female potency.

For a poet who wants above all else to be original yet anointed at the same time, the poetic negotiations between parental claims upon desire are of an urgent order. Desire at its most potentially explosive appears to be encoded female to Wordsworth, perhaps in part because of the overwhelming power that must accrue to the energies he puts into repression of his own too-early-absent mother, a theme well-treated in earlier criticism.[7] But, more generically and generally, as a poet of Romantic desire, Wordsworth logically elevates the idea of woman as the location of the purest poetic reproduction, for in modern Western culture desire lends itself to pursuit of the female as a subject prior to linguistic indebtedness. In objectifying the "original" silent subject, therefore, one becomes a true poet of the primitive that Wordsworth's preface to the second edition of *Lyrical Ballads* and, by implication, his *Essays upon Epitaphs* extol, and that Shelley's *Defence of Poetry* alludes to as well. Lacan states that desire becomes human when language subjects needs to the signifier and unveils the excesses of demand that cannot be captured in the phallic linguistic mode. Desire slides incessantly as the play of signifiers, moving as if in hopes that it can finally locate the moment of phenomenal fullness (however illusory this eidetic memory really is) present in the maternal dyad. Still another complication is the paradox that language also teaches the subject what to desire. The trick or antinomy: language brings into play a desire that seems predicated precisely on its exteriority to language—its lack that language creates and can never fill—while at the same time desire seems defined, in its objects, by that same alienating language. And because, as Lacan says, "the Other . . . [is] the locus of the deployment of speech," and desire is the effect of the subject's need "[passing] through the defiles of the signifier," the subject's "desire is the desire of the Other" (*Ecrits,* 264). Since the Other in its cultural norms valorized fullness, however, the desiring subject is

---

enabling polarization he would impose upon it, a codification that would allow him to draw in a neat economics from two discrete genders, if not sexes.

7. See, for example, Lindenberger, Onorato, Schapiro.

taught to value that which is complete, so that the ascendancy of the very medium that divides the self—the symbolic order—leads to a retroactive valuing of the mirror gestalt.[8]

For the Romantic poet, engaged in the exploration of origins and language, this assumption of the Other's desire translates into an ostensible overvaluation of the feminine organic wholeness so touted as part of the Romantic project. At the same time, the preoccupation with the fragment points instead to the layers the poets have stripped away from the cultural myth of wholeness.[9] The model of organic fullness in the Romantic period is to a large extent a defensive reaction to a darker knowledge that such plenitude was available only without language, before its onset—the very condition that would obliterate the poetic medium. In fact, the diasparactive nature of so much of the poetry—even Wordsworth's continual revision of *The Prelude*—suggests the possibility that fragmentariness subverts the binding claim of the Other; that a poetry-of-becoming thwarts the Law that would impress its desire for linguistic authority upon its unwilling, indebted subject.

The Hegelian dialectic of desire, as interpreted by Lacan through his own dependence upon Alexandre Kojeve, serves the critical explication of Wordsworth particularly well. Desire moves toward transforming its object, a paradigm of destruction that Wordsworth applies, for example, to "Nutting." He comes to learn, however, that if this desired "non-I" is thinglike (or "natural"), then the "I," through its negation of it, experiences itself as thinglike (or "natural") and achieves not self-consciousness but at best the mere sentiment of self that characterizes an animal. Hence, for the "I" to experience itself as self-consciousness, the non-I toward which its desire is directed must be another self-consciousness, another desire (Richardson and Muller, 20).[10] Thus Wordsworth imbues nature with a female presence in order to wed his search for poetic motivation to his sentimental attraction to an Edenic past prior to language. And now, as he seeks to consummate his desire through the desire of an other, he creates the potential for endless movement, for the refusal of resolution that will allow his poetry

8. This explanation comes from Kaja Silverman, *The Subject of Semiotics*, 176–78.

9. See, on this topic, Anne Janowitz, *England's Ruins*; Marjorie Levinson, *Romantic Fragment Poem*; and Thomas McFarland, *Romanticism*.

10. I am well aware that not all Lacanians agree with Richardson and Muller's explications of Lacan, but I have felt free to appropriate their insights that are congenial to my own reading of Lacan.

eternal voice. It is difficult to take deliberately as one's vocation the activity of writing, which recognizes in every trace it leaves the paucity of its offering versus the unwritable—even unrecognizable—truth anterior to it. Defensively, therefore, Wordsworth uses mother nature both as an emblem for and displacement of his need to write from an original voice. Embedded in this solution, however, is also a potential destruction through the desire of the female other, or at least absorption by her, a necessary risk as the poet seeks recognition by this outside self.

Not only is Wordsworth's ambivalence over the location of power one of the most complicated dynamics of his poetry: it enables its richest, most rewarding tensions—tensions that readers have been tempted to explicate (and sometimes expiate) in almost any terms other than sexuality and gender, unless such discussion is conducted in the familiar cast of oedipal crisis and parental deaths. Wordsworth usually tries to cast his gendered myths of desire in categories, preferring to construct binary locations even though such distinctions rarely hold and in fact often collapse into an explosive self-consciousness that proves propaedeutic to the insight of the poem. Such a taxonomic breakdown could with equal ease be termed androgynous, genderless, or urgently gendered in a clearly defensive, definitional moment that, paradoxically, in its very extremity gives the lie to polarized gender identification. We return to the question implied at the beginning of this chapter: does power reside in a mythical, maternal, preoedipal world of nature, which the poet constructs for himself in the hope of finding female sexuality or "essence" silent, or in his fantasized paternal fallen world of the poet-in-language?[11] Wordsworth believes that to succeed in his quest for origin, he will end up in the imaginary realm of the mother and thus find the authenticity for true poetry that he seeks. But—and deeply problematic—the castration of (illusory) fullness that the father's name imposes functions as a protection of poetic voice. What at first sounds like the vitiation of the self through language becomes instead the salvation of the writing self: "The symbol manifests itself first of all as the murder of the thing, and this death constitutes in the subject the eternalization of his desire" (Lacan, *Ecrits*,

---

11. As Langbauer reminds us, "Representation and essentialism go hand in hand: to depict something is to place it within sexual difference" (217).

104). And this paternal linguistic protection is our purchase upon a new perspective on an old Wordsworth: his writing is determined by familial paradigms, yes, but from the beginning it is undergirded at a foundational level by an insistence upon a subjectivity calibrated by an alternately anodyne and astringent masculinity.

Wordsworth enacts Lacan's hierarchy of power: the woman has no penis to "mortgage" as she enters the phallic potency of language, and thus, to Lacan, she implicitly both retains the imaginary fullness of the prephallic stage and remains excluded from the privileges and powers of the cultural Law. At the same time that Wordsworth's fear of a phallic woman invades his poems, we also sense a subtle denial of women's social power in such complex texts as the Lucy poems, for example, where Lucy is assigned repeatedly to a mute, presocial order. No one but the speaker knows Lucy—no one but Mother Earth. It is Lucy's threat to burst into meaning—to laugh, as the woman of "To Joanna" does, in a betrayal of her proper place—rather than remain content to be assigned to "Being," that activates the keen sense of anxiety in these poems. If woman, here functioning as emblem of primal fullness, refuses her position, such authenticity as the poet bespeaks in his great Ode loses its existential grounding. And woman keeps threatening to speak in Wordsworth. The patriarchal use/abuse of language for male ends so often present in Lacan's own confusion of phallus with penis (a confusion the psychoanalyst denied) dovetails neatly with Wordsworth's location of woman as on the other side of discourse, the most oppressive gesture of Wordsworthian gender notations.[12] It is in fact this movement that best justifies the uneasiness some otherwise sympathetic feminist critics feel at junctures in Wordsworth's canon.

Nonetheless, it remains important to note the very real difference between Wordsworth's belief system and the mythic constructs he felt necessary to develop his voice; the biographical evidence does not

12. See Silverman, *Subject of Semiotics*, 189, for a cogent discussion of Lacan's blindness on the exclusion of the female subject to which his phallus/penis distinction leads. In addition, I should note here that I myself employ a vocabulary of gender and sexuality in the mythical ways in which the poets themselves conceive them, so that while I use, apparently unselfconsciously, such phrases as "the woman," or "nature as female," I am doing so in a bid to replicate the kinds of psychological gestures constitutive of the poet's mythologies. That there will at times appear an inconsistency of usage is perfectly congruent with the slipperiness of the subject, especially in the complications of desire that so worried the would-be fixed poetical/textual functioning of gendered categories of meaning.

suggest that Wordsworth feared the castrating powers of "real life"
women in any particularly dramatic way, yet he seized upon the poetically functional nature of such a psychological drama. He allowed such
a myth to structure his desire in language and his search for poetic
power.[13] For textual affirmation of the poet's fear of the potential
castrating powers of "the woman" (woman encoded as a mythic space
irretrievably outside the self), we do well to open to our Lacanian gaze
the texts of Wordsworth's "Poems on the Naming of Places," written,
for the most part, within the two years before his 1802 marriage to
Mary Hutchinson.[14] The poet's anxiety over getting married is not
unrelated to the act of naming. It is Mary who will henceforth name
herself by appropriating the poet's proper sign. As Walter Ong remarks: "The most widespread name acquisition in Western culture
thought of as the 'taking' of a name is the bride's 'taking' of her
husband's name. There is plenty of literature, much of it highly defensive, edgy humor, making clear that the 'taking' of her husband's name
can come across as an act of possession, a taking possession of him: she
has 'got' her man" (74).

In this short collection of poems, Wordsworth obtains revenge
against any would-be female arrogation of him, whether the actual
medium be woman or nature. These poems all convey a peculiarly
unsettling tone, set in motion by the odd, almost arrogant act of
appropriation announced in the preface to the set: Wordsworth and his
kind will name the unnamed and thus give them life.[15] In contrast to

13. As always, to assume parallels between artistic postures and the ideologies sustaining
one's daily choices is to beg many questions about the imbrication of art and life, interesting,
even compelling questions at that, but surely not answered yet to everyone's satisfaction.

14. Theodor Adorno ("Lyric Poetry") argues that a truly new critical reading of a poem,
executed with an acutely sensitive attention to the words on the page and the stylistic
elements that configure them, leads outward into a full appreciation of a poem's social
history. While the type of conclusion I pursue through my formalist readings here differs
from the historical largesse that Adorno suggests, I think his point applicable as well to the
idea of illuminating the gendered, personal history of that poetic voice which is "original
owner," however guiltily we cover up such knowledge of that originary presence.

15. I am grateful to Frank Jordan for suggesting the relevance of these poems to a
Lacanian schema, though I am not at all sure he would agree with my conclusions. Geoffrey
Hartman, while acknowledging the commemorative, elegiac aspects of inscription, nonethe-
less takes a stance opposite to mine, when he claims that in "the 'Poems on the Naming of
Places' . . . naming is a joyfully spontaneous act that almost escapes elegiac implications"
(*Beyond Formalism*, 222n.). It seems to me that Hartman is accepting too readily an explicit
text that yields itself more fully if we read through its author's defensive denials. David
Simpson is one of the few critics to have commented on this set of poems in more than a
cursory fashion. His discussion teases out the historical and economic situation of the individual pieces; see his *Wordsworth and the Figurings of the Real*, 31–34, 37–38, 41.

his announced project, however, the poet names the places to subordinate them to his own powers in an almost sinister subtext of desire inscribed in this sequence of seven poems. "The Poems on the Naming of Places" articulate that to name is to kill, to ascribe to oneself an authority that at the same time stops the play of desire. Wordsworth juxtaposes images of death and the grave with the act of naming the place—inevitably with a woman's name.

Inherent in Wordsworth's celebration of those mute inglorious Miltons who do not speak their poetry is a serious ambivalence. To leave the moments of "spontaneous overflow of powerful feelings" unmarked is to allow them to escape the poet's inscription. Whenever power is inherent in a natural scene, Wordsworth will not be content to leave it untouched; he will subsume it through his own word. The independent *jouissance* of nature flouts the need for the male pen, so that the sexuality of woman and wilderness threatens to overwhelm Wordsworth's tongue. Thus he must fix the free play or ecstasy of nature through his mark. He will kill the very spontaneity he lauds in the preface to these poems on naming ("places . . . where little Incidents must have occurred, or feelings been experienced, which will have given to such places a private and peculiar interest") as he provides monuments, or epitaphs, for these spots of time. Yet as he "renew[s] the gratification of such feelings" (preface, "Poems on the Naming of Places") he will establish the grounds for endlessly repeating memories, the substance of his poetry. He will fix the moment, thereby destroying the very immediacy of experience that he will spend his poetic life trying to recapture with his word. Wordsworth manipulates the repetition compulsion into a mainstay and deliverance of his poetic voice.[16] He uses it, however, as a first principle, unlike Shelley,

16. Repetition in language occupies Wordsworth often. The preface to "We Are Seven," for example, invokes a long story of Coleridge's *Ancient Mariner,* a poem whose structure replicates its central thematic curse: the infinite man, the Wandering Jew, must repeat infinitely. He cannot stop telling his story; in other words, he functions as emblem of entrapment in speech; his existence, definition by speech. The compulsion to repeat aims at exorcising speech, at reducing tensions to an inorganic stasis. It is interesting that in the preface to "We Are Seven" Wordsworth very nearly boasts of his contribution to Coleridge's poem as he cites particularly "two or three lines at the beginning of [*Ancient Mariner*]": "'And listened like a three years' child; / The Mariner had his will.'" In addition, the last line of "We Are Seven"—written, Wordsworth tells us, first—invokes the issue of will-in-language and truth, of control, in a gesture reminiscent of the mariner's co-option of his listener's will in Coleridge's poem as well. In the preface to "We Are Seven" the narrator listens, reduced to the level of the eight-year-old of his poem—dumb and spellbound as the Ancient Mariner's three-year-old child: the child has his will. But what crime has the

who will surrender to it only as a last hope, and in contrast to Byron, who will celebrate its tendency toward deferral as the triumphant trick of language.

The location of poetic power is at issue in the third poem of this set, "There Is an Eminence." Wordsworth translates a peak "so distant in its height" (line 6) into the source of a mysterious regenerative power, somewhat akin to Shelley's economy in "Mont Blanc."

> [It] often seems to send
> Its own deep quiet to restore our hearts.
> The meteors make of it a favourite haunt:
> The star of Jove, so beautiful and large
> In the mid heavens, is never half so fair
> As when he shines above it. (Lines 7–12)

The peak is, "in truth / The loneliest place we have among the clouds" (lines 12–13), so its solitude seems part of its primal strength. In a strangely defensive gesture, the narrator immediately turns to the woman dwelling with him to claim her abilities at warding off solitude:

> She . . . whom I have loved
> with such communion, that no place on earth
> Can ever be a solitude to me. (Lines 14–16)

The narrator has not suggested that he feels himself in isolation, and thus the avowal appears, to some degree, a non sequitur. The lines, however, prove overdetermined, for it is precisely the "agreement" to

---

child/mariner committed to force it to "repeat"? None: it is the auditor now who asks the child speaker repeatedly to repeat its wisdom—as if the movement of the eight-year-old, who speaks a wisdom not of the world of her fathers, signifies a compulsive tugging from an earlier, more "authentic" realm. Furthermore, the last paragraph of the preface to "We Are Seven" passes for an odd, disconnected aside on Wordsworth's acquaintance Jem (James Tobin), wherein Wordsworth commends the digression as being, potentially, worthy of our notice. Yet on the face of it, the lines are completely anecdotal and personal. The submerged importance, however, is to imply that to name is to master, as well as to give life, two contrary traditions. Coleridge and Wordsworth define Jem poetically ("A little child, dear brother Jem")—and make him "ludicrous," as Wordsworth himself avows. Later Jem objects to that very poem on grounds that it will hurt Wordsworth's "good name as a writer." But by naming Jem—even if, as Wordsworth claims, it is Coleridge's idea—there is created a proleptic naming of all possible critics of the poem. Wordsworth has taken care to maintain his "good name as a writer": he has mastered naming by other would-be Jems. No wonder that the poet admits to enjoying "the joke of hitching-in our friend['s] . . . name."

live in communion, in language, that has stripped the poet of the illusory claims to be the original "Eminence," or phallus, which the poem anxiously explores. Yet the peak also serves as a sign of the plenitude of a maternal, untouched nature, just as the mountain in "Mont Blanc" shifts in its gender significations.[17] Thus community deprives him of the sole possession of an Edenic presocial order as well as of a preeminent claim upon the phallus.

In a maneuver typical of the circumventions of anxiety in these poems, Wordsworth displaces his wish for originality onto the "She" (woman or nature) whom he has loved with such communion; in her proper appreciation of the man before her, she accords him the enabling phallus: she allows him to escape solitude yet retain original voice, by giving "to this lonely summit . . . my Name" (line 17). By articulating a woman's voice who names him as the full phallus, Wordsworth appropriates unto himself the powers both of nature and the Law: he can have it both ways.

Nature leads the speaker back into a deep, secret recess in poem 5, "To M. H." It is hard not to see the "spot" as a condensation of Mary herself (to whom only the poet will have access) and unclaimed wilderness:

> The spot was made by Nature for herself;
> The travellers know it not, and 'twill remain
> Unknown to them. (Lines 15–17)

But the very act of the poet's naming the place, thereby robbing it of its secret existence, violates the sanctuary marked for the lovers alone. To write is to deny any possibility of innocence, and in the following congruence of death and remembered image, we see this covert wisdom acted out.

> [If] a man should plant his cottage near,
> . . . .
> He would so love it, that in his death-hour
> Its image would survive among his thoughts. (Lines 18, 21–22)

---

17. For an illuminating discussion of Romantic gender confusion and collapse, see chap. 3, "The Feminine as the Crux of Value," in Cooke, *Acts of Inclusion.*

As Frances Ferguson has illustrated, for Wordsworth the onset of language, in the mode of the epitaph as inscription upon a grave's monument, coexists with knowledge of death. These last lines suggest that the image of the speaker's inscribed secret spot will mystically outlive his actual death as the image is absorbed into others' memories of him and repeated in epitaphic rememoration. By naming it, the speaker has penetrated and thus incorporated into himself this nature, a metaphor substituting for his anticipated appropriation of Mary. Language and sexuality together guarantee the further indebted progeny who will continue to commemorate their father's name. "[M]y sweet MARY, this still Nook, / With all its beeches, we have named from You" (lines 23–24). Once again through a maze of relationships between nature and the word, Wordsworth ensures the sustenance of his poetic voice through the woman's power.

Just as the nook in "Nutting" marks the intersection of nature, woman, and sexuality, so in "To M. H." they become entwined into "a thick umbrage" (line 3) that connotes a potency that Wordsworth fears. Shelley's contempt for Wordsworth's timidity in *Peter Bell*, his reluctance to "lift the petticoat" from nature, turns out to be a fair assessment at points. As Wordsworth approaches unmediated joys that exist outside language, he intuits a death at the heart of things, until he finally appears more afraid of the silence inhabiting the imaginary than he fears the preemptiveness of language. He fights his battles for voice against the mother, with the ironic result that he becomes named a poet of nature.

Certainly it is not incidental that all but one of the six poems on naming explicitly call upon a woman to mark the place. One of Wordsworth's modes of disavowing the claims of an anterior originary potency is to appropriate images through his own gaze, taking the field of the Other into himself and calling it his own, and thereby "reconciling [at least] the male subject to symbolic castration by situating him in a position of apparent discursive potency" (Silverman, "History, Figuration," 27). Thus in poem 1, after the confusion of nature's signs ("Green leaves were here, / But 'twas the foliage of the rocks" [lines 30–31]), which presages vision proper for Wordsworth, he "gazed and gazed," and reassures himself that "Our thoughts at least are ours" (lines 37–38). But what he arrogates unto himself through the gaze and the word is the Otherness of woman/nature/mother, a power he dreads at times more than the word itself. His thoughts will incorporate, overcome this plenitude outside the proper and at least knowable boundaries of language; he attempts to allay his awe or desire for this never-to-be-recaptured Edenic nature, this maternal fullness, by capturing it, or encapsulating it, with his word. Hence the next line: "and this wild nook, / My EMMA, I will dedicate to thee" (lines 38–39). He will name her there, and in such marking of nature's effusions ingeniously further the illusion of fullness in the poet's word.[18]

"Soon did [Emma's] spot become my other home" (line 40) the poem continues. The speaker tells "this fancy" (line 44) to the Shepherds who see him there, and who,

> perhaps,
> Years after we are gone and in our graves,
> When they have cause to speak of this wild place,
> May call it by the name of EMMA'S DELL. (lines 44–47)

Through his story he has created this fearful scene as text, doomed to be repeated, to be spoken, and originally named by him. He has absorbed what preceded him and yet taken the name of its creator.

"To Joanna" contains the most shocking revelation of the ambivalence toward gender that underscores the poems on naming; its malicious treatment of Joanna surfaces only through a richly overdetermined system of symbols. Under the guise of a story to win Joanna—autobiographically a "real" member of the Wordsworth family—back to nature and to the bosom of the Wordsworth circle, the poet narrates to her (vis-à-vis his narration to a third party) the story of his revenge upon her castrating truths.[19] The oft-quoted lines from the Isabella Fenwick

18. As Kaja Silverman claims, "The assimilation of . . . form into . . . surroundings attests to [the] viewer's or maker's nostalgia for an 'intact state' of things—for a moment prior to differentiation." This mechanism functions to disavow "the male subject's symbolic castration—a device for covering over the self-alienation induced in him by the entry into language. Woman-as-intact-state makes good male lack through the fantasmatic restoration of phenomenal plenitude" ("History, Figuration," 27).

19. For an astonishing example of how two readers can create opposite meanings from the same text, compare John Hodgson's interpretation of this poem ("Wordsworth"), wherein he reads a Wordsworth intent upon gently teaching a family friend lessons about nature, with my own. Hodgson's reminder that Wordsworth's contemporary manuscript note on "To Joanna" is a rare case of the poet explicating his own poem is well taken, though I obviously feel that it further supports my own sense that Wordsworth entertains tremendous anxiety about this particular piece.

notes point to Wordsworth's difficulty at separating himself from the prelinguistic wholeness wherein he felt all objects part of himself. "I was often unable to think of external things as having external existence, and communed with all that I saw as something not apart from, but inherent in, my own immaterial nature" (Wordsworth, *Poetical Works*, 4:463). Joanna unhappily reminds Wordsworth of the impossibility of claiming nature-as-mother for the grounds of his poetry.[20] Through inscribing the death-dealing power of the word, the poet retaliates against the renunciation of plenitude. If poetry cannot create origin, he writes, it can name the end.

"To Joanna" has, as its manifest content, the narrator's account to Joanna of his recent meeting with a mutual friend. But the sexual currents of the text belie this innocent account. We encounter a lover's thinly veiled tale (recounted to the parson) about the place of sexual liaison: the rock where Joanna teased, where Joanna, looking into his eyes, "beheld / That ravishment of mine" and "laughed aloud" (lines 52–53). The ensuing echoes establish the rhythm of increasing sexual desire reverberating off the mountains. Echoes contiguously issue from peak after peak, "A work accomplished by the brotherhood / of ancient mountains" (lines 69–70), but the poet will claim the primacy of his phallus alone—he will mark nature himself, chiseling, "like a Runic Priest, in characters / Of formidable size . . . / Some uncouth name upon the native rock" (lines 28–30). Joanna is apparently as well known as she is too knowing, as the incredulity suggested by the vicar's "grave looks" (line 26) presage his ability to smile in the story-teller's face as the tale of sexual experience is ineffectually displaced onto terms of nature's innocence. The latent content of sexual games, read through the screen memory of nature's emblems, contributes to a more sinister third discourse: authority over the father effected by access to the mother after all. The question of power, of power relations, structures this poem. "Joanna" is a delicate conflation of woman, mother, and nature, a unity circumscribing the imaginary realm fraught with danger to the son, because that realm cruelly both creates the poet's earliest sense of potency and casts her son out of that Eden as

20. The master-slave relationship that Wordsworth tries to establish in this poem is illuminated by Jessica Benjamin's analysis of such a dialectic: "Erotic domination (by a man over a woman) represents an intensification of male anxiety and defense in relation to the mother. The repudiated maternal body persists as the object to be done to and violated, to be separated from, to have power over, to denigrate" (77).

soon as he eats of the tree of knowledge. He can never (ful)fill the mother as those who knew her originally. But he ravishes Joanna instead.

From the opening, where Joanna is odd (wo)man out, disapproval keeps threatening to erupt. "Amid the smoke of cities did you pass / The time of early youth" (lines 1–2), the speaker reminds her, circumstances Wordsworth considers ill-favored. Indeed, because of this unnatural occupation, Joanna's "heart / Is slow to meet the sympathies of them / Who look upon the hills with tenderness," (lines 5–7). Unlike the implicit aloofness that the city breeds in Joanna, those in the country still "love [her] well" (line 11), though we soon learn that Joanna has not visited her friends in two years. As the narrator claims to try, through his memory of the shared times with Joanna, to reinsinuate himself into her affections, we sense an undercurrent of censure and covert purpose: Joanna must be "taught" (line 15) her proper place by the poet who writes, inscribing her there.

It is striking how closely the salient episode in the narrator's walk with Joanna parallels structurally the first poem of naming. As the speaker comes upon a lush scene of nature, discrete entities collapse into a kaleidoscopic scene. The delight the scene engenders in "To Joanna" as the narrator traces the "tall rock" (line 42) or "lofty barrier with my eye / From base to summit" (lines 44–45) leads him

> To note in shrub and tree, in stone and flower,
> That intermixture of delicious hues,
> Along so vast a surface, all at once,
> In one impression, by connecting force
> Of their own beauty, imaged in the heart. (Lines 46–50)

But the act of looking suggests that the "connecting force" (line 49) is the scopic gaze, appropriating the other scene into itself. Indeed, it is "when I had gazed perhaps two minutes' space" (line 51) that Joanna—by "looking in my eyes" (line 52) and beholding "That ravishment of mine" (line 53)—laughs. Joanna, the pariah who dares claim the superiority of the city, looks at the poet during his vision and calls him absurd. Her laugh denies him the power to appropriate nature, the feminine power to create; but her gaze fixes him into her own discourse, traps him into the object status he would fix upon her.

As if in a nightmare, the mountains and sky echo back the laughter, repetition that mocks the poet's ability even to fix vision with his word.

The narrator's response to the ringing in the hills is an astonishing *méconnaissance*: He turns to the vicar, "our cordial Friend, / Who in the hey-day of astonishment / *Smiled in my face*" (lines 66–68, emphasis mine). That is, he mistakes his audience's incredulity as munition for his side. He assures the vicar that even if the thunderous sound he but "dreams" and "visionary impulses" (line 71) to the poet "alone [are] imparted" (line 72), nonetheless "there was a loud uproar in the hills" (line 73). In the story the narrator tells the vicar, Joanna now draws to his side, "as if she wished / To shelter from some object of her fear" (lines 75–76): the gaze has reversed itself yet again, with the speaker incorporating the laughter of the Other into his own defense arsenal. The very nature in which Joanna as woman felt at ease as a proper subject frightens her—will keep her from returning— as it becomes appropriated by a male voice that will inscribe her against her will in a text she did not want to write.[21]

For Joanna is right to be afraid. Eighteen months later, when memory has defended the poet through its plastic revisionism, Joanna's friend (and the real Joanna's brother-in-law) will create his poetry to commit to the ages. "In memory of affections old and true" he will chisel out "in those rude characters / Joanna's name deep in the living stone" (lines 81–83), and name the place "JOANNA'S ROCK" (line 85). He will defile the rock that "took up the Lady's voice, and laughed again" (line 55) and avenge himself upon it and Joanna by marking this monument as an epitaph, inscribing the death of the woman who will fail to return. What this unsettling misogyny points to in Wordsworth is not so much a virulent sexism as the Romantic intuition of the oedipal terms of even or especially linguistic equations, of the gender oppositions that infuse the very language the poet would call universal.

21. Comparing "To Joanna" with an early version of "Strange fits of passion have I known" yields a possible new vocabulary with which to explore the enigmatic Lucy poems. In a letter to Coleridge, Dorothy Wordsworth transcribes an initial rendering of the manuscript that assigns to Lucy the role of tauntingly laughing at the narrator's dream of her death which he confides to her: "I told her this; her laughter light / Is ringing in my ears; / And when I think upon that night / My eyes are dim with tears" (Alexander, 149–50). This Lucy, "strong and gay" in this version, left fantasized dead in the final edition, surely prefigures the Joanna whose laughter occurs at the wrong time and whose power to overwhelm the poet must thus be defensively captured by his pen.

Wordsworth's poetry is a brilliant dance of Lacanian desire as it seeks an androgynous zone of meaning safe from familial claims. Freud too called upon the myth of Plato's Androgyne (*Beyond the Pleasure Principle*, 57–58) as he sought to explain the "totalizing intent" of desire, the need to restore life to an earlier unified condition (Brooks, 106). Shelley was shortsighted in believing Wordsworth to be sexless; he was instead anxious about sexuality displaced into his texts. As in so many acts of repression, however, the displaced anxiety results in Wordsworth's often elevating the very mother and father he would rather disavow, a tension central to his poetic quest to bring to birth his own voice.

The "Runic Priest" as poet, creating an epitaph for a sinner, now neatly repeats the earlier "Vicar from his gloomy house" (line 21) whose "grave looks" (line 26) proved the inciting gaze for the poet's story. Although poetry can only repeat, and memory be pure only as it bypasses the word, at least poetry has the power to kill by naming, a power that at times must seem to reinact a primal potency. If "Peele Castle" recounts Wordsworth's mature, psychologically integrated acknowledgement of illusion, "To Joanna" is his subterranean answer to the question of how power and poetry—and men and women who threaten his tropic use of gender as they become sexually real—are related.

Poem 6 (unnamed) extends this subtext of a nature that betrays. The first third describes nature's refuge of a "stately Fir-grove" (line 9), where the poet spent "full many an hour" (line 32) in tranquility. But nature threatens to overrun Wordsworth and so he quits this haunt; in various manuscript variations, he cannot find a place where he can walk "with back and forward steps" (*Poetical Works* 1:120), for the grove is so thick that it lacks "a length of open space" (line 37), a space, we might say, in which to write. Wordsworth's brother visits the same spot, however, and this communicant with the infinite sea, the man Wordsworth will soon call the "silent poet" in line 80, surveys the scene "with a finer eye" (line 60) and thus wears away a track in the wood that his brother cannot create. Wordsworth's fear of losing his mandate to write as he locates it in nature was projected onto Joanna's laughter, while nature's echoing laughter subtly tormented the poet. In this poem he projects onto his brother John a oneness with nature that implies its "contagious" closeness to Wordsworth as sibling too.[22] He can learn from John: John is rewarded because he is patient and "had surveyed [the grove] with a finer eye" and "had worn the track / By pacing here" (lines 61–63). John lacks the power of the word his more eloquent brother possesses (even on ship, John is "muttering the verses I muttered first" [line 99]), but through the power of memory he enters the realm of poetry himself:

> to the sea [thou] hadst carried
> Undying recollections; Nature there
> Was with thee; she, who loved us both, she still
> Was with thee; and even so didst thou become
> A *silent* poet. (Lines 76–80)

Now it is Wordsworth's memory of his brother's holy treatment of and by nature that restores him to his faith in nature's originally pathless ways. If Wordsworth can stay bound to this silent poet, he will provide the brotherly mantlepiece to their mutual love of maternal nature, as Wordsworth busies himself with "timing my steps to thine" with "a store / Of undistinguishable sympathies" (lines 106–7). It is memory of John, of course, that will also finally destroy the poet's always tenuous hold on nature's promise of bonding and kinship, as the unhappy postscript to this poem, "the lamented Person not long after perished by shipwreck" (*Poetical Works* 1:123), motivates Wordsworth's most crippling insight. The sea can "cease to smile" ("Peele Castle," line 19); the "loss [of John that] will ne'er be old" (line 39) "hath humanized [his] Soul" (line 36) so that a poet must return to his own "Kind" (line 54), abandoning nature as too threatening a force to infuse his poetry.

Wordsworth's strong attraction to a self-constructed though culturally indebted Mother Nature therefore coexists uneasily with his fear of being reabsorbed by her, an ambivalence acted out in gender ascriptions enabling, for example, Emily to integrate and illuminate the men in *The White Doe*. For to gain the special potency of a preoedipal order,

---

22. David Simpson provides a reading of this poem that is congenial toward while certainly not totally congruent with my own (*Wordsworth and the Figurings of the Real,* 31–38).

Wordsworth might risk losing the speech of a poet.[23] At the same time, as Sarah McKim Webster acutely analyzes in one of the initiatory studies of the female in the male Romantic text, women are "sources of power" for Wordsworth and Coleridge as well; they "generate models for imaginative expression" (56–57), often escaping circumscription by the male poet's pen (and thus generating poetic anxiety).[24] Such a psychology motivates the seemingly inexplicable tensions of some of Wordsworth's most difficult texts, for example, the curiously unsettling "The Thorn," where the poet entangles maternal fullness with death, an eventual awareness of desire's predicament that to ensure its host's life it must arrest the move toward satisfaction. Edenic fullness can silence the poet.

In the prefatory note to "The Thorn," Wordsworth asserts the need for an introductory poem preceding this one. In this same preface he justifies his use of tautology and repetition, an argument Coleridge will attack on the grounds that portraying a repetitive character by repeating, is, in fact, merely boring.[25] But Coleridge misses Wordsworth's larger point, which does not pertain to character but to what we might call today the Bloomian perspective that every poem is another poem, that imbedded in one is the other. In this case, Wordsworth points to the impossibility of happy resolution that he seeks through fixing upon an object. For "The Thorn" tells us that birth and death are indistinguishable. The thorn, pool, and moss all mark the possibility of both a beginning and an end; but neither attempted arrest of meaning is sure, nor distinguished from the other in time, and the images are repeated as if to get a "fix" on the truth. "Our birth is but a sleep and a forgetting": it is as if the reader and the poet of "The Thorn" are doomed to repeat because they cannot remember that utopian, organic fullness in Wordsworth's great Ode, which preceded the "human" birth of being delivered into the world of language where "Shades of the prison-house begin to close / Upon the growing boy"

23. Reeve Parker locates Wordsworth's anxieties over gendered functions in/of language in his statement, "Narrative itself [is] the usurping father" (*Reading Wordsworth's Power*, 312). Thus to write is to be male—and inauthentic.

24. For an argument complementing Webster's own comments, see Claridge, "Pope's Rape of Excess."

25. Jerome Christensen, in an illuminating discussion of Coleridge's dissatisfaction with "The Thorn," reminds us of the Lockean psychology of desire that underwrites this poem, wherein "narrative craving is the manifestation of an uneasiness caused by the incapacity of language to communicate passion" ("Wordsworth's Misery," 278).

(lines 67–68). In "The Thorn," Wordsworth subtly suggests that the imaginary maternal world he would seek is a fictive fullness and, most importantly, that he limns it from this early time in his career as a world whose bequest is already complicitous with the father.

To understand the rich psychology of "The Thorn," we do well first to insert into our critical inquiry at this point an account of the ways in which familial desire is configured through linguistically derived paradigms. A common psychoanalytic situating of desire and desire lost is the child at the woman's breast, an emblem recurrent at strategic points in Wordsworth's canon. As several recent studies have emphasized, the pleasures of the breast are peculiarly sadistic in that the infant gets "hooked" only to be educated into autonomy through weaning.[26] Thus the very emblem of a mutuality that staves off death, mother and infant as one, already implies its opposite, a betrayal of that communion. At the same time, if the (for Western society) normative oedipal sequence is not followed with the child's innocence forfeited to the symbolic order, then she or he forecloses on the order of language— poetry. To go further: Lacan allows for a deictic stabilization of meaning in the anchoring of "positions of narration," shifters such as personal pronouns, which "enforce a curb on the infinite textual regress opened by difference" (Davis, *Lacan and Narration,* 854). Thus the otherwise inevitable *glissement* of the signification is short-circuited, with a signifier fixed, to some extent, through its engenderment by the Other. In the oedipal triangle when the father fails his proper insertion into the mother/child dyad, the mother is unanchored from the real world and the child cannot speak properly from his Name-of-the-Other. It is a similar failure of both the symbolic and imaginary orders that motivates the repetition and tautology in "The Thorn," that vexed poem whose economies have so cagily evaded critical commentary on its strangeness, enacting in this opacity to exegesis its own internal psychology of resistance to the normative operations of language upon the real.

One of the first oddities of "The Thorn" occurs in the introduction of Stephen Hill as an appropriate fiancé for Martha Ray—"friends and kindred all approved / Of him whom tenderly she loved" (109–10);

26. See, for example, Goodman. For a general psychoanalytic situating of the importance of the breast to the developing identity of the child, see Laplanche's study on the aggression that founds and sustains life.

after this recommendation, his egregious carelessness that so quickly follows the community affirmation seems oddly abrupt and facile:

> And they had fixed the wedding day,
> The morning that must wed them both;
> But Stephen to another Maid
> Had sworn another oath;
> And with this other Maid, to church
> Unthinking Stephen went. (Lines 111–16)

But "The Thorn" focuses on function, not character, and the male failure here causes madness, as the woman is "with child" (line 128) and alone. Phallic fulfillment is denied to both mother and child, so the child is not forced from her by the "properly" intruding father but instead is absorbed back into her in an enactment of the Words-worthian fear that nature can devour the potential poet. As important to the old sailor's narration as the mother's implied guilt is the paternal default: "O guilty Father—would that death / Had saved him from that breach of faith!" (lines 131–32).

Even the superstitious narrator becomes implicated in the process of oedipal identification, as he displaces his desire toward what he believes to be either a deranged or a possibly bewitching creature onto a story about her instead. He allows himself both an attempt, at least, at objectivity:

> if a child to her was born
> No earthly tongue could ever tell;
> And if 'twas born alive or dead
> Far less could this with proof be said. (Lines 148–51)

and an implied agreement with the prevailing wisdom:

> all and each agree,
> The little Babe was buried there,
> Beneath that hill of moss so fair. (Lines 207–9)

The woman's hold upon the narrator (he mistakes her for a "jutting crag" [line 186] and runs to her for shelter) is associated with the mesmerizing power of the pool upon its spectators.

> Some say, if to the pond you go,
> And fix on it a steady view,
> The shadow of a babe you trace,
> A baby and a baby's face,
> And that it looks at you;
> Whene'er you look on it 'tis plain
> The baby looks at you again. (Lines 214–20)

The gazer becomes both the locus of the Other, the speaker-in-language who failed the babe that needed to gain his identity from that Other; and the gazer becomes the baby (it "looks at you" [line 218]), locked in the mirror of a pond because its mother failed to provide a mirror in which the baby could know itself as exclusively hers. Nonetheless, the only identity the ghost baby possesses is linked with the mother's, so the hill of moss madly shakes off its predatory grave diggers as if to ward off a naming or discovery whose presence is too late.

Emblem of origin and end, birth and death, the mother is closely aligned with the thorn "bound / With heavy tufts of moss that strive / To drag it to the ground" (lines 233–35), as the narrator in the very next sentence shifts to the pronoun "She" without any putative antecedent but the thorn. This pulling back toward the ground, away from life, suggests the dark side of origin, with the repetition "'Oh misery! oh misery! / Oh woe is me! oh misery!'" (line 241–42) rehearsing Freud's myth of the repetition compulsion moving us toward death. Wordsworth writes his own story, however, so that both mother and father share complicity in dooming desire to be endlessly articulated and never located, as the father's refusal of phallic responsibility creates an impotence in the mother. In an impulse integral to the psychological vision informing Wordsworth's view of relationships and power, Martha Ray "possesses a power which the people—or at least the narrator—cannot contain." But because that potency exists "in relation to the community" (Webster, 58) to the extent that the townspeople's words drive Martha to self-destruction, even the sexual force that clearly unsettles this text through its infusion of Martha proves inadequate for the task of regeneration.

Still, "The Thorn" defers the issue of the father and mythologizes most persuasively the inadequate mother. The repetition that Wordsworth's own preface emphasizes—the stuttering of passion—suggests an inability on the speaker's part to allow the incarnation of language to occur, the very incarnation to which Wordsworth appeals in the third essay of his *Essays upon Epitaphs*. Repetition in Wordsworth, as Geoffrey Hartman avows, maintains the absent as absent: "[In] poetry we often sense a word under the words. This *paragrammatic doubling*, which may induce a *doubting* of the literal or referential meaning, can be compared to what happens when the boundary between living and dead becomes uncertain in the mind of the mourner. The poet feels that what is lost is in language, perhaps even a lost language: under the words are ghostlier words, half-perceived figures or fragments that seem to be at once part of the lost object yet more living than what is present" ("Touching Compulsion," 359).

Yet the speaker's inability to "get beyond" the mother's own blocked speech implies the threat as well as the joy of a maternal bonding that is successful: a symbiotic union where a blissful silence might overcome the imperative to talk. Thus the mother loses either way: her complicity—however unintentional—with the father robs her of authenticity, and an alternate solitude threatens the poet's word. Wordsworth's poetry is rammed throughout with this aweful paradox of the poet's would-be original voice: "To speak or not to speak" as it creates a Lacanian homology by implying "To be not where I speak, or to be where I refuse the word."

I want to conclude this chapter by enlisting several now canonical insights on *The Prelude* in the service of sketching the economy of my own critical grammar as it would be enacted across that large work. I do so not as any totalizing claim upon *The Prelude* but tendentiously to serve my interpretive project elsewhere in this study. Since *The Prelude* serves me well as a text extensively read and explicated in terms of desire and familial compulsions, I can use these critical coordinates to map out tensions that will appear throughout Wordsworth's great decade. Thomas Weiskel's brilliant analysis of the Simplon Pass episode, for example, further illustrates Wordsworth's anxiety over getting what he thinks he wants—desire fulfilled, the bliss of unmediated communion—and his subsequent contradictory need to keep the silent mother absent after all. One of the most powerful passages in Wordsworth's canon, this passage from book 6 gains its strength and tension

from just such anxiety over nature's claims upon poetic voice. A domesticated version of Weiskel's analysis would read something like this:
Wordsworth and Robert Jones did not really miss the crossing of the
Alps. Geographically, the dramatic descent into Gondo Gorge follows
almost immediately the passage of the summit, so even allowing for
Wordsworth's missteps, the crossing and the descent were close in
time. The spectacle of the "woods decaying" (1805, 6.557) in the gorge
served as Wordsworth's source of keen excitement from the onset of his
memories, as he wrote his sister of the Alpine crossing three weeks
after it had occurred. The letter suggests no sadness or disappointment
at a perceived missed crossing. Yet as he writes this episode of *The
Prelude,* probably in 1804, he not only makes central his disappointment over missing the crossing but he also prefaces his description
with the avowal that he approaches this story with "deep and genuine
sadness" (1805, 6.492). Why the poet would have aligned a memory of
the spectacular nature of Gondo Gorge with disappointment is puz-
zling, until we see that the sadness over the trumped-up missed crossing acts as a screen memory for the overwhelming of self that actually
occurs in the spectacular gorge. As Weiskel notes, Wordsworth's use
here of "Apocalypse" is the only explicit reference to that word in his
canon. "The types and symbols of eternity / Of first, and last, and
midst, and without end" (1805, 6.571–72) that greet him in the gorge
are nature confronting the poet with its real powers of sublime vision
that efface the word.

It is a scene that strips Wordsworth of any self-determining power,
as the man sees face-to-face the power that the child suspected the
mother always had, the power to swallow him whole. As Wordsworth
gazes upon a scene in nature where all signifiers meld into one indistinguishable eternity, where difference (writing) is no longer necessary
for meaning, he loses his position as signifier. Such an induction into a
signifier-free world, or at least a world in which an apocalypse fixes the
slippage of desire, must, paradoxically, terrify the would-be visionary
poet. For ultimately it is the *glissement* of meaning that allows him the
luxury of an unending poetic quest. It is as if the terrible moment when
Wordsworth comes face-to-face with that which he seeks—an original
language that subsumes both absence and presence—so overwhelms
his imagination that the episode must be fictionalized, displaced, tex-

tualized, in order to be under his control again, under the control of
the word.[27] Surely this is an uncomfortable truth for Wordsworth:
nature may deliver more than one bargains for.

A commonplace of Wordsworth criticism holds that the poet's oft-
attempted collapse of subject/object intends to bypass mediation and
arrive at ultimate fullness. It is, however, the poet's belief that he must
draw upon authentic experience—the material made spiritual—as the
grounds for representation that gives him pause. The fullness of a prelinguistic space suffocates, a position several times enacted metaphorically through Wordsworth's representations of a child nursing at
the mother's breast.

In the 1805 *Prelude,* for example, the Infant Babe section in book 2
posits an intermingling of mother and child wherein the infant incorporates the mother's soul along with her body, an identity that will
henceforth guide "soul-bonds" with others:

> blest the babe
> Nursed in his mother's arms, the babe who sleeps
> Upon his mother's breast, who, when his soul
> Claims manifest kindred with an earthly soul,
> Doth gather passion from his mother's eye. (2.239–43)

The 1850 version places the babe more fully within the scopic gaze of
the woman looking down, in a subtle shift in emphasis from the reciprocity of the relationship to the power obtaining in the mother:

> blest the Babe,
> Nursed in his Mother's arms, who sinks to sleep
> Rocked on his Mother's breast; who with his soul
> Drinks in the feelings of his Mother's eye! (2.234–37)

More interestingly, what developed from the 1805 verse is the
resultant power of the infant to envision all part-objects as a coherent
whole; the power he gains from incorporating the mother allows him
the knowledge of plenitude:

---

27. I am heavily indebted to Weiskel's description of Wordsworth's "screen memory"
(195–204), both in its analysis and in the conclusions to which it has led me.

> hence his mind, . . .
> . . . .
> Is prompt and watchful, eager to combine
> In one appearance all the elements
> And parts of the same object, else detached
> And loth to coalesce. (2.245–50)

This important passage is omitted totally in the 1850 version, replaced
with the immediate succession of the lines on the transcendent vision
resulting from the mother's love:

> For him, in one dear Presence, there exists
> A virtue which irradiates and exalts
> Objects through widest intercourse of sense. (2.238–40)

It is as if Wordsworth's evolving exploration of the source of visionary poetry moves toward locating the tremendous determining powers
of the presymbolic order squarely beneath the gaze of the mother-as-
Other. In 1805 the poet at least intersperses several lines on the quick-
ening powers of the youth before he avows the vision granted by the
mother. But the revised order of sentiments in the later version are true
to the poet's constant covert fear, now articulated, that authentic (for
example, maternal) vision always escapes his pen—even his own eye.
Attendant upon establishing priority in the mother and, by analogy, in
nature is the worry that the cost of collapsing into her, as the condition
for oneness with first principles of meaning, is poetic bankruptcy. In
this startling reversal of the oedipal dilemma, it is nature, or the mother, that threatens to castrate the writer; the father gives life or at least a
tool. Thus the following passage, in which the poet ostensibly mourns
the loss of the mother and the advent of the Law, represents the
projection of his hope as a poet. In a typical displacement of his real
fear, Wordsworth proffers as anxiety-free the period of absorption by
the mother and worries over his need to make his own way in the
world—a need that he immediately suggests is his license to write:

> For now a trouble came into my mind
> From unknown causes. I was left alone
> Seeking the visible world, nor knowing why.
> The props of my affections were removed,

And yet the building stood, as if sustained
By its own spirit! All that I beheld
Was dear, and hence to finer influxes
The mind lay open, to a more exact
And close communication. (1850, 2.276–84)

Wordsworth's assertion in the third essay of *Essays upon Epitaphs* that words must be an incarnation of thoughts, not clothes to adorn them, emphasizes the same desire to fix the sliding signifier that informs his love of nature—until nature really does overwhelm the signifier. Born into the symbolic order, of the law of language, the child wishes for a wholeness previously feigned, at least, by his union with the mother, a wholeness that is now driven underground. Language, as it hollows being into desire, divides up—articulates—the fullness of the imaginary so that we will never be able to find rest in the single object, the final meaning. Desire is born from the newly felt lack—the fractured state the human must inhabit as language promises more than it can deliver, thus maintaining a constant state of desire. Lacan, of course, speaks in linguistic terms; Freud would have spoken of the pleasure we seek in stasis or in returning to an inorganic, untense level of existence, so that the death drive and pleasure principle join hands. But language is empty because it is only an endless process of difference and absence, and the child of language will now simply move from one signifier to another along a relentless linguistic chain.

Reflecting (as well as helping forward) a line of thought that currently holds sway over our reading of Wordsworth, Frances Ferguson lauds Wordsworth's enlightened attitude toward language versus nature. She believes his position to be an enabling one, as he asserts the inevitable humbling through the inescapable nature of linguistic binding. Even in *The Excursion,* fascinated "with language and reading" he courageously "refuses to allow any 'erected spirit' to believe that he can ever renounce enough to stand beyond language or the world" (*Wordsworth,* 24)—a conclusion, as we will see in the last chapter, that was articulated by the time of *Peter Bell.* For while this stationing of Wordsworth's later linguistic position is surely correct, the cost of getting there is too easily forgotten. The poet himself believed, however superstitiously, that it was access to a pre- or antilinguistic realm that enabled his visionary voice, and when he could no longer lay claim to a desire that could at least feign potential consummation, he defined himself self-consciously as now, a mere inheritor of tradition, no longer a prophet. The notion of reading "Peele Castle" as a personal statement strikes many readers in today's critical climate as unnecessarily sentimental, akin to reading Shelley's *Triumph of Life* as deliberately, rather than fortuitously, his last work. Yet for such an avowedly autobiographical poet as Wordsworth, it may well be naive instead for us to suppress the philosophical coloration of "Peele Castle," whose concluding stanzas are read, biographically, as an aubade to Wordsworth's claim upon the visionary as he tacitly acknowledges that the poet he would be requires an inner illumination not appropriate for the real, versus the imaginary, world, an arrogance, even, to the realities of the world:

> Farewell, farewell the heart that lives alone,
> Housed in a dream, at distance from the Kind!
> Such happiness, wherever it be known,
> Is to be pitied; for 'tis surely blind. (Lines 53–56)

The "fortitude" and "patient cheer" (line 57) he welcomes in the place of anointed vision severely compromise what his most famous critics through the years have characterized as Wordsworthian voice, for it is a voice predicated upon a mythic, imaginary female as Wordsworth would have her represented by nature. Wordsworth retreated because that mother figure could become a Medea as well as the madonna of the word that he preferred; he relinquished her and sought a (paternal) life-giving word that would keep desire alive even as it revealed first and last things.

Chapter 2

Transgression or Transcendence: Voicing Desire through Silence

In Wordsworth's efforts to mediate the complications of a self-occluding desire, he constructs fictional human relationships that act out sometimes baroque libidinal economies underwriting authorship itself. Different from the often-allegorical relationships in Shelley as well as from Byron's mobile familial figurations, his narrative moments depend heavily upon a gendered desire that disrupts what might otherwise be sentimental themes of suffering and redemption into unsettling records of identity formations fettered by law and liberated by silence. I want now to turn to two of Wordsworth's long, underinterpreted narrative texts, *The Borderers* and *The White Doe of Rylstone,* both of which rather neatly frame the celebrated decade of his most productive period, and both of which hold as central to their work the familial economies of power and identity.[1] In addition, these two texts do share a certain appearance of thematic accessibility. In explicating at length two obviously historical or extrinsically political Wordsworthian texts, I am swerving from the recently dominant trend of treating these kinds of texts from a historically contextual basis, and addressing instead what I take to be the omitted psychological, personal politics that become translated into working metaphors for social relations at

1. Important, extended explication of *The Borderers* has recently appeared; see Liu, *Wordsworth,* 225–310, as well as the Fall 1988 special issue of *Studies in Romanticism* dedicated to this play.

large.[2] In doing so, I mean to explore the ways in which Wordsworth creates gender paradigms that adjudicate his own psychical tensions and which, all to our good, animate his poetry.[3] Furthermore, I raise here the question of fair treatment: do his models appropriate what he deems the female at her expense? How does he treat the male?

My deployment of two cases of Wordsworth's silent women is tactical, an attempt to examine the possibility that what would, at first nod, appear to be yet another sexist or at least romantically oppressive move could in fact form a tributary to a different discourse, wherein Romantic attempts to speak outside of both the symbolic and the imaginary orders of subject constitution (to escape the limitations of signifying systems as we can describe them) might inflect Wordsworth's corpus as well as, more predictably, Shelley's textual practices. We tend to locate Wordsworth in a maternal realm wherein he either seeks to domesticate the threat of the female or to manipulate the image into one of madness. I would suggest instead the operation of a kind of *théorie distraite,* through which the poet plays almost absent-mindedly with a theory of silence that would save by means of an apocalyptic mystagogy—if only it could be constituted without mediating the margins of discourse (the silent women) through such tools as the patronymic staff in *The Borderers* and the recursively embroidered banner in *The White Doe of Rylstone.*[4]

Driving these two narratives are Wordsworth's efforts to voice male phallic claims upon the contingencies of meaning, even as he tries to

2. It is noteworthy, for instance, that in the excellent special volume of *Studies in Romanticism* devoted to Wordsworth's play, there is little treatment of the textual dynamics not determined by external political or historical concerns. To the point here is Marjorie Levinson's observation that she treats of Keats's romances because their "peculiar transparency [is] a quality that renders them strangely opaque" (*Keats's Life of Allegory,* 32), a position I maintain—toward obviously different critical ends—for these two narratives of Wordsworth as well. A similar condition attenuates treatment of Byron's explicitly political plays, a case again of critics taking the poets far too readily at their word. What such nonetheless important explication fails to yield, is, to put it in language by now a truism, the personal dimension of all that is political. Recent trends in Romantic criticism emphasize the political element as constructing the personal and downplay the impossible complication of the self from the moment of biological conception as a space also constitutive of society.

3. At what level of artistic consciousness, of a knowing self-agency, these gender stratagems were deployed seems of little importance to me. Indeed, we surely no longer believe that Wordsworth's poems tell only one story; and, perhaps more to the point, why should they? "The greatness of works of art lies solely in their power to let those things be heard which ideology conceals. Whether intended or not, their success transcends false consciousness" (Adorno, "Lyric Poetry," 58).

4. I borrow here from Jacques Derrida's self-examination in *Psyche,* 9.

preempt the voice of an enabling "female principle" through, paradoxically, silencing her. Wordsworth appears, at different thematic levels that compete for interpretive significance, to grant silence as a reward, or to exact it as punishment. As Freud insisted, silence—even if it become a mental illness blocking all social communication—can be a protest against a Law, a phallic power disenfranchised persons at once recognize they do not really possess anyway, or they possess in such small degree that their portion assigns them to serve the larger master, an alienated language of others' cultural, material, and psychological power.[5] Outside of *The Borderers* and *The White Doe,* there exist few other places in Wordsworth's canon (perhaps the Lucy poems could compete) where the tensions of male-versus-female sexual potency (mythically encoded surrogates for the procreative act of poetry) become so prominent an element in the poem's actual composition. At the center of both narratives is the false father of Freud's family romance, the man on whom inadequacy must be projected. In *The Borderers,* for instance, Herbert cannot be allowed to deserve Idonea. Rather than protecting his progeny against the poisoned world, he immures her in it through his own inability to take care of himself. Because the patriarch is set up as undeserving, the other Freudian family myth—the primal scene—is enacted with less anxiety.[6]

A central question becomes—in both narrative poems—who gets the woman, the daughter functioning as a displaced wife? This question will be repeated in major Romantic texts, as, for example, in

5. Nonetheless, one could protest a certain Freudian error in locating individual authority as totally as he did—as writers tend to do—in language. Although, on the one hand, Freud came very close to recognizing the cultural role in women's hysteria—the fact that by not having the phallus, we would say today, women are silenced, and that hysteria is a reaction-formation to that silence—he also, by virtue of his role as patriarchal healer, insisted that nice women would open their mouths to him: they would speak to him his (and their) name. We can think of this model enacted in the literary realm: of Thomas Hardy's Tess reluctantly acceding to this paradoxical "niceness" that will prove her undoing as she opens her mouth to Alec's strawberries; and we can all remember hearing the names used for a woman who will not open her mouth, will not speak or smile her assent to a language of co-option, to the patriarchal man who would have her: the kind of angry male response to female recalcitrance or, worse, indifference. The insistence on the part of strongly patriarchal men—or women, probably—that women in their field of vision open up to them is a strongly appropriatory act, the knowing move of a Cenci father who would force complicity upon his daughter.

6. In one of the few "intrinsic" textual explications of *The Borderers,* Reeve Parker offers a particularly sensitive criticism of the father-daughter relationship ("Reading Wordsworth's Power").

Byron's *Marino Faliero,* which, for all the overtly political allegory, depends for its dramatic motivation upon a son's claims to the paternal wife; or, as in *The Cenci,* where, similar to Wordsworth's conclusions, silence is the only way the woman lays claim to authentic, unfathered voice.[7] Like the other major Romantic poets, Wordsworth, as several of his most sophisticated recent commentators have amply demonstrated, was hardly naive to the ways in which language constituted sense, so that, for him, if meaning is indeed differential, it is inevitably constructed therefore through relationships.[8] Yet the collapse of gendered categories that lay claim to a neat taxonomy of lived experience is also best represented by the effacement of difference that incest, or at least a fantasized too-close familial relationship, suggests.

Written in the aftermath of his disillusion with the French Revolution, *The Borderers* records as early as 1796 Wordsworth's anxiety over the source of authentic poetic power. Although, as Carl Woodring asserts, *The Borderers* marks "no revolutions in language" (94), recent assessments by Peter Thorslev (*Romantic Contraries*) and Reeve Parker locate in the text signs of Wordsworth's interest in language as a medium for study. One fruitful way to extend prior analyses of this play, then, is to cast its underlying impulse as the conflict between a stolen speech and an authentic silence, or, a satanic subversion of the Law versus the solitude of "the woman." In the end, the father's conservative claim to be the rightful name of the Law convinces the poet, as he comes to believe that phallic regeneration of a bequeathed language is the only ground for a poetry consonant with a normative civilization. Wordsworth, far more than Shelley, doubted the possibility of a truly original voice, in spite of the fact that Shelley's *Defence* pays homage to tradition, while Wordsworth's preface of 1800 grounds his poetics in an unsullied beginning of language. In both cases, it would seem that the constative dimension of the intellectual discourse transforms itself adversarily in the performative work of poetry.

The creation of his own world motivates the satanic Oswald of *The Borderers.* Discussing Oswald's unfathomable evil deeds, one of Marmaduke's band claims:

7. Although outside the scope of my project here, it might be worth exploring the significance of these examples belonging to the genre of drama, best suited for dialogic exploration of voice.

8. Particularly see Hans Aarsleff.

> Power is life to him
> And breath and being; where he cannot govern,
> He will destroy. (Lines 1432–34)

A companion answers:

> He recks not human law; and I have noticed
> That often, when the name of God is uttered,
> A sudden blankness overspreads his face. (Lines 1437–39)

This is a man who has escaped fealty of any sort, creating his own "uncouth superstition" (line 1441) and swearing, instead of oaths to kings, the "strange answer" that "I hold of Spirits, and the sun in heaven" (lines 1446–47). Marmaduke's credulity in the face of Oswald's slandering of Herbert follows naturally from Marmaduke's admiration of strength. Trusted friends warn the younger man against Oswald, though when they claim Marmaduke should not love him, their leader responds:

> I do more,
> I honor him. Strong feelings to his heart
> Are natural; and from no one can be learnt
> More of man's thoughts and ways than his experience
> Has given him power to teach. (Lines 32–36)

But what Oswald would teach his admiring companion is the need to slay the father in order to free the self, a lesson that to Marmaduke will spell silence in the end, a freedom not worth the purchase. Oswald disavows the worth of "old venerable" (line 922) Herbert: to murder the Greybeard is but to "kill a worn-out horse" (line 927). In urging Marmaduke to bloody his own hands, Oswald seeks to initiate him into the postlapsarian world of the man who would call God's bluff. Marmaduke's passions "have too long, / . . . diverted wish and hope / From the unpretending ground we mortals tread." So Oswald will "shatter the delusion, break it up / And set him free" (lines 931–35).

Complicating Marmaduke's final guilt upon his desertion of Herbert on the moor is the extreme paternal goodness that informs Herbert's character, a love that will have to be exposed as inadequate. If Louis XVI was an unfortunately benign king to behead, Herbert acts as a particularly benevolent parent, saving a babe from flames and incurring her endless devotion. Thus when Oswald encourages the overthrow of this father's claims, we encounter a more ambivalent paradigm of power relations than, say, in Shelley, where the father almost always deserves to have his fire stolen. Oswald essentially makes the claim against Herbert *faute de mieux*, as a general vendetta against the chains of tradition; he tells Marmaduke, upon the latter's struggle with guilt:

> To-day you have thrown off a tyranny
> That lives but in the turpid acquiescence
> Of our emasculated souls, the tyranny
> Of the world's masters, with the musty rules
> By which they uphold their craft from age to age:
> You have obeyed the only law that sense
> Submits to recognise; the immediate law,
> . . . .
> Upon an independent Intellect. (Lines 1488–96)

Oswald acknowledges as his own motivation toward evil the sedition of his ship's crew and captain. "I was the pleasure of all hearts, the darling / Of every tongue—as you are now" until the "foul conspiracy / Against my honour" occurred, in which the captain played the chief part (lines 1687–88, 1690–91). Conflict over whose word will prevail results in Oswald and his "comrade" (line 1717) leaving the captain to starve to death on a remote rock. Rock as epitaph: the monument to the totemic killing of the father by the sons. The man is "left without burial" (line 1728), that is, in an open grave, a reflection whose psychological veritability, reflected in Lacan's poetics, haunts our efforts to put the discourse of the Other once and forever to rest. This bereft father calls upon his murderers to have pity upon him, in powerful cries that "might have stopped the boat / That bore us through the water"—but those he had commanded "scoffed at him with hellish mockery" (lines 1733–34, 1736). When Oswald avows that the captain was really innocent, that the crew merely wanted to "rid themselves, at any cost / Of a tyrannic Master whom they loathed" (lines 1758–59), Marmaduke insists that the man must have been "marked" with "guilt" (line 1751). He cannot bear the thought of a parricide undeserved.

But Oswald takes with him from this illicit theft of power the lesson that the world of "words and things" (line 1775) comprises "A slavery compared to which the dungeon / And clanking chains are perfect liberty" (lines 1777–78). This founding knowledge becomes for him now an ontogenetic terminus a quo: he renounces the world, where in sickly egoism men love only what images themselves, and he learns from the "mighty objects" (line 1809) of nature how ill it is for so mighty a Being as himself to "perish self-consumed" (line 1813). His contempt for the world allows him to inhabit "a region of futurity, / Whose natural element [is] freedom" (lines 1818–19). Until we dare to assert our own laws, Oswald tells Marmaduke,

> "We subsist
> In slavery; all is slavery; we receive
> Laws, but we ask not whence those laws have come;
> We need an inward sting to goad us on." (Lines 1856–59)

Wordsworth's only clearly conceived Satan figure congratulates his epigone for having "cast off the chains / That fettered your nobility of mind" (lines 2248–49), as if the renovation constitutes a new Prometheus. Yet in Oswald's earlier sinister pronouncement—"My Master shall become / A shadow of myself—made by myself"—we get a truer sense of the economy of this relationship. Oswald enters into a Hegelian struggle of master/slave with Marmaduke, paying ostensible homage to Marmaduke's superior status, while desiring most of all to be desired of the Other. In Lacanian terms that illuminate the interactions between the two leading characters, "desire may be 'of the Other' . . . insofar as, given his finitude, the subject thinks he can achieve the self-awareness appropriate to him only in recognition by the Other that simulates and in a measure restores, the radical affirmation of a primordial unity" (Richardson and Muller, 282). Marmaduke's earlier halting recognition—"You do but echo / My own wild words?"—points to the eventual absorption of one murderer into another. In this particular master/slave dance of desire, however, the victory is too complete; in the end neither master nor slave can claim any ground other than impotence from which to speak.

Interrogation of structural positions in relationships occurs too in what appears, upon casual reading, as the idyllic parent-child relationship of Idonea and Herbert.[9] Implicit in procreation is the child's accession to the parent's place: as Herbert confronts old age and death, he at times (Oswald's villainy aside) seems determined to drain his daughter of her vitality. When Idonea falls silent as she and her father rest upon their journey, Herbert claims to "divine the cause" (line 132): his daughter's reveries about Marmaduke, the man she has given up for her father. Much as she loves Marmaduke, the father's word weighs more with her: "I pondered patiently your wish and will / When I gave way to your request" (lines 133–34). As a result, "the name of Marmaduke is blown away" (line 138). But Herbert's immediate response to his daughter's protestations of loyalty suggests his unconscious realization of the family psychodrama:

> a faintness overspread
> My frame, and I bethought me of two things
> I ne'er had heart to separate—my grave,
> And thee, my Child! (Lines 141–44)

The urge to encounter her as his wife rather than daughter surfaces explicitly in the lines following Idonea's efforts to reinvigorate her father:

> I should be as cheerful
> As if we two were twins; two songsters bred
> In the same nest, my spring-time one with thine.
> My fancies . . . are such
> As come, dear Child! from a far deeper source
> Than bodily weariness. (Lines 149–54)

Thus Oswald's slanderous insinuations that Herbert's child rearing allowed for illicit sexual encounters (lines 266–95) find an uneasy home in the familial underpinnings of this play as well. For the dominant narrative line to hold, it is necessary that Herbert be vindicated in

9. Many studies of *The Borderers* touch on the family configurations in this play, though none pursues the play as part of Wordsworth's attempts to locate and to gender voice; instead, familial invocations tend to serve larger historical locations. See, for example, the special issue of *Studies in Romanticism* (cited above): also, particularly see Liu, *Wordsworth*, 225–310, and Storch. Liu's extended treatment is especially impressive in its evocations of a densely textured cultural (heavily economic) environment, though for that very reason it worries me that the psychological province of the textually motivating anxieties that figure voice disappears under the weight of the sociological.

the end—all his rights as ruler and proper father are reinstated from unimpeachable sources—but the entire stability of a patriarchal world is severely decentered as Wordsworth weakens Herbert's claims upon our sympathy.

Why, though, with little evidence, is Marmaduke so extraordinarily quick to translate the man he previously admired into a vicious deceiver of an innocent girl? As he repeatedly hesitates to murder the old man, we receive our answer: reminiscent of Hamlet's inability to kill Claudius, the "stutter" suggests a covert guilt Marmaduke experiences as he recognizes, at some level, the man who stands in the way of the sexual relationship he seeks. Oswald impatiently waits for Marmaduke to deny this guilt—to throw off chains that enshackle him to ordinary mores and to become satanically free of societal codes. But Marmaduke hesitates:

> Why do I tremble now?—Is not the depth
> Of this Man's crimes beyond the reach of thought?
> And yet, in plumbing the abyss for judgment,
> Something I strike upon which turns my mind
> Back on herself. (Lines 780–84)

Even Herbert hints at a strange kinship between Marmaduke and himself in the dungeon scene reminiscent of *King Lear*, when Tom-o'-Bedlam ministers to the storm-ravaged king. Since Herbert is blind, he fails to perceive the dismal nature of his imprisonment, and he is free, unlike his sighted companion, to claim a grateful affinity with him:

> a roofless rock had been a comfort,
> Storm-beaten and bewildered as we were;
> And in a night like this, to lend your cloaks
> To make a bed for me! (Lines 814–17)

Manuscript 2, representing the completed original text of 1797, includes another explicit linkage omitted in Wordsworth's later versions. Herbert tells Marmaduke (here named Mortimer):

> "I never shall forget the shuddering
> that seized you when you led me over the torrent; but for you there
> had not been a hair betwixt my death and me." (II.iii.16–18)

The old man fails to understand, of course, that the shuddering issues from Marmaduke's indecision, his fear at killing someone to whom he feels so inexplicably close. Tom's role in *Lear* is clear; Marmaduke, however, cannot decide his allegiance.

"Which way soe'er I turn, I am perplexed" (line 878), the Wordsworthian Hamlet claims. Every time he attempts to kill the father he feels Idonea's presence. Contemptuous of the repeated failure, Oswald accuses Marmaduke, "You thought his voice the echo of Idonea's"—to which Marmaduke assents: "And never heard a sound so terrible" (lines 887–88). Marmaduke deeply fears the totemic act; he convinces himself of the older ruler's effete state, his effaced word, as he springs "to grasp his withered throat," but immediately weakness overtakes him until he almost falls asleep upon Herbert's breast. Marmaduke feels himself the thieving son, the slayer of his father and appropriator of his father's wife, who is in this case the overdetermined Idonea, functioning as mother, wife, and daughter to Herbert. In spite of an apparent total acquiescence to Herbert's putative guilt, Marmaduke continues to intuit the illicit nature of his mission.

> 'Twas dark—dark as the grave; yet did I see,
> Saw him—his face turned toward me; and I tell thee
> Idonea's filial countenance was there
> To baffle me. (Lines 984–87)

As if staging the Freudian primal scene, the band of "brothers" returns and gathers around Herbert, hearing Oswald proclaim that "We recognize in this old Man a victim / Prepared already for the sacrifice" (lines 1092–93). Oswald's further statement that "his death will be a monument for ages" (line 1124) conflates competing wisdoms, for the very epitaph that marks the father as dead elaborates the recuperative mode of rememoration. To be dead is to be remembered —and, if a death is never properly mourned, doomed to be repeated. In a last displacement of the subtext of desire informing Marmaduke's story, the narrative shifts to the fantasy Oswald spins of the fraternal sharing of the father's female bounty. In a voyeuristic gaze, he takes in the spectacle of Lord Clifford's savage companions celebrating the kill:

>   wreaths
> Of flowers were in their hands, as if designed

> For festive decoration; and they said,
> With brutal laughter and most foul allusion,
> That they should share the banquet with their Lord
> And his new Favorite. (1202–7)

Achieving the phallic voice depends, it would seem, upon the use of woman as commodity. Woman as mysterious other affords a counterpotency to the satanic subversion of that Law the Name-of-the-Father would impose. Implicit in the indebted male word that bequeathes the Law from generation to generation is an inherent tendency toward duplicity, as it struggles to displace too-determining structures. Thus the meretricious word deceives even while it glitters in its ingenuity. As Oswald plots to win Marmaduke to himself, he decides:

> now
> For a few swelling phrases, and a flash
> Of truth, enough to dazzle and to blind,
> And he is mine for ever. (Lines 562–65)

When, however, the male word reflects the feminine, its slipperiness evolves into stasis. Hearing the echoes of Idonea in Herbert's voice, for instance, plunges Marmaduke into an agonized period of inaction. When the male word collapses into silence through the apocalyptic powers of nature, the realm Wordsworth so closely identifies with woman, it finally approaches the aporia of vision—a truth where words fail—until it is once again appropriated by the male:

> When, upon the plank,
> I had led [Herbert] o'er the torrent, his voice blessed me:
> You could not hear, for foam beat the rocks
> With deafening noise,—the benediction fell
> Back on himself; but changed into a curse. (Lines 744–48)

Finally, the life-engendering impetus of the female word is foregrounded when Matilda, in the earlier version of the manuscript, intervenes to rescue the murderer of her father from being murdered himself: "Save him, save him," she calls out to the unheeding men who kill Oswald (V.iii.258).

At least to some extent, masculine value inheres in being the recipient of this commodity or signifier of worth. The question of who gets the woman covertly mediates the power struggle that subtends the male relationships in *The Borderers,* but, just as important, it is a question that ultimately underscores the inadequacy of all men in the play. Oswald and Marmaduke describe the slander Idonea hears as born "of [Herbert's] own coinage" and as that which "[Herbert] coins himself" (lines 257, 262). Implicated in this coinage is Herbert's ostensible exclusive claims upon Idonea ("Yet that a father / Should in his love admit no rivalship" [lines 268–9]), as well as the villainous Clifford's designs upon the girl. But even Marmaduke's rights to possess the woman are questioned, and not only because he kills his lover's father. After all, in act I this "open-hearted Leader" abuses the ostensible trust of the beggar woman, who, when she tries to tell Marmaduke of her infant's trials, is preemptively admonished, "We have no time for this, my babbling Gossip" (line 407). The woman soon accuses Marmaduke, "You Sir, should be kinder," to which he responds, "Come hither, Fathers, / And learn what nature is from this poor Wretch!" (lines 443–44). Lack of charity, however, is exactly what motivates the woman's condemnation of Herbert—"He is a most hard-hearted Man"—a judgment to which Marmaduke accedes, as he fails to see himself mirrored in her words.

Stationing woman as anterior to patriarchal figurings of political realities—even as she therein "feels" comfortingly exoteric to moral dilemma—subordinates the generative male exchange of power to the woman's function as a pure signifier, an unfilled, slippery word. Idonea, paradoxically, engenders "deaths" of some sort for the three leading characters, and thus the play unveils the very delicate nature of any phallic arrest of meaning; potency can be attenuated by the very woman who lacks its fullness. At the opening of act II, Oswald depends upon his own phallic word to capture forever the "modest Youth" (line 552): Marmaduke will respond quickly to "a few swelling phrases" and be in Oswald's power "for ever" (lines 563, 565). But upon Marmaduke's entrance, we hear his preoccupation with the almost hypnotic silence of Clifford's coerced mistress: "These ten years she has moved her lips all day / and never speaks!" (lines 566–67). Oswald responds in kind; he too has seen her, pacing around the graveyard, "Upon the self-same spot, still round and round, / Her lips for ever moving" (lines 578–79). Her curse of silence produces a keen anxiety in Marmaduke, for he extracts from her the threat of female "otherness":

> At her door
> Rooted I stood; for, looking at the woman,
> I thought I saw the skeleton of Idonea. (Lines 579–81)

Woman's speech has the power to redeem wickedness, but only at a cost. It is after Herbert blesses his daughter's guidance that Marmaduke exclaims, as reason for his reluctance to cut off the old man's breath, "The name of daughter in his mouth, he prays!" (line 1377). Like Hamlet, the would-be murderer resists a sinner potentially saved at his prayers, but finds thereafter "my wrath is as a flame burnt out, / It cannot be rekindled" (lines 1402–3). As Marmaduke abandons Herbert to the lonely moor, he assures the old man that if he is innocent, his daughter "from the utmost corners of the earth / . . . will come o'er this Waste to save thee" (lines 1410–11). Looking at the staff that leads the blind father, Marmaduke notes that it is "carved by her own hand" (line 1412) in these words: "I am eyes to the blind, saith the Lord. / He that puts his trust in me shall not fail!" (lines 1413–14). Adding that "God and that staff are now thy only guides," the unwilling murderer leaves the man alone. Neither God nor the staff will keep death at bay, however, as the daughter fails to rescue either her father or Marmaduke from the ultimate silencing of their voices, even as the men are unable to arrogate unto themselves her silent purity. Her engraving of male words envelops their strength in a female invagination that preempts the stick on which they are written; they function as a noncopula in contrast to the phallic signifier. The words inscribed on the staff therefore become a female silent message in the desert, with the blind man unable to appropriate them through his eyes, and with no one to sustain their sound for him through his trial. Idonea stays innocent in the snares of her would-be despoilers; but the men, even Eldred, all end inscribed by corruption.

The early version of the manuscript contains an extraordinary sequence omitted from the published version of 1842, a sequence that completes the meaning of the later expurgated text. In the 1842 text, Marmaduke laments his inability to force himself upon Idonea's vision; she will refuse to believe him the murderer of her father no matter what he says: "[She will] say no blame was mine—and so, poor fool, / Will waste her curses on another name" (lines 2243–44). The 1797–99 edition adds the following line: "And this will be when I am in my

grave" (V.iii.179). The refusal of the woman to recognize the theft of
the paternal word nullifies the feat; it becomes essential that Marmaduke receive "credit" for his blame. "I'll prove it that I murdered
him—I'll prove it / Before the dullest court in Christendom"
(V.iii.180–81). Marmaduke/Mortimer drags Eldred/Robert to the
court of justice, with the latter insisting upon Marmaduke's innocence
(impotence) in causing the father's demise. It was nature, not man,
who killed Herbert. In a wonderful conflation of meaning the old
man's staff blocks Marmaduke's way: the staff, inscribed with Idonea's
mediation of patriarchal words, serves as the bar denying access to that
which is the father's, the word and the woman.

> There is something
> That must be cleared away— . . . That staff
> Which bars the road before me there.—'Tis there,
> 'Tis there, breast-high and will not let me pass. (V.iii.197–200)

The conclusion of the initial manuscript embraces a demonic rite of
passage for Marmaduke that is effaced in the later version. After the
storm scene, when Oswald/Rivers returns to his protégé, the two men
"mutually fasten their eyes on each other for some time," and Mar-
maduke/Mortimer avows "I am a man again," to which Rivers replies,
"Nay, something more" (V.iii.224–25). Rivers is pleased that Mortimer is "Almost as quiet" as the dead man inside the cottage, for it is as
he has "prophesied" (V.iii.228). It seems that through Mortimer's
finally successful extinction of the old father's voice, he has exorcised
the claims of all earthly language upon him, in the process achieving a
satanic newness. In the published version Oswald rejoices,

> You have cast off the chains
> That fettered your nobility of mind—
> Delivered heart and head! (Lines 2248–50)

In both the published version and its predecessor, Marmaduke/
Mortimer justifies his actions toward the betrayed man as unassailable
in the end, because, he reasons, death is only a continuation of the lack
of vision with which we live: "Twas nothing more than darkness deep-
ening darkness, / And weakness crowned with the impotence of
death!" (lines 2253–54).

This assessment, however, vitiates the patricidal enterprise: the epi-taphic monument raised on the "dreary waste" to "record my story" (lines 2294–95) marks Marmaduke not as sole possessor of phallic brilliance but as a man doomed to be repeated and repeating, reenact-ing in his time the story of the grave he just tried to cover over. As he had recognized earlier, "We all are of one blood, our veins are filled / At the same poisonous fountain" (lines 1738–39). Like the Ancient Mariner, this slayer of innocence becomes doomed to travel endlessly in search of expiation—"a wanderer *must* I go" (line 2312)—but he finds himself robbed of any tongue in which to speak to others: "No human ear shall ever hear me speak" (line 2314). For while the "incar-nation of language" that epitaphs suggest may fail to "reincarnate the dead subject," it does in fact point to absence—the absence of the dead father, the speaker who is always made present by the rememoration of the epitaphic mode. The epitaph, the monument to death, "reveals a time lag within the feelings which makes them more capable of fidelity to absent than to present subjects" (Ferguson, *Wordsworth*, 32). Thus the very death Marmaduke effects puts into place a signifier always rising up from the grave—the echo Wordsworth the poet unhappily invokes only to displace so often in his textual maneuvers to domesti-cate death in the service of poetic liberation.

The conclusion to *The Borderers* finally teaches us that Words-worthian vision demands that for one to be a communicant—very specifically, a man speaking to other men—he must accept belatedness as the condition for voice. A successful castration of the very signifier that bears one into the world of language leaves the unshackled Satan bereft of communicable words. One cannot risk the freedom of Pro-methean theft nor, it would seem, the virginal embrace of womanly silence, presenting its own threatening claims upon male voice. One never can, that is, possess the woman, only acquiesce in being the recipient of a, to put it indelicately, hand-me-down phallus. This par-ticular mythology, the wisdom of the countertext in much of Words-worth's canon, sustains his poetry's ability to yield pleasure to feminist readers, for the possession, the appropriation, is always forestalled. Whatever authenticity Wordsworth the poet locates is borrowed, never stolen. Thus, in contradiction to the perhaps too-energetic espousals of Wordsworth's poetics, wherein the mandate to write in the voice of original man (which originally the poet acts out only in his desire for the female) compels his explanations, his play legitimizes phallic regeneration as the only real grounds from which the (male) poet gains license to speak.[10] And to some extent, we might argue that to a man whose gender fantasies translate into particular poetic possibilities, it is inevitable that the poet of the Real be a man speaking to men. Pneumatic woman (and I play here upon that odd doubling of Webster's definition, wherein "pneumatic" can mean either "spiritual" or—on the seemingly quite disjunctive other hand—"of the well-proportioned" female figure, with special reference to her full breasts) is the Imaginary Poet "by nature" who therefore has no compulsion to recreate originality through voice.

> Suffering is permanent, obscure and dark,
>   And shares the nature of infinity.
>
> *—The Borderers,* 1797

> Suffering is permanent, obscure and dark,
>   And has the nature of infinity.
>
> *—The White Doe,* 1807–8

Suffering and poetry are obvious mates, for poetry recommemorates the death that resulted from the human's new ability to mark difference, the discovery that the percept of a unified self is always consolatory sham. In a condensation of cause and consequence, we can emphasize the price of the knowledge Eve gained by giving way. That is, she became able to know both good and evil, to create meaning by learning to differentiate—and this linguistic sine qua non extends an invitation to the Word that would be both exogenous and intrinsic to subject definition at the same time. The Logos enters human time to redeem those beings who have left the deathless realm of wholeness for the delineated history where one names to make sense. Such naming, however, acknowledges finitude.[11] To the degree that Wordsworth

10. Indeed, as Reeve Parker suggests, the structural trope of this play is repetition, as the "characters . . . develop . . . through the tales they hear," with a "ventriloquistic network" resulting ("Reading Wordsworth's Power," 126).

11. For a finely nuanced discussion of the ways in which "the disjunction between the divine logos and the disparate words of human language [develops into] an acute problem" in at least another Romantic's poetics, see Ferguson, "Coleridge."

views suffering as the existential performance of inhabiting one's own fallenness, it is also the irrefragable branding of the loss through which humans are born into a network of predetermined desire. Suffering as redemption consists both of its hold on truth—its "permanence"—and of the "gracious openings" through which it allows the soul to see a transcendental exterior to life (epigraph, *The White Doe*), an escape from the grip of signifiers as the soul "rise[s] with sure ascent / Even to the fountainhead of peace divine" (epigraph).[12]

Those "gracious openings," as we might expect, turn out to be moments of inspired poetry that function as a kind of metalanguage incorporating all other communication. In *The Borderers* Wordsworth experimented with a frontal attack on the father's claims to linguistic power; he negotiated a Promethean theft that resulted, nonetheless, in a stifled voice that allowed for no "gracious openings" to occur. Oswald's and Marmaduke's Faustian appropriations of knowledge became the intertext for *The White Doe of Rylstone,* as Wordsworth places in relief alternative responses to the poet's indebted condition, whereby he is now more willing to let a female alterity carry the day.[13] Emily does not kill the father; she quietly incorporates him and all maleness into herself, ending up the victor through a paradigm of female power even as she appears most acquiescent to the paternal rule.[14] Her story becomes a poem, as the mythological marker of the white doe repeats the effective silence of suffering every time the animal lightens the chapel at Rylstone. With the doe's translucent brilliance suggesting a transformed, visionary state, Emily lives on after her death in an em-

12. All citations from *The White Doe* come from Kristine Dugas's edition unless the line numbers are preceded by a C, denoting Alice Pattee Comparetti's edition instead.

13. For a sense of the foundation that enables his whole poetic enterprise, we could profitably explore in the preface to the second edition of *Lyrical Ballads* the linguistic fodder for Wordsworth in his opposition of suffering to action. The permanence of suffering partakes of the epitaphic mode through which language bespeaks itself and through which it commemorates those "absent things as if they were present." In its long-suffering aspect, poetry gains access to a kind of permanence that preoccupies the Wordsworth of the *Essays upon Epitaphs,* for instance. And it is an easy step to associate the Emily, the doe, and the production of this poem (as well as the stuttering text of Idonea in *The Borderers*) with such a poetic, memorializing function. For a conceptualization of Wordsworth's easily overlooked marriage of death, silence, and language, which, while not "gendered," is congenial to my own, see Ferguson, *Wordsworth.*

14. Such a power dynamic may well give us pause, in light of the current critical emphasis on the opposite dynamic of Romantic poetry. See, for instance, on the notion of Romantic introjection of the female, Knoepflmacher in Claridge and Langland, Richardson in Mellor's collection, and, for a sense of the larger argument sustaining his book, Ross in the same volume.

blem of suffering obviously reminiscent of the incarnated Logos. And in Wordsworth's experiment to situate an anxiety-free infinitude in the woman, Emily represents both the negative emptying out, or hole-ness/holiness that Wordsworth ascribes to nature, and the overdeter-mined wholeness that results from the collapse of everything anterior into the female's clasp.[15] This wholeness, of course, implies the weak-ness inherent in claiming voice through nature: the poet is not granted an exception to the all-encompassing embrace.

Certainly Wordsworth elevates Emily and denigrates the men in this poem. The paternal presence in *The White Doe* functions almost exclusively as an oppressive Law that overrules a priori the desires of others.[16] "Fearless Norton" enacts the role of a heedless God who is willing to sacrifice his children for the sake of establishing the proper name on the throne. "From his Son whose stand / Was on his right" (662–63) the father takes the banner of Christian typology, woven by Emily—just as Herbert's staff was inscribed by Idonea in *The Borderers*—and he proclaims,

> "behold . . .
> The ransom of a sinful world;
> Let this your preservation be,—
> The wounds of hands and feet and side,
> And the sacred Cross on which Jesus died!" (Lines 665–69)

15. I offer the following contrast to this Wordsworthian construction of silence versus voice. In 1790, Maria DeFleury, who had been a rapid anti-Catholic propagandist for the Gordon Riots, published her well-received *British Liberty Establish'd, and Gallic Liberty Restor'd*, in which she uses the idea of woman as religious icon, a function Wordsworth implicitly assigns Emily through her later association with the Sunday doe; but through DeFleury's recreation of a bride of Christ, she redoes history, rewriting it as progressive liberation and recuperating the abstraction of freedom into a self-constructed position of real freedom. (I thank Stuart Curran for this particular explication of DeFleury.) Surely it is interesting to speculate on the different ways these two poets, one male, one female, figure female freedom through religious iconography. To the man writing, the freedom is the relief immanent in silence; to the woman, it is the ability to write her own story: almost as if each gender wants what the other is eager to discard.

16. My explications of Wordsworth assume, of course, that the epistemological enterprise is deeply entrenched in familial discourse, an issue disputed by those (e.g., Gilles Deleuze and Felix Guattari) who would socialize desire in a dialectical movement bereft of a personal subject. In contrast, a Lacanian scheme posits the paternal, Lawgiving signifier as finding its support by, however impossibly, both evoking and invoking a female "opposite" as lack, so that "it is only through the mother's desire that the cultural primacy of the phallus can be established and maintained, and that the discourse of the patriarchal family can be perpetuated" (Silverman, *Subject of Semiotics*, 189).

But this is the Word that leads to murder and bloodshed: "all the multitude / Who saw the Banner reared on high / In all its dread emblazonry" (lines 681–83) will use its inspiration as incentive to kill.[17] Indeed, an emphasis on owning and sacrificing his children often accompanies mention of Norton:

> these eight are mine
> Whom to this service I commend;
> Which way soe'er our fate incline
> These will be faithful to the end;
> They are my all. (Lines 617–21)

Norton burdens the one son who will be granted freedom after the battle with a suicidal charge of laying down the banner, while he defends what he considers his holy mission in a classic denegation:

> There let at least the gift be laid,
>   The testimony there displayed;
> Bold proof that with no selfish aim,
> But for lost Faith and Christ's dear name,
>   I helmeted a brow though white,
> And took a place in all men's sight. (Lines 1312–17)

Suggestions of divine authority cling to Norton: "the monumental pomp of age / Was with this goodly Personage" (lines 744–45). He has

> Magnific limbs of withered state,—
> A face to fear and venerate,—
> Eyes dark and strong. . . . (Lines 750–52)

Norton thus easily inhabits his role as possessor of God's holy word; caught in his own megalomania, he courts a sure defeat as his small band stands against a thousand foes. "A rescue for the Standard!" he cries, but "the sacred Standard falls" (lines 1158, 1160). As a result of Norton's frequent juxtaposition of banner and Emily, the emblems she embroiders seem imbued with her presence, as if her purity will vali-

17. Tangential to my concerns here, but nonetheless a study I see as necessary to release more fully the complexity of this poem, is an intertextual explication of Wordsworth's poem by reading it through Spenser's *Faerie Queen*, which Wordsworth's dedicatory piece claims as *The White Doe*'s analogue. See Kristine Dugas's illuminating introduction for the starting point for such a study.

date the father's enterprise and thus protect his clan. Norton bars her
from the active participation she seeks yet exploits her by stealing her
ability to create meanings. As if to show that woman will not be
silenced, Emily's words turn back on the father, not saving him but
making herself present through her marks in such a way that the taw-
driness of the father's proud sacrifices is inscribed by the absent, obedient daughter. Norton insists that had his word prevailed, there
would have been "a renovation from the dead" (line 1279), a claim we
know to be untrue even as Francis carves out his father's word and
thereby is killed himself.[18] The father planned to claim the world by his
word: the "spring-tide of immortal green" (line 1280) would see

> New life in Bolton Priory;
> The voice restored, the eye of truth
> Re-opened that inspired my youth. (Lines 1287–89)

But for all his bombast, his word is already indebted to the female,
predicated upon Emily's toil—and he dimly senses that it is so. His
frequent application to her name betrays a reaction-formation to his
fear of the passive feminine powers suggested in his "wise" (line 1114)
son, Francis, but most of all in his daughter. Even as he boasts of his
sacrifice of filial blood he asserts he must keep Emily at a distance,
leaving "the name untouched" (line 1322) of the one child at home.

Strangely, it is the daughter's loving obedience to her father that
helps render him impotent. He forces her to participate in an imagery
she feels to be illicit, and then he revels in her act. The banner is

> An unblessed work; which, standing by,
> Her Father did with joy behold,—
> Exulting in the imagery;
> A Banner, one that did fulfil
> Too perfectly his headstrong will:
> For on this Banner had her hand
> Embroidered (such was the command)
> The Sacred Cross. (Lines 350–57)

18. While outside the scope of this project, it would illuminate Wordsworth's poetic
trajectory to pursue Susan Wolfson's reminder (126) that *The White Doe* was, in its first
"finished" published form, roughly contemporaneous with *The Excursion*, which is marked
itself by an interrogation of voice and silence. We could fruitfully start such an inquiry by
reading Frances Ferguson's study of *The Excursion* (*Wordsworth*) across the funereal inscriptions of *The White Doe*.

But the patriarchal co-opting of his daughter's voice weds unlike things together, so that Emily's pacifism is forever—fatally—embroidered in the banner proclaiming the father's arrival. The verse builds to a foreboding silence as the emblem of what Emily's sign will effect:

> that same Banner, on whose breast
> The blameless Lady had exprest,
> Memorials chosen to give life,
> And sunshine to a dangerous strife;
> This Banner, waiting for the call,
> Stood quietly in Rylstone Hall. (Lines 375–80)

The banner, "unhallowed" (line 505) becomes an emblem of rape, of illicit claims; Francis begs his father "most of all, for Emily" (line 398) not to touch it. Since a babble of words fills the hall as Francis entreats Norton, the older man cannot hear his daughter's name, "pronounced with a dying fall" (line 401), as if to name her is to align her with death. Norton's fatherly devotion (similar in its effects to Herbert's for Idonea) unsettles the reader as his anticipated triumph on the battlefield invokes almost sensual feelings associated with Emily's embroidered banner:

> on the banner which stood near
> He glanced a look of holy pride,
> And his wet eyes were glorified. (Lines 403–5)

Incest, of course, was at least a covert concern of much Romantic literature; we have Shelley's oft-cited reference to the subject in a letter to Maria Gisborne of 16 November 1819: "Incest is like many other incorrect things a very poetical circumstance. It may be the excess of love or hate." Such a complication of opposite emotions motivates the Wordsworthian father-daughter relationship in *The White Doe*.

What Norton feels most deeply, however, is his inability to keep woman as signifier barred from the meanings he would create, the wars he would wage in opposition to female desires. He raises the banner only to experience the "Imagery" (line 867) shedding "Despondency unfelt before" (line 869), with the thought that while Emily "did in passiveness obey" (line 876), "her Faith leaned another way" (line 877), a way that spells emasculation for him. For like Shelley's Count Cenci, this oppressive father acts as if "there exists a causal, almost mystical relationship between words and events" (Worton, 112), and thus Norton desires full control over his daughter's speech. The idea of Emily evokes his wife, who will not stay buried; she has influenced her daughter in her castrating direction:

> Her other Parent, too, whose head
> In the cold grave hath long been laid,
> From reason's earliest dawn beguiled
> The docile, unsuspecting Child:
> Far back—far back my mind must go
> To reach the well-spring of this woe! (Lines 887–92)

The mother's word—its consecration by her children—undoes the father, as if in this poem it is the woman's word that is always already there, however silent she may appear to be.[19] If there is a mediatory position between the father's violence and Emily's silence, Francis holds that place. He is the compromise—the son who would save, not slay, his father. Such a solution, however, will not work; Norton, even as he dies, will oppress Francis with the paternal imprint to the point of causing his son's death as well. In the sense that the sibling communion between Emily (the "solitary Maid" [340] and "solitary One" [1556]) and Francis suggests an uncommon closeness, there hovers again, as in *The Borderers,* the covert suggestion that the men—father against son—are competing for the woman.

At times Norton, Emily, and Francis seem engaged in an unspoken power struggle that subtends the narrative antagonism over proper obedience. The narrator wonders what will become of the "fortitude / Of this brave Man" when he sees "That Form" and knows it as Emily (lines 443–45). A formal property in her ability to be present to all who rely upon her Banner, she becomes a producer of meaning, as the literal art of her sewing the Banner translates itself into a symbolic preserve of her spirit. In his letter to Wrangham, 18 January 1816, Wordsworth alluded to *The White Doe*: "Throughout, objects (the

19. Marshall Brown points out that "the exact center of *The White Doe* of Rylstone [*sic*] is Emily's vision of her mother" (168); it might be useful to append Reeve Parker's observation of *The Borderers,* equally relevant to this narrative, that "the repression of the mother coincides with the usurping of self that gives birth to narrative" (*Reading Wordsworth's Power,* 308).

banner, for instance) derive their influence not from properties inherent in them, not from what they are actually in themselves, but from such as are bestowed upon them by the minds of those who are conversant with or affected by those objects" (*Letters*, 276). Emily, as the transcendent signifier that effaces the father, serves as a touchstone for Francis's attempts to circumvent that father's gaze. Thus he goes to her when he thinks he has escaped the Other's discourse; though even as he notes the consistency with which the "Sire and Sons" (line 475) "have their desire" (line 459), he ascribes his decision to rest with the quiet Emily to the need to comfort her.

We know instead that Francis goes to Emily for himself; he positions himself in her unsullied wisdom in an effort to fortify his necessary claims against the father: "Might ever son command a sire, / The act were justified to-day" (lines 455–56), he tells himself as he approaches the maid. He feels himself "by the right of eldest born" (line 488) and, more significantly, "in a second father's place" (line 489) to bear the responsibility to dissuade his family from battle. Just as he approaches success with one of his brothers, however, Norton's gaze claims itself as imprimateur on any speech acts: "[the younger son] . . . would have laid his purpose by, / *But for a glance of his Father's eye,* / Which I myself could scarcely brook" (lines 496–98, emphasis mine). Norton, this "withered" (line 750) old man with "Eyes dark and strong" (line 752) reminds us of Coleridge's Ancient Mariner, with the glittering eye that, fixing upon its victim, could stay his course. In a fruitful coincidence of Lacanian terms, we are told that in his attempt to persuade the Earl to his cause, Norton "fixed at his demand, / His eye upon Northumberland" (lines 641–42). The Lacanian gaze that would appropriate the other into the onlooker's own discourse suggests as well the lack at the base of Norton's desire: he claims he wants justice for the throne of England, but the inability of demand to speak all of desire suggests the surplus of meaning in his actions. In Norton's insistence that he wants only to obliterate "strife and factions desperate" (line 646) at the state level lies a clue to the psychic underpinnings of his actions: he seeks an end to all tensions inherent in familial paradigms, especially in that his own so strikingly echoes, in the relations of fathers, sons, and daughter as displaced wife, the composition of Freud's primal scene.

Francis can reinsinuate his own ocular power, however, one that is potentially liberating, since he sees "With un-participated gaze" (line

761). While Norton's look is proprietary, Francis's appears to be one of concern:

> his eye
> Is pregnant with anxiety,
> While, like a tutelary Power,
> He there stands fixed, from hour to hour. (Lines 773–76)

Yet, as if his self-proclamation of his "second-father" status were a proleptic definition of his relationship to Emily, Francis, for all his pacifistic tenderness, seems unable to avoid acting out the very role he would shun. At the moment when Emily prays that her mother's "radiant ministry" (line 1053) will "Descend" (line 1054) upon her brother, Francis appears in thought to her as the Other who will bar his sister's identity from herself, forcing her to live in an alienated form untrue to the mother's wholeness that Emily would emulate. Rather than follow her own dictates of conscience—to go to war and perhaps command her father through the mother's intervening grace—Emily becomes the subject barred from her own desire, Lacan's $, "She meets the insuperable bar, / The injunction by her Brother laid" (lines 1064–65); and thus "*Her duty is to stand and wait*" (line 1070, Wordsworth's emphasis). Though this turn of events is an uncomfortably nasty twist, we cannot help then wondering at the nature of the following victory: she finally "secure[s] / O'er pain and grief a triumph pure" (lines 1071–72). The subsequent verses tell the story of Francis's death, a narrative development necessary for Emily, as the only, and only pure, signifier of its phylogenetic history, to enlaurel the Norton family.

Francis functions as a tension between possibilities, a role particularly interesting as it points to Wordsworth's drive toward a compromise. On the one hand, Francis suggests a Christ figure; he tells his father to trust his son, for "If God so will," this son will effect the father's mission (line 1327). Yet at the same time he enacts the part of a monument to his family, as the banner he carries becomes an epitaph, embroidered with the Logos reminiscent both of Christ's wounds and the Norton family's death. As the family marches to their execution a soldier taunts them by placing the banner in their path, and Francis reacts as if to a challenge as he rides away after seizing the cloth. (The 1815 version, written when Wordsworth was working on his *Essays upon Epitaphs,* actually substitutes the word "monument" for the earlier word choice, "banner.") If Francis had "braved / This insult" (lines 1366–67) like Christ and refused further participation in the secular renovation of his father's name, paradoxically he could have saved it, for he would have lived to carry on the Norton heritage. Instead he extends the father's curse through guaranteeing the banner's life and thereby engineers his own death.

What Francis should have fulfilled is a role similar to Emily's; in terms redolent of the Holy Spirit we are told,

> Thoughts of love
> Should bear him to his Sister dear
> With motion fleet as winged dove. (Lines 1391–93)

He should appear to her "like a heavenly Messenger, / An Angel-guest wing" (lines 1393–94). Though less obvious than in Byron or Shelley, Wordsworth agrees that in sibling incestuous passion inheres an ability to ward off the alterity present even at the heart of subjectivity; one mysteriously becomes more present to oneself as different branches of the same familial tree act as undifferentiated union. Francis is Wordsworth's experiment to create a male Emily. Like Emily, he should become a dove; like Christ, victorious even as he appears vanquished, he should take on the self-immanence that marks both the translucent doe and his sister, in that they appear meaning-full in and of themselves. Thus the confusing emphasis in *The Borderers,* repeated in the epigraph to *The White Doe,* on the superiority of infinite suffering to transitory action begins to make sense: it is the extraordinary presence-to-oneself that Christ's "infinite" suffering afforded him—the confrontation of his own divinity contingent upon an ascesis through which the rest of the world would pass—that Wordsworth privileges over action.

An authorial fear underwriting this poem is that Francis, branded as a participant in the male line, may lack the capacity to assume the feminine role he desires. As Lacan posits:

Symbols in fact envelop the life of man in a network so total that they join together, before he comes into the world, those who are going to engender him "by flesh and blood'; so total that they bring to his birth . . . the shape of his destiny; so total that they give the words that

will make him faithful or renegade, the law of the acts that will follow
him right to the very place where he is not yet and even beyond his
death; and so total that through them his end finds its meaning in the
last judgement, where the Word absolves his being or condemns it.
(*Ecrits*, 68)

Francis's inability to escape his father's determination figures the
conviction that shapes much of Wordsworth's poetry as it founds itself
on his claim to an authoritative voice. The 1815–32 renditions, collapsed in Alice Pattee Comparetti's edition of the poem, emphasize an
ambivalent son surprised to find himself holding the banner after the
father's death:

> Finds he the Banner in his hand,
> Without a thought to such intent,
> Or conscious effort of his own. (C, lines 1415–17)

He cannot understand how the banner has "Clung to the hand to
which it passed / without impediment" (C, lines 1415–17), and the
sheer force with which this paternal imprint—though translated
through the inscriptions of the woman—imposes itself leads him to
submit "will and power / To the stern embrace of that grasping hour":
"No choice is left, the deed is mine" (C, lines 1430–32). Unlike Shelley's triumphant hero, Francis as a would-be Prometheus will choose
action over renunciation and thus install a genealogy that bequeaths
the curse of an all-determining word onto those he would save. It is
vital to Wordsworth's purposes, however, that the curse's perpetuation
work against the real intent of his protagonist:

> He looked about like one betrayed:
> What hath he done? what promise made?
> Oh weak, weak moment! to what end
> Can such a vain oblation tend,
> And he the Bearer? (Lines 1413–17)

Once again Francis is identified in Christological terms, as his
brightness sheds such "overcoming light" that his enemies are temporarily stayed (line 1474). And again, like Christ, Francis is censured
by soldiers indignant at his subversiveness: he does not fight like other

men, but walks "aloof," unarmed, threatening always to overturn the natural law through his unorthodox, pacifist ways (line 1466). In the later versions, as Francis lies dying, a soldier rushes in to steal the power of the banner in a scene reminiscent of the biblical tossing of dice for Christ's robe. As the radiant son, "a glimmering sense still left" (C, line 1492), watches, his blood blends with "the wounds" (C, line 1497) embroidered by his sister, in a comingling of their purity: "Thy fatal work, O Maiden, innocent as good" (C, line 1498). With the secondary suggestion of the casting off of the merely human bonds, Francis may stand in Wordsworth's canon as an emblem of the most that a male protagonist can realize in terms of freedom.

It is to Emily, as her identity coalesces with the doe's, that Wordsworth accords the ability to achieve immortal status. The doe, "soft and silent as a dream" (line 59), is marked by the qualifier that describes Francis and his sister—the "solitary" one (line 60). The "lustre of a saintly show" (line 104) that illuminates the places that the doe touches, emboldens the narrator to bury the dead and outcry the living, if only for a moment: "Lie silent in your graves, ye dead! / . . . / Ye living, tend your holy cares" as "I with this bright Creature go" (lines 69–71, 76). The priory frequented by the doe suggests both the mother who inspired Emily as well as Emily herself—it is "The Lady's work" (line 238), and it is the sorrow of these women that mysteriously is kept alive by the doe, with her predictable, repetitive Sabbath utterance of their memories.[20] The doe's commemoration of pain, however, seems peculiarly uncontaminated by the ordinary emotion: it is "spotless, and holy, and gentle, and bright— / . . . / And glides o'er the earth like an angel of light" (lines 242–44); this is the doe that can pry

20. The literary and social constructions that defensively substitute silence for the almost overwhelmingly definitional powers of the maternal have been well glossed by feminist scholars of the last decade, among them Sarah Kofman, who argues, "[We can] recognize how much is owed by speculation, by rational, masculine theory—that of psychoanalysis— to the visual demonstration produced by a woman, the mother; it is to recognize that this celebrated 'progress of civilization' could not have been accomplished without the perceptible mediation of the mother. The pedagogical order is as rigorous as the natural order, it governs the necessary passage through the senses and through myth, through maternal education: this latter anticipates the science to come, in which men merely formulate, formalize, what women have always known though they have been unable to say it, only to show it, reduced as they have been to silence (in the dream the mother does not speak), reduced to taking the place of death in culture" (76). I would simply reassert my own sense that Wordsworth goes about something related to tapping into the potentially liberating effect that historical marginalization confers on these veiled female conduits of culture.

"into the darksome rent" (line 259). The mysterious sympathy between Emily and the animal is reaffirmed when the "single One" (line 1662) returns after several years absence and "fix[es] its large full eye / Upon the Lady Emily" (lines 1663–64). These lines are followed by a description appropriate to the immediate antecedent (Lady Emily) as well as to the animal itself: "A Doe most beautiful, clear-white, / A radiant Creature, silver bright!" (lines 1665–66); "Joined are they" now (line 1689).

If at times both Emily and the doe seem a mere transparent medium through which the word can pass, at other moments they become so radiantly luminous that they shed light upon the ground they tread. While the male epitaphic monument recreates memory and thereby inevitably effaces the materiality of the one whose absence it marks, the doe, as she "lays her[self] down" (line 143) on Emily's grave, functions as a grave marker that absorbs absence into itself until that absence shines forth as newly transformed, incarnated presence. The doe and Emily become metaphors of presence in a linguistic paradigm predicated upon a purity outside of and previous to language. Together— and reminiscent of Wordsworth's Lucy—they represent something eminently desirable that can make absence present, something that locates an authenticity prior to one's alienation from the grounds of being.[21] We know where we are—in the land of Wordsworth's "Intimations Ode"—when we read of the boy who blushes for joy when he sees the doe, finding her "Bright . . . as in dreams / [he] had seen her,—yea, more bright— / But is she truly what she seems?—" (lines 195–97). The doe is that poetic content always spilling over its form, the erotics of the aesthetic: the desire that as it goes unnamed is a "whisper soft [that] repeats what he / Had known from early infancy" (lines 193–94). The doe—and Emily—are the ideal enabling female that Wordsworth wants nature to be.

As close as Francis comes to being a Christ figure, then, it is Emily who enacts the complete transformation: when her brother leaves for battle, he tells her to "fill thy destined place," which, as he presumes to

21. Lacan describes the lack inherent in subject formation as the absence always subtending any signification in which the self would come to know her or himself as such, a phantom structure that, I think, informs the desire of others for Emily's "pure" silence: "When, in love, I solicit a look, what is profoundly unsatisfying and always missing is that—*You never look at me from the place from which I see you*" and "*What I look at is never what I wish to see*" (*Four Fundamental Concepts*, 103, Lacan's emphasis).

name that place for her, is "the purest sky / Of undisturbed humanity" (lines 589, 591–92). But Emily's vision surpasses his own. We are told that "He ended,—or she heard no more," and then three lines later, he kisses "the consecrated Maid" (lines 593, 596). Emily inhabits a realm far beyond her brother's attempts to define her, his word irrelevant to her as she is consecrated into a transubstantial copresence with the divine. Her iridescence allows the true Word to speak through her, so that any lesser paternal language loses its power to fix its meaning upon her. Still later, as Emily awaits the outcome of the battle, she is called again the "consecrated Maid" (line 998) as she emerges into the "open moonshine, where the Doe / . . . is laid" (lines 1001–2). Emily, as she is elided into the doe's magical Sunday appearances after the maid's death, becomes the Logos to be repeated in the Eucharist celebrated at Rylstone chapel.

Yet Emily's appropriation of this holy role provokes certain anxieties in Wordsworth. In a letter to Robert Southey in 1816, the poet answers a critic's charge that the word "consecrated" appears often and meaninglessly in relation to Emily.

> The name Emily occurs just fifteen times in the poem; and out of these fifteen the epithet ["consecrated"] is attached to it once, and that for the express purpose of recalling the scene in which she had been consecrated by her brother's solemn adjuration that she would fulfill her destiny. . . . The point upon which the whole moral interest of the piece hinges, when that speech is closed, occurs in this line, "He kissed the consecrated maid"; and to bring this back to the reader I repeated the epithet.
> (*Letters*, 325, emphasis mine)

One is forced to wonder at the "whole moral interest" that hinges upon the brother's kissing of the maid, an action redolent of the Sleeping Beauty story, with the prince's kiss as signifier that allows the woman to live. Indeed, the 1815 version of the poem suggests the poet's conjuring her up, as if he speaks in the role of a high priest, effecting the transformation of word into Word:

> But where at this still hour is she,
> The consecrated Emily?
> Even while I speak, behold the Maid
> Emerging from the cedar shade. (C, p. 165)

Emily's claim to solitary powers must be circumscribed—inscribed—
by the poet who would, after all, give voice to her.

In the end, however, Emily outlives all male determination as she
sees the familial law undone: the "Norton name" becomes "unknown";
the "waste" seems "under her dominion placed" (lines 1592, 1599–
1600). Like Marmaduke in *The Borderers,* she has been doomed to
silent wanderings; but unlike him, she returns home finally victorious
in her silent suffering. Against the phallic power that led, in this poem,
to the bloodshed of Elizabethan England, but that found contemporary echoes in the French Revolution, Emily retains her integrity and
remains "awfully impenetrable" (line 1647). She achieves what Wordsworth explored in Marmaduke/Oswald, and found impossible: by her
own thoughts she is engendered and therein immortal. Worldly claims
matter to her only in the most superficial ways; "The feeble hath
subdued her heart" (line 1801), and thus to that extent her brother's
prophecy is fulfilled. But the doe's signifying presence "disproves"
(line 1808) the majority of his prescriptions so that "If tears are shed,
they do not fall / For loss of him—for one or all," but for her animal
counterpart (lines 1810–11).

If, as in Shelley's *The Cenci,* the father robs Emily of her power to
speak her own word, this Beatrice ends triumphant as she becomes the
signifier par excellence, a brilliant light that contains all that goes before and after, as she incorporates the doe's visionary powers in the "reunion / [that teems] . . . with high communion" (lines 1699–1700).
Emily and the doe are seers of "Endless history" (line 1735) even as
they escape the "trouble-haunted ground" (line 1720) of the paternal
nook (line 1707). The doe that marks Emily's grave has "filled a holy
place" (line 1894), "And bears a memory and a mind / Raised far above
the law of kind" (lines 1896–97). Both *The Borderers* and *The White
Doe* fantasize escaping the bloodthirsty power of the word, the alternative to appropriation by a mythical, preoedipal female nature-without-
words; only the latter poem suggests a way out, through silence, still
"essentially" female in Wordsworthian mythology. Wordsworth's sense
that phallic voice is inferior to the desire that is the silent woman causes
him to cast as male the story of "prostrate altars" (line 1909) and
"fractured cell, or tomb, or vault" (line 1913). But the vessel for the
endless transmission of Truth, the conflated image of the doe and
Emily—and, at last, the poem itself—remain insistently female in a line

that seems to herald Keats's Grecian urn: "Thou, Thou art not a Child of Time, / But Daughter of the Eternal Prime!" (lines 1928–29)'.

Still, Wordsworth is too honest a poet to pretend he can annex such an emblematic female to his purposes while retaining the pen. Emily, in all her whiteness, suggests a kind of sterility unsuitable to the real world, for she generates no text except the one through the doe, one which continues to be self-reflexive. If, as the preface claims, "suffering has the nature of infinity," it does so because it perpetuates, unendingly, the human condition, not because it is sealed off from it. Visionary poetry, inspired through a particular Wordsworthian grid of desire, threatened the poet with its fundamentally antisocial impulses. A certain ethical dimension obtained in Wordsworth's psyche to the extent that he refused to spend the mature part of his life recasting the tensions of locating authentic voice for himself. This subsequent repositioning may well be felt to be his readers' loss, given the conviction of many that he did have *The Recluse* within him; but such a refusal also reminds us of the representative psychological energy, for good or ill, necessary to sustain the kind of poetry we have valued as high Romantic.

Chapter 3

Safe Sex: The Collapse of Gender into Re-generation(s)

Indebtedness engenders filial energy when it transforms the anxiety of influence into the legacy of tradition. Wordsworth straddles the fence; unlike Shelley, who refuses the father's name, and in contrast to Byron, who accepts the presence of that name as a just premise for his own iconoclastic voice, Wordsworth vacillates between isolating the paternal grounds as the source of his poetry or as its death. In the end, the father's inadequacy yet inevitability will prove the psycholinguistic position most enabling for Wordsworth's poetics—if not his poetry— as it allows him a legal space from which to compete. In this battle between father and son, the paternal corruptness of linguistic begettings is finally irrelevant, as the text that is safe enough to stay Words- worth's anxieties demands the irrefragable, even if rebarbative, as- sumption of the legally relegated father's word, the quarry after all. I want now—moving rapidly and accretively in several places—to jux- tapose two sections in this chapter, with the first meant to calibrate the filial anxieties which we have heretofore seen subtending the Words- worthian writerly position of lack, and the second to provide poetic models of the affiliation (with its strongest literary translation occur- ring in that unlikeliest of poems—*Peter Bell*) that functions as the terminus ad quem of his conflicted desire for a self-engendered, or silently inspired, poetic story.

Perhaps one of the strongest, though unlikeliest, poetic recountings of Wordsworth's confrontation with paternal generative power occurs in the "Vaudracour and Julia" section of the 1805 *Prelude,* where, as Kenneth Johnston suggests, Vaudracour "is driven mad by his failure to resist parental power" (180). The 1850 text excises this episode, and although its now "respectable" author may indeed have been chary of the account of youthful sexuality, it seems more likely that Wordsworth wants, even to himself, to demote its significance to a poet now, after all, firmly entrenched in the tradition of his fathers. In any event, upon scrutiny, "Vaudracour and Julia" appears to be not so much a story about lovers as about a father and son bound inextricably to each other.[1] The emphasis from the beginning upon the father's contempt for the lovers' union suggests the Name-of-the-Father as a mark of institutional authority.[2] Because Julia's family lacks social prestige,

> The father of the young man, who had place
> Among that order [of nobility], spurned the very thought
> Of such alliance. (Lines 568–70)

The father's disapproval is in fact actually used to justify Vaudracour's illicit unwedded passion; we are told that if the father had cooperated, marriage would have precluded the dishonor. But to some extent, the narrator's strong language and extraordinarily convoluted long sentence suggesting the need to thwart the father confuse the direction of Vaudracour's real desire: the girl or the father?

> This state was theirs, till—whether through effect
> Of some delirious hour, or that the youth,

1. Although they do not engage in detail with the question of silence and voice, there now exists a sizable number of important interpretations that bear tangentially, at least, upon my own explication. Richard J. Onorato's important discussion, while setting the stage for all later psychological inquiry into the episode, assumes that "Vaudracour . . . does not want to be like his father" (329), a conclusion whose starkness I find problematic, as my own treatment will make clear. Ronald Paulson renders the tale as a son's struggle as well, but he annexes the paradigm as a useful historical analogue to Wordsworth's revolutionary days (265, 268–69). Alan Liu, on the other hand, still believes the tale can best be understood in the social terms of Romeo and Juliet, a position that leads him to conclude, "Vaudracour changes scripts entirely to become villain rather than victim" (377), a real interpretive loss, I think, to the significance of the silence that ends the tale. Similarly, Mary Jacobus, in her finely calibrated study of this segment, in which she does engage in some detail with the possibility of paternal transgression, believes that "Vaudracour and Julia" "stops short of questioning the law" (*Romanticism*, 204).
2. See Jacobus, *Romanticism*, 190–91.

Seeing so many bars betwixt himself
And the dear haven where he wished to be
In honorable wedlock with his love,
Without a certain knowledge of his own
Was inwardly prepared to turn aside
From law and custom and entrust himself
To Nature for a happy end of all,
And thus abated of that pure reserve
Congenial to his loyal heart, with which
It would have pleased him to attend the steps
Of maiden so divinely beautiful,
I know not—but reluctantly must add
That Julia, yet without the name of wife,
Carried about her for a secret grief
The promise of a mother. (Lines 596–612)

The context of desire in this poem dictates that Vaudracour prefer the sonship of inheritance rather than arrogate paternal rights unto himself. A son may inherit the prison of fabricated meaning, but he inherits the father's pen as well; the rebel inherits an iron prison where he can speak in blissful solitude, but no one will hear him. The narrator tells us that his story is that of Romeo and Juliet's, but that he cannot indulge in relating much of passion. Rather, he must "tread / The humbler province of plain history," and, most significantly as it presages the motive of obedience, "without choice of circumstance, submissively / Relate what I have heard" (lines 642–43, 644–45). The emphasis on duty is important, especially in that it deconstructs the putative analogy between Shakespeare's play and this poem. For in *Romeo and Juliet,* the lovers create their own meaning; if they obey laws of nature at times, they seek often and energetically to defy them. Romeo and Juliet choose death, finally, as their stand against the fathers, and in that choice they determine paternal law, as the fathers' feud is ended. The lovers in this poem effect no such resolution, however, as Vaudracour acts out the role of son far too thoroughly to challenge tradition. Even as he stays at home to earn money for a lovers' retreat, Vaudracour *deliberately* antagonizes his father in a way that will ensure his ultimate capture and retention by paternal powers.

Equally impressive as Vaudracour's covert movement toward retaining son status is his father's viciousness. "Incensed" at his son's effrontery—his protestations of the wrong love—the father imposes a law even greater than his own: "by a mandate / Bearing the private signet of the state / He should be baffled of his mad intent" (lines 666–68). In fact, Vaudracour's parents actually set up his arrest by the state, as they withdraw "Upon some feigned occasion" which allows "three armed men, / The instruments of ruffian power" to seize their son (lines 673, 677–78). Partially as a result of murdering one of the men, Vaudracour

> peacefully resigned
> His person to the law, was lodged in prison,
> And wore the fetters of a criminal. (Lines 682–84)

Vaudracour's father serves, therefore, as a kind of Cenci paternal monster, in this case willing to sacrifice his own son because that son speaks against him. As in *The Cenci,* the potential cost of daring to fight against corruption is silence, imposed on Vaudracour and Julia at different intervals throughout the poem. Even when a friend who has an "in" with the authorities obtains Vaudracour's release from prison, the premise for that "freedom" is that the son "sit down / Quietly in his father's house"—a "hard law" (lines 698–99, 701). Oddest here, however, is the suggestion of relief on Vaudracour's part; having acceded to an admissible guilty conscience vis-à-vis the ruffian's murder, Vaudracour assures the pregnant Julia that a "right is gone" from him: she "cannot love" him (lines 707, 709). In an amazing skewing of appropriate sympathies, Vaudracour checks Julia's predictable indignation at her lover's father; he

> would [not] hear of this, for thought
> Unfilial, or unkind, had never once
> Found harbour in his breast. (Lines 715–17)

The son's loyalty seems ill-directed in light of the paternal vendetta against him. The father issues a mandate "to arrest him on the spot" (line 728), but either "through the father's want / Of power, or through his negligence" (lines 754–55) the son at least remains free of a literal prison. The narrator announces that he will omit part of the tale that would illustrate how much the man "Was traversed from without" (line 746) and the apparently attendant mental confusions he experiences in this period. The "dark and shapeless fear of things to come" (line 749) reminds us of the anxiety Wordsworth felt as a boy in the early theft scenes of *The Prelude*. "Vaudracour and Julia" recaptures the conflict between outwardly determined authority and the will to action from within. That the biographical chronology of this poem marks it as a rite of passage into manhood speaks significantly to the Wordsworthian quest to locate a poetic voice. We can predict from this conclusion to the book whose larger context is the French Revolution that Wordsworth will not, like Shelley, try to steal the phallic fire for his own self-birth. In "Vaudracour and Julia" the child actually requests that his father disinherit him, as if such an act would leave him free; but this unyielding parent even refuses "from the birthright of an eldest son / [To] exclude him" (lines 832–33).

Still, sons do not gain freedom by asking for it, and what Wordsworth the poet seems to be acting out in this story is his own mutual desire and refusal to slay the father and co-opt his voice by occupying that space where paternity staked itself—or to lay claim to the mother occupying the position through which voice issues, belatedly, out of silence. Even as the other texts from these fruitful years of his great decade emphasize his anointing by nature, Wordsworth points in this dislocated autobiographical sketch to his strong intuition that, for him, the cost of sustaining an iconoclastic or female-fathered poetry would be too high in light of the psychological normalcy in "real life" that he would value.

At times Vaudracour clearly prefers disinheritance. After all, to the extent that the father bars him from fully possessing the phallus, he is doomed to a life of lack in language, a life of infinite desire, a potentially fertile position for the poet writing Vaudracour's story. And in assuming the position of father, the new authority becomes stationed in line to be deposed in the unending cycle of parricide and guilt-engendered voice. Thus at times Vaudracour seems happier being the castrated rather than the one who threatens to castrate, the spoken rather than the speaker. Gayatri Spivak's insight that in books 9–11 "one may find textual signs of a rejection of paternity, or a reinstatement of the subject as son (rather than father) within Oedipal law, and then, through the imagination, a claim to androgyny" (47) is particularly relevant for the lovers' tale in book 9. One suspects, in fact, that if there is any justice in Shelley's claim that Wordsworth was a sexless poet, it lies in Wordsworth's flinching from sexual struggle, a swerve that vitiates his potency as a result. The seductive opacity of the seemingly (at first reading) limpid Lucy poems, the vitality of "Nutting" and of "To Joanna" and the boat-theft scene of *The Prelude,* all displace a sexual tension that energizes Wordsworth's poetry at its best. When the poet represses rather than displaces this tension, however, a certain vitality is lost to the literary manifestations of his desire.

Vaudracour's only attempted appropriation of phallic preeminence occurs as he tries to force his father to accept, through the birth of the son's own child, that Vaudracour has the phallus now. That is, Vaudracour appropriates the phallic fullness of childbearing unto himself, as he resolves that the baby's presence will move the father to treat him as an independent man. The child does bring Vaudracour temporary renown: whenever he appears at the window with his child, "immediately the street [is] thronged," as the "whole town" (line 821) sympathizes with him in his misfortunes (line 825). Julia, however, becomes a commodity; her function is to produce a signifier that the male can insert in the symbolic order as he pleases. We are prepared for Julia's final loss of her child by the language describing her confinement before childbirth: she is "herself a prisoner" (line 770) who announces nightly to the kind housewife attending her, "you are coming then to lock me up" (line 775). After the birth, her lover tells her that she must return to her home with "your child" (line 801), or "your boy" (line 805); the child is another possession assigned to one lover at a time. It is because "all hope to move / The old man's heart proved vain" that Julia must be "immured" in a convent, and even as she insists upon a "mother's rights / To take her child along with her," she is refused (lines 838–44). Vaudracour's inability to convince the father that he as son now possesses the power of speaking as a man dictates that Julia must give him the female phallus, the child. This child offers Vaudracour one last chance to appear to be his father's match without doing things his father's way.

In this last attempt Vaudracour will actually assume female identity; he has silenced the Other, and now, since he becomes the mother, identification with the female or with (mother) nature allows him the symbolic function of phallus as lack, the very grounds for desire. This identification depends upon the female condensation of opposites: the fullness of bearing a child, and the emptiness of not having the penis.

Upon Julia's removal, Vaudracour enters into an extraordinarily intense union with the baby. He subverts paternal omnipotence by becoming a mother, as he spends all day "beneath the roof / Where now his little one was lodged" (lines 865–66). When he moves the child from its town, he cannot avert his gaze from the boy, "nor would [he] permit / The hands of any but himself to dress / the infant, or undress" (lines 884–86). But the other father still refuses to acknowledge his son's phallic claims; even the feminized filial form, ostensibly reduced in its direct threat to the father, is unable to win him over. It is, however, the phallic signifier of the baby himself that is barred; at the father's house, we are told, "to the innocent child / Admittance was denied" (lines 891–92). The child, through Julia's legacy, marks a socially signifying class system inferior to the patriarch's, and it is this threat of being determined against his will—a determination motivating Vaudracour's actions—that the older man strives most to keep at bay.

The intractable father causes Vaudracour to set up housekeeping in the country, tending, except for the help of "an aged woman" (line 904), to his baby all by himself. In an unsettling, even shocking, abrupt denouement, we are told that the child "after a short time, by some mistake / Or indiscretion of the father, died" (lines 907–8). The sons cannot escape a system of meaning into which they are born; both nature and culture are scandalized when a man retreats into the woods to bring up baby. Wordsworth's own history provides an illuminating analogue: Caroline did not die, but her father *metaphorically* left her for dead in her infant stage, fulfilling little parental function until he came to accept determination of his rightful place by the English society that had bred him.

It becomes oddly important to the narrator/Wordsworth at this point that the unhappy conclusion be ascribed to powers beyond the storyteller's control, to a system that fosters such conclusions:

> The tale I follow to its last recess
> Of suffering or of peace, I know not which—
> Theirs be the blame who caused the woe, not mine. (Lines 909–11)

The son's hope of bypassing the problem of the father through the mediating presence or illusion of the mother comes to nothing.

Vaudracour's sentence for failing to resolve his place within the system is his loss of voice, a literary moment that helps us understand Lacan's insistence that silence is the result of a foreclosure of the Oedipus complex. "From that time forth he never uttered word / To any living" (lines 912–13). The chance for feminization to engender original voice collapses when Vaudracour is robbed of his maternal role. As we have already seen, if Wordsworth fears the father, he trusts the mother's constancy far less, even as he covertly locates the source of his real power in her nature.

"Vaudracour and Julia," ostensibly a romance, opens to a subtext of filial responsibility, the story of a son's conflict between proper inheritance and a self-engendered language. Book 3 of the 1805 *Prelude* neatly illustrates these contrasting emotional impulses. In 1805, Wordsworth's hopeful response to being weighed down by family expectations of academic, institutional success is that he is "a chosen son," endowed with holy powers that escape systematic determinations (3.82). Yet by 1850—when the "Vaudracour and Julia" episode becomes, somehow, superfluous text—that subversive status is changed; no longer are the daring words "chosen son" invoked, and though holy powers still move the poet, they work in conjunction with "reason" and "moral law" (3.84–85). Thus the poet acknowledges the incorporation of the father's word into a superego, a strong conscience that will propel Wordsworth into the role of a more dutiful son, a role that already covertly informed—perhaps motivated—"Vaudracour and Julia," even as the poet tried to escape his destiny. Although he is commenting on *The Borderers,* Michael Friedman speaks elegantly to this point: "Wordsworth gives up his attempt to break through the restraints his internalized father had placed upon him. He gives up his attempt to destroy this father. He relinquishes his attempt to attain effective power. Instead, he accepts the moral and social world that the image of the father represents" (127).

Most impressive, therefore, in Wordsworth's account of voice in "Vaudracour and Julia" is its own unintentionally epitaphic wisdom. The apparent flouting of the father's desire coupled with Vaudracour's refusal to hear ill spoken of the older man implies a passion of son for father in keeping with Freud's definition of the moral masochist, "whose need to be punished is closely connected to the wish to have passive sexual relations with the father" (Bersani, 83); to be, we might say, the female phallus for the father. But the need to be punished therefore also reflects the desexualization of the father, the resolution of familial desire by introjecting him as one's conscience (Bersani, 83); to accept, that is, the father as barring one's original desire. "Vaudracour and Julia," both in its textual conclusions and its extratextual allusions to the poet's own history, suggests Wordsworth's reconciliation to his status as son, fearful that any other subversive language of "holy powers" (1805, 3.83) will fail him, leaving him not a speaker of weak words, but a poet with no voice at all.

The paternal intertext that fathers—literary or familial—create for their sons functions at a foundational level in "Guilt and Sorrow," the early and much-revised poem that never pleased Wordsworth, a poem that seems to hang fire as it never quite gets to the point. If the metaphor dominates rhetorical tropes in *The White Doe*, "Guilt and Sorrow" is based, both in its grammar and semantics, on the powers of metonymy. Wordsworth worried that the separate tales of desertion and failure remained unrelated, but even allowing for the forty years of reweaving separate texts into a whole, this concern was a case of the artist's (deliberate) lack of insight into his own motivation to write. This is a poem that, as Wordsworth himself suggested, at least partially succeeds by virtue of the contiguity of characters' emotions: "[its hold on the mind] is effected by the identity of moral intent that places the two personages upon the same footing in the reader's sympathies" (Perkins, 179). The narrative line proceeds, not by virtue of literal connections among the unfolding stories, but by compulsively repeating, as if variations on a theme, a basic story, four times in this one poem. Repetition marks, among other things, a resistance of the subject, a refusal to dwell on the grounds upon which his or her alienation occurs. It also marks a conflation of the death and life instincts, the reduction to zero of all tensions that we have noted elsewhere—but also an immediate return of the excitability (pleasurable to a point) that will demand extinction again. Thus repetition lies at the heart of any psychic grid of desire. The poet especially can grasp victory from the compulsion to repeat: repetition becomes the governing mandate from which to write, Wordsworth's right to write. In his endless expiation of guilt over the son's attempted Promethean thefts of genealogical power and the father's inevitable failures as well, Wordsworth justifies himself as a poet.

The most salient motif of "Guilt and Sorrow" is the potential disaster that accompanies determination by forces outside one's control. The sailor "forced away / By seamen" (lines 51–52) is implicated from the beginning in a wicked history compelling even his captors against their will, since they too "perhaps themselves had shared / Like fate."[3] The "helpless prey" is taken "Gainst all that in *his* heart, or theirs perhaps, said nay" (lines 51–54). For years following his kidnapping "the work of carnage did not cease" (line 55), yet as soon as he is released the sailor hopes to reestablish his previous innocent love of his wife and children. He has been spoken by others, however; the "fraud [that] took all that he had earned" (line 64) serves subtextually as a reminder of the ego's imaginary basis from its beginning as it is formed on an image of the Other and fractured from self even further by eruption into the linguistic system. Displacing his own self-division onto a material event that he can determine, the sailor murders a traveler, an action that now provides focus for his alienation:

> From that day forth no place to him could be
> So lonely, but that thence might come a pang
> Brought from without to inward misery. (Lines 73–75)

The immediate "sound of chains" (line 77) that alerts him to the nearby human body swinging in irons expresses metonymically the murderous power of the ironclad social system that defines cultural possibilities from birth to death.

Seeking shelter at Stonehenge, the sailor hints at a nostalgia for the original word of plenitude. But too soon the landscape's stony giants become reminiscent of Freud's primal scene, the first parricide that issues in a guilt that will forever keep the father's tomb empty and threatening, the father's name barring the son from a completed desire.

3. Stephen Gill gives a detailed account of the stages that mark the composition of "Guilt and Sorrow" before it saw its first publication in 1832. I am using the finished text of 1832, but I rely upon its essential completion as story by the 1799 "Adventures on Salisbury Plain," since the alterations into "Guilt and Sorrow" are basically of a technical sort (Wordsworth, *Salisbury Plain Poems*, 16). Thus I treat "Guilt and Sorrow" as revelatory of Wordsworth's psychological concerns during his great decade.

This mysterious monument is "so proud to hint yet keep / Thy secrets," secrets that include having watched over "the giant wicker rear /
For sacrifice its throngs of living man" (lines 118–19, 122–23).

As the sailor's failure to "father" his family well is repeated in other
stories, it becomes clear that paternal complicity in creating familial
desire always involves sacrifice of others. Four cases of paternal failure
occur in this comparatively short poem, and it is their apparent lack of
connection that leaves Wordsworth displeased with his poem's dis-
unity. But the different episodes all depend upon the metonymic displacement of the sailor's abuse of the innocent. Each case implies, as a
pivotal line in the poem obliquely suggests, "strange repetition of the
deadly wound / He had himself inflicted" (lines 491–92).

We have already noted the sailor's betrayal of his family—a betrayal
nonetheless wrought by the system the sailor inhabits, as even his
destitute wife acknowledges at the end of the poem:

> "[People said that] *he* had done the deed in the dark wood—
> . . . but he was mild and good;
> Never on earth was gentler creature seen;
> He'd not have robbed the raven of its food." (Lines 607–10)

Because her husband fails his family the woman is forced to seek her
"father's door" (line 579), but the paternal failure put into play by the
sailor curves back upon itself: she is unable to reach him before she
dies.

Fate wreaks havoc in the family constellation of the soldier's widow
as well. Her reliance upon her father's protection is highlighted by the
juxtaposition of his virtuous life and his pious injunction that she kneel
in prayer to God nightly. Her "good father" (line 204), however, sees
his "substance [fall] into decay" (line 229) through "severe mischance
and cruel wrong" (line 228): again, this future is determined from
without, as the family discovers that "vain were wishes, efforts vain as
they" (line 232) and that they all must leave the father's "old hereditary
nook," when "the summer came" (lines 233–34). The daughter turns
to another man to save her family, and in the role of husband, he at first
provides the security they have lost. Yet again, the family is threatened
from without as war engenders an "evil time" that allows them "no
relief" (lines 271–272). As the "noisy drum" of war "beat[s] round to

clear the streets of want and pain" (lines 273–274), the young father runs off to join the soldiers, and his wife and children become embroiled in "Disease and famine, agony and fear" (line 299) until, husband and children dead, the woman awakes, as if from a trance, "on board / A British ship" (lines 305–6), emblem of the war that robs her of her family. The most dramatic paternal betrayal occurs when both storytellers, sailor and widow, encounter on their joint walk a father viciously beating his small child. The boy had "in a simple freak of thoughtless play / . . . provoked his father," who then "as if each blow were deadlier than the last, / Struck the poor innocent" (lines 472–75). As the abusive parent scornfully inquires of the sailor "What kind of plunder he was hunting now," for "The gallows would one day of him be glad" (lines 483–84), we recognize the putative "plunder"— absolution through a vicarious repetition of his crime with the chance to change the ending this time. The sailor effects in his tears the boy's salvation:

> The stranger's looks and tears of wrath beguiled
> The father, and relenting thoughts awoke;
> He kissed his son—so all was reconciled. (lines 500–502)

In the process the sailor paves the way to his own redemption in the proleptic empathetic suffering that prepares us for the absolute identification of the final story with the sailor's own life. Most important, he also points to the generative, as well as degenerative, nature of paternal acts that otherwise encode only a relentlessly muscular process of accommodation to the depletions of the law.

It would seem that the sailor has earned his release; as he and the soldier's widow separate, a new and redeemed existence might appropriately ensue, especially as their parting sight is of the "cottage children" clustered around his knees (line 537). But while the widow will escape this poem intact—she who has wounded no one and who in many ways is yet another negotiation of the same position Emily and Idonea enacted—the man still must pay for the improper execution of his male vocation, for his inability to sustain the life-giving nature of his word as well as its ability to mark death. From the beginning of his encounter with his dying wife, her silence is stressed; her "voice [will soon] be dumb" because the husband's "loving kindness [that] stood between / [her] and all worldly harms and wrongs" proved inadequate (lines 611–12). Yet even on her deathbed "the Wife's lips move his name to bless / With her last words" (lines 616–17), and as the sailor cries out his anguish, the wife is transformed by joy at his voice.

The female forgiveness works on several different levels. For the soldier's widow, it is a life-engendering breath. Throughout the poem the reader is tempted to marry her to the sailor, somehow interpreting the two stories as half of the same marital tragedy. Yet now, thanked by the sailor for the "pious care" (line 641) that allowed his wife to die in his arms (line 643), the widow can linger in the cot (line 640) and exit unremarked from the story. For the woman here has no guilt, *but it is at the cost of possessing no voice.* When one assumes voice, one inherits debt, a position worried in Shelley's *The Cenci* and exploited as the very structure and story of Byron's *Don Juan.* Where Wordsworth's fear surfaces is in the strength of the female forgiveness that undoes the curse, a forgiveness or blessing that as male both Coleridge in *The Rime of the Ancient Mariner* and Shelley in *Prometheus Unbound* invoke, one more optimistically than the other, in order to locate repetition as grounds for a justified poetry. Wordsworth fails in the late revision of the poem to totalize its parts because his conclusion subtly undermines his earlier generative ending in the 1799 version.[4] "Adventures on Salisbury Plain" (1799) ends cyclically, with the sailor hung in the same iron case that so haunted his own imagination earlier. "Festive booths" (line 822) are placed beneath his body, so that celebration and death comingle. And any "kindred sufferer" (line 825) in the future will be caught up in the dead father's gaze, as "Upon his swinging corpse his eye may glance / And drop, as he once dropp'd, in miserable trance" (lines 827–28). Neither the father nor the poet can stay the slippage of desire through confessing his sin: the debt is not so easily paid, and the important lesson of "Guilt and Sorrow" is that paternal inadequacies ensure one's place in the text, bearer of the ever-empty word. In contrast, the 1842 version, which presents the sailor's dignified execution by the authorities, allows Wordsworth to close the poem artificially in the name of formal coherence as he flinches from his own earlier

4. An interesting shift in focus occurs as Wordsworth reshapes his earliest version of the poem into his 1799 text: the emphasis turns to the sailor and his problem of fitting into society, versus the former center of the female vagrant (Gill, 13).

intuition. He would sidestep the burden that recursive male voice is often en-gendered by acts of failure and sanctified by the female phallus as lack, just the lack Vaudracour tried to appropriate from Julia.

Still, Wordsworth's economy in "Guilt and Sorrow" (though undercut in its final form when a father, not a son, is writing) is directed toward an acceptance of debt in both the poetic enervations and engenderments that debt instigates. Imbedded in the displacements of tale upon tale is the idea of the eternal slippage of desire along the chain of signifiers, as the poet repeats the word even as he seeks the Word, the father's attempt to fill in the gap built into language and life. The structure of this poem, so troublesome to author and critics alike, merely acts out Wordsworth's own uneasy peace with the paternal law, however inadequate, and its reification into a generational community wherein each inadequate word passes on to the next yet another chance to speak the desire.

If we are allowed nowadays once again to read the man through the poetry, as well as the poetry through the man, then we can claim to have traced the trajectory of Wordsworthian desire during his great decade through the conflicts of the highly social versus vatic voice, which invest his career even as they prove unsustainable tensions. The rapprochement with the father inevitably moves the poet toward a socially integrated vision. As we have seen, Wordsworth tends to equate voice with guilt, and one way by which he sustains that guilty knowledge— extremely important to both the man and the poet who would evolve over the years—is to diffuse it by displacing an investment in the personal vatic voice onto communal bonds of responsibility instead. Two early poems emphasize the belief in community that issues from a peace made with paternal inheritance, a belief that plagues any attempt Wordsworth makes to carve his word in the wilderness instead. "Simon Lee," a poem popularly anthologized and commonly glossed as a paeon to human suffering, more significantly insists upon society as the very condition for meaning and thus serves as a useful intertext for the larger and underinterpreted project *Peter Bell*. Started the same year that Wordsworth wrote "Simon Lee" (1798), and probably best known for the contempt it aroused in Shelley, *Peter Bell* indeed opens to a reading antithetical to Shelley's own poetic impulse: a common social order constitutes the only safe grounds for a poetics. Particularly when we recall that Wordsworth labored for years over *Peter Bell*, so that more than twenty years passed from its inception to its publication, we can claim a particular authority for the position struck in this poem (*Peter Bell*, ix), a position whose importance has been occluded by the poem's low position in the Wordsworth canon.

"Simon Lee" asserts that meaning is generated through social bonds; a solitary individual cannot signify without implicating the entire social order of language. Simon "is the sole survivor" (line 32) of his master's world. The servant outlasting his betters is exposed as a Pyrrhic victory, however, as Simon is incapable of engaging life fully outside of community; he needs some prop more than the "One prop he has" (line 37) in his aged wife. Simon is dying in part because he is disengaged from community, from the social order of people and their words, of "men, dogs, and horses" (line 31), groups that called upon the powers of Simon's "horn" at the hunt in the old days. What the narrator sadly accepts is his own burden of human responsibility, the requirement that he step in as "master" and generate a dialectic of meaning for the old man again. In order to maintain his desire as fully human, the narrator is doomed to repeat the function of those recalled from the past who fulfilled meaningful social roles in Simon's life.

Even as he recognized its cost, Wordsworth himself felt strongly his responsibility for cooperating with the social order, an impulse whose tensions benefited Milton and, some would argue, vitiated Wordsworth, and which coincides with the continual flinching at nature, which Geoffrey Hartman fingers as the culprit in what he and many sympathetic to the later poetry nonetheless consider Wordsworth's poetic decline. If "the gratitude of men / Hath oftener left [the narrator] mourning" (lines 95–96) than have unkind deeds, it is the burden of acceding to the social order, a duty (implied in that gratitude) that bears regret, a duty interrogated in Byron's *Don Juan*. Certainly the narrator tries to justify his position as an isolationist, as he suggests the couple's resistance to outside influence. After telling us that "From labour [you] could not wean" (line 54) them and that death is imminent to the old man, the narrator suddenly turns to his reader and gently admonishes her for expecting a meaning-full tale. This rather unaccommodating narrator places the burden of closure, of making sense, on his audience, implicating the readers in the metonymic chain of desire he is about to instigate through repetition of storytelling.[5] That is, though he has just avowed Simon's recalcitrance toward others' attempts to help him, it becomes clear that all the narrator has to do is to note how "overtasked" the huntsman is and to ask for his "tool" (line 82) to find himself "gladly" (line 83) received. "With a single blow" (line 85) the narrator severs the tangled root at which Simon works—and, we might add, the nodal point of a trumped-up defense on the speaker's part against an insistent social engagement.

Thus the narrator reverses his relation to Simon from the isolation early in the poem to his intervention after he invokes the reader. By feigning a closure when the narrator preemptively turns to the reader, Wordsworth further involves us in that social order, implying that to make meaning of what he says, we too fall under the compulsion to repeat the human condition of indebtedness to o/Others. And in his authorial claims upon the tale, which he has nonetheless implied only we as readers can create, he suggests our ever-shifting relationships of master and slave to the text, reminding us therein of our inescapable involvement with a system of limited possibilities for meaning. To create sense, Wordsworth believes, we have to write against and therefore into the midst of others. With "Simon Lee," then, as our intertext of the clearly emphasized priority of community—one that takes on a feel of androgynous gendering—we can open *Peter Bell*, the more ambitious poem, to an enlarged perspective that will suggest, I hope, the less marginalized position it deserves.

The closest to a complete early copy of *Peter Bell*, written in 1798 but not published until 1819, is inscribed, according to John E. Jordan, with "Mary Hutchinson—Gallow-hill"; Jordan speculates that the poem may have been part of Wordsworth's courtship of his future

5. The true open-endedness of poetry versus the apparent closure the dictates of form suggest undergirded the Romantics' poetics to an extent just now being recognized. In *The Rime of the Ancient Mariner*, written concomitantly with Wordsworth's early canon, Coleridge dealt with the paradox that language always precedes the poet and thus inscribes his words before he gets the chance. In his brilliant sidestepping of indebtedness, Coleridge relies upon repetition as a governing trope, as Jerome McGann explores in his unlayering of the poem ("Meaning of the Ancient Mariner"). McGann demonstrates that instead of claiming the illusion of fixing the word, Coleridge, through his tripartite text, points to the method within Higher Criticism of generational interpretation of meaning. Thus the Mariner provides one story, the scribe purveying the gloss a second, and the poem-giver (Coleridge himself) a third. The successive audiences would, of course, allow for infinite unveilings of meaning, so Coleridge gathers to himself the slippage of meaning as the very trope for interpretation.

wife (Wordsworth, *Peter Bell,* 6). Particularly when we recall that the "Poems on the Naming of Places" were written in conjunction with his impending marriage, the treatment in *Peter Bell* of the claims of community and tradition upon a would-be iconoclastic voice gain in interest. The prologue, an oddly discordant frame for the rest of the story, positions the narrator in a boat, a female vessel that tries to convince its passenger to eschew the earth below and make supernatural haunts his home instead. The boat conveys only the passionate: "Frail man ne'er sate in such another" (line 22), and the boat and man make a very compatible duo: "Each is contented with the other" (line 25). But an odd cross-genderization occurs. The "canoe" (line 17), like the female "crescent-moon" (line 7), stirs fear in the hearts of the narrator's friends; yet in contrast to these fears, the narrator, "untroubled" (line 16), admires the canoe's "pointed horns" (line 17). This image suggests the boat's maleness, akin to Timothy Bahti's aligning of the "elfin Pinnace" in the first book of *The Prelude* with a "little Penis" (115). The strange, aggressive lines that follow, in which the narrator stresses his temptation to "laugh" (line 20) at his friends till his "ribs ached" (line 20), encourage us to read the horns as the emblem of a cuckold.

But who is the cuckold here, and who makes him one? If we allow for a displacement of anxieties in this section, we can better understand the lines that contextually seem an oddly placed apocalyptic description of nature: "The woods, my Friends, are round you roaring, / Rocking and roaring like a sea" (lines 11–12). They imply the power of the "natural" female space outside language to rob the poet of his male voice while promising, at least, something original in its place. The speaker's bravado in ascribing the apprehensiveness at the "noise of danger" (line 13) to his audience, and then asserting his own impulse to laugh at them, highlights his tension over acceding totally to the imaginary realm. He may be the cuckold—nature may betray him after all, laughing at him, even as the woman does in "To Joanna," just as the promise of apocalyptic powers seems his. His insistence upon his lack of concern where others are fearful cleverly negates the anxiety that generates this poem, an anxiety that leaves the boat's passenger disoriented as he starts his down-to-earth tale of *Peter Bell*. The narrator has flirted with the idea of writing a different poem—an *Alastor* where the boat and its passengers indeed would "know the secrets of a land / Where human foot did never stray" (lines 96–97), the explicit tempta-

tion this canoe extends. But Wordsworth is more earthbound than
Shelley, and he senses that in the passions of unknown lands he would
lose his way, and lose what he can now avow as his responsibility to
write:

> Then back to Earth, the dear green Earth:—
> Whole ages if I [in heaven] should roam,
> The world for any remarks and me
> Would not a whit the better be. (Lines 51–54)

The narrator asserts a benign, passive "mother-earth" (line 133)
against the libidinous powers of the moonlike skiff, and with this
domestication of nature is allowed back into the community to tell his
tale of a common man. But this descent into the tea party also marks a
reassuring reentry into the world of words, a place where the inscription of tale within tale—the narrator's prologue, the narrator's story
of Peter, Peter's "tale" to the widow, and the subtitle of *Peter Bell* ("a
tale")—works against the lure of origin with which maternal nature
seduces the poet, and affirms instead the infinite regress of words, the
necessary lifeline of the poet's desire.

That tension over proper location of voice motivates this poem is
further suggested in the last stanza of the prologue, where the anxiety
reminds us of that attending the three theft scenes of Wordsworth's
boyhood in *The Prelude*. The narrator tells his friends that through his
story he will quickly repay them "the well-remembered debt" (line
185), but his obligation to his party seems ambivalently assumed, as he

> spake with faltering voice, like one
> Not wholly rescued from the pale
> Of a wild dream, or worse illusion;
> But straight, to cover my confusion,
> Began the promised tale. (Lines 186–90)

Hesitation over speaking surfaces in the later 1827 manuscript as the
narrator claims that "Breath failed me as I spoke" and that he is "somewhat out of voice" (line 338). The narrator's disorientation results in
Peter Bell's story confusing its listener at first, as it opens abruptly with
Peter's aggressive cudgeling of a mute ass. As if the repeatedly "heavier
weight" (line 194) with which Peter strikes the animal falls op-

pressively on the audience, the squire immediately intervenes and requests an end to this decentering; he prevails upon the speaker to "start from the beginning" (line 200)—a request that integrates the speaker back into the ordinariness of community discourse and retrieves his breath for him as well. The community pulls the narrator/Wordsworth back into the (unoriginal) but verse-engendering realm of real story-telling.

Peter himself, a "wild and woodland rover" (line 207), functions analogically as the one poetic alternate to both paternal and domestic maternal claims, as Peter tries lawlessly to live anterior to both powers: he will have to learn that there is no "outside" in which genealogy—and therefore responsibility—is not already implicated. In lines easily parodied by Shelley the revisionist, the narrator asserts that

> nature ne'er could find the way
> Into the heart of Peter Bell.
>
> In vain, through every changeful year
> Did Nature lead him as before;
> A primrose by a river's brim
> A yellow primrose was to him,
> And it was nothing more. (Lines 244–50)

In the preceding incongruous words that sound oddly laudatory, we heard that "Sure never man like him did roam!" (line 235), a description recalling the narrator as passenger in the boat. Much later, when Peter reacts to nature's powers upon his mind, we again get another description in a variant of manuscript 2 (*The Poetical Works*)[6] that links Peter with the narrator who relinquished his moonlike boat's lawless powers in order to return to earth:

> For Peter Bell he looks I vow
> With his dull face of ashy white
> Just like a creature that pertains
> To some strange world of silent pains
> A creature of a moonlight night. (*The Poetical Works* 2:366)

When a solitary or particularly distinctive life functions negatively in Wordsworth, the fault lies either in the attempt to escape entanglement

---

6. I cite manuscript variants by volume and page number.

with community and its already-written words or in the disloyalty to the potential life-giving force of nature. For example, the poem begun in 1795, "Lines Left upon a Seat in a Yew-tree," already implies Wordsworth's suspicion of autonomous claims upon power and thus throws light upon *Peter Bell*. Like the narrator at the beginning of *Peter Bell* the protagonist of "Lines" is unwilling to suffer the tedium of real engagement with the world in which he finds himself. He lives not to serve, but to be served, service he thinks befitting a man of his great talents. Reality intrudes:

> The world, for so it thought,
> Owed him no service; wherefore he at once
> With indignation turned himself away. (Lines 20–22)

Although, in his self-imposed exile, the man turns to nature for succor, he mistakes his place here too, as he turns his "gaze" (line 33) onto her and finds himself not overpowering her, but overpowered by her: "nature had subdued him to herself" (line 38). A "lost man" (line 44), with his would-be masterful eye streaming instead "with tears" (line 46), he is captured by the gaze of the Other, as nature becomes his only epitaph: "In this deep vale / He died,—this seat his only monument" (lines 46–47). The poet, however, is the monument-maker; unlike the self-focused protagonist of whom he writes, it is the poet's very immersion in the social world of words that allows him to inscribe the dead man's absence from a vantage point exterior to the untrammeled nature that the grave marks.

Wordsworth consistently experiments, then, with exaggerating the claims of nature until she blanks out the word; he pushes toward the sublime only to reappropriate voice in the very process of redomesticating nature. Thus we see the narrator in *Peter Bell* suggesting how Peter misses the real source of original potency, since nature can fix signification and stop the incessant sliding of meaning that Peter would dominate with his "lawless life" (line 276), this pretense at an original phallus unbeholden to the Law:

> On a fair prospect some have looked
> And felt, as I have heard them say,
> As if the moving time had been
> A thing as steadfast as the scene
> On which they gazed themselves away. (Lines 266–70)

Peter wants to claim phallic power as his strength while he manages to escape both nature and humankind. He is the most "lawless" of all wild men; he is a thief even of the father's word, a word neither earned nor yet bequeathed. Wordsworth clearly disavows here any Promethean claim to stolen voice, for in *Peter Bell* the would-be possessor must come face-to-face with the dead, lost, and wrongly displaced father. He must learn through Mother Nature, however, the lessons that allow him to restore the dead father to his proper grave and to assume the rightful signs of a living father himself.[7] Peter, we might say, must be castrated by nature for being too harsh a phallic signifier, an outlaw phallus that constitutes a man so savage that "To see him was to fear him" (line 285). Peter must earn the right to signify, and earn it through the mother's lessons on acceding to the lawful legacy.

Peter Bell's trip in the dark maternal woods brings him, for the first time, an awareness of death. In the midst of the "woods, / And rocks that spread a hoary gleam" (lines 391–92), Peter comes upon the ass, a male beast that again becomes a conflated sign of gender as it also suggests the female, both in its muteness and in its physical attenuation of a "proper" male animal, the horse. From this point on, Peter will confront the Other through the stubborn beast that plots his itinerary for him. Peter at first worries that stealing the ass may cause his own imprisonment, but the narrator assures us that Peter "need not fear" (line 390). For while Peter thinks he controls events, he is instead under the determining gaze of the Other and the oedipal dynamics of coming into one's proper signifying function. Reminiscent of the Ancient Mariner's use of his glittering eye, the ass establishes territoriality by turning his eye on Peter. This is the ass's zone, and the outlaw's stick will not preempt the Other's prior claim, regardless of the beatings Peter inflicts. The narrative proceeds by interspersing episodes of

7. Wordsworth appears initially to have hoped that *Peter Bell* located a poetic voice for himself beholden neither to nature nor the law. In 1798 he read the "finished" manuscript to several friends, among them William Hazlitt, who was struck by Wordsworth's own valuation of the poem: "'His face was as a book where men might read strange matters,' and he announced the fate of his hero in prophetic tones" (*The Poetical Works* 2:528). This poem pleased Wordsworth so greatly because he managed to take from Mother Nature just enough to leave Peter Bell free of the father's word, yet not so much that he feared absorption by the mother. Peter Bell returns to society, and the narrator, after being shown his "specialness" vis-à-vis the canoe, is released to tell his story of ordinary man. But Wordsworth's relief is superficial, and the honesty that compels him in "Peele Castle" to renounce the poet's dream of visionary poetry anterior to loss and sorrow also plagues his tentative gestures toward publishing *Peter Bell* until twenty years after its completion.

the ass's gaze with Peter's fear of demonry. An earlier manuscript reads "And now the ass through his left eye / On Peter turned most quietly / Looked quietly in his face" (*The Poetical Works* 2:347); the final version substitutes the ass's ear as the odd signifier that compels Peter to think "Some ugly witchcraft must be here!" (line 417). As Peter "in the pride / of skill" delivers another "sturdy blow" with his staff, "the patient Beast on Peter turned / His shining hazel eye" (lines 423–24, 425, 434–35). The ass then switches his gaze from Peter to the river, tracing the trajectory of identity Peter must follow.

The Lacanian gaze surprises Wordsworth in the role of voyeur as he seeks to define self versus other. Whenever there appears an overly determined description whose emotional content is in excess of its narrative, we witness the poet peeping through the keyhole and being confronted by the gaze of the Other, as in the theft scene of *The Prelude* described above. Here in *Peter Bell* a similar capture by anterior self-defining structure exists. In manuscript 1 we read that with the ass prostrate before Peter, "But one impression did remain / Of his large and shining eye" (*The Poetical Works* 2:350). In the published manuscript, the ass's bray underscores Peter's inability to "break the chain, / In this serene and solemn hour, / Twined round him by demoniac power" (lines 472–74).

The demoniac power is nature's ability to transform Peter even against his will, for nature has his will. A clue to Wordsworthian desire is what Thomas Weiskel calls a "kind of death by plenitude," wherein meaning is overwhelmed by an overdetermination that in its "extreme threatens a state of absolute metaphor," "a universe in which everything is potentially identical with everything else." Weiskel concludes, "Such a state is apocalyptic: a word or signifying segment seems to contain so much that there is nothing we cannot read into it—the word dissolves into the Word" (26). Peter's perceptions of nature slip into illusions of apocalyptic powers, as the

> moon uneasy looked and dimmer,
> The broad blue heavens appeared to glimmer,
> And the rocks staggered all around. (Lines 483–85)

As Peter regains control of himself, the moon appears steady, and nature must saturate his word with her own overripeness again as she

attempts to bring Peter to the self-knowledge of a proper son. The
dead man in the river forwards Peter's own emptying out or ascesis in
the mock death he must experience in order to assume a legitimate,
always alienated self. Peter's "death" to himself is in one sense a reverse
of the aphanisis that marks for Ernest Jones and Lacan the "disap-
pearance of the subject"; Peter's signifier has become too oppressive,
too "materially present" to allow for the breath of a subject at all.
Hence he must lose, temporarily, his signifying phallic function in
order to regain his "self." When "a startling sight / Meets him, among
the inverted trees" (lines 499–500), Peter's reaction is determined by
the gaze of the Other located in an overdetermined nature that has
subsumed all powers of differentiation or distinction unto herself:

> He looks, he cannot choose but look;
> Like some one reading in a book—
> A book that is enchanted. (Lines 518–20)

But in this very collapse of discrete signifiers lurks the threat not
only of nature's extinguishing Peter's present presumptuous voice, but
of her castrating him too thoroughly, which might leave him forever in
silence as well. Nature will be no final resting place for voice. When he
rouses from his first faint, Peter "feels the glimmering of the moon"
and then wakes to find himself "with glazed eye" (lines 537–38). Only
the sight of his staff—his "treasure" (line 542)—reminder of "where
mortals dwell" (line 544), saves him from a second swoon. Yet any sign
of male potency hardens Peter against the identity nature would teach
him, and so, after talking himself out of repentance yet again, he
knocks upon the lid of his "shining horn tobacco-box" "in a light and
careless way, / As men who with their purpose play" (lines 817–19).
Suddenly, as if in response to the manly bravado, the mute, signifying
ass "turned round his head and *grinned*." The narrator admits it is an
"appalling process," a hideous spectacle (lines 825–29). The grin is
contiguous with the rumbling of the earth, and in short order Peter
Bell must confront his evil past and become a new man, determined
against his own will. The sinister association of laughter and reforma-
tion already has occurred in the prologue, of course, where the narrator wants to laugh at those friends who fear his sallies in supernatural
heights. The juxtaposition also appears in "To Joanna," where Joanna's

laugh seems a superior dark knowledge set against Wordsworth's desire to align nature only innocently with rekindled voice.

When Wordsworth locates desire in nature, a metonymic subtext
connects her wisdom with an initiation into her own limitations as she
points back to the human as the source of poetry. Nature's conferral of
death through plenitude turns out to have been a necessary ablution
for Peter, then, as a prelude to a proper anointing by his paternal
lineage. The description that opens the third part links the saturation
and collapse of meaning (the mysterious word that appears in the
darkness and educates its reader [lines 754–55]) with nature's final
inundation that teaches Peter his identity at last. The word in the
Godly book that opens the third part echoes the words that nature
imposed on Peter earlier in the enchanted book that forces his gaze
(lines 518–20).

Peter is ascending to the place of the lawful paternal signifier, as his
journey on the ass mimics "that day / When Jesus humbly deigned to
ride, / Entering the proud Jerusalem" (lines 976–78). He has sensed a
relationship to a dead father early, as he puzzled over the reflection in
the water. He literally becomes more entangled with the dead man as
he entwines his sapling among the man's hair and pulls him out of the
water, recognizing in the act that the man must have been the master of
the ass, a position Peter will now assume. As the ass carries Peter to the
dead man's home, the daughter mistakes in yet another metonymic
displacement: "My father! here's my father" (line 1005). We already
know, through the son's earnest search for him, of this dead father's
proper paternal nature. In manuscript 4 the father's goodness is even
more strongly emphasized:

> Poor Robin loved his Father well
> For often by the hand he led
> Sweet Robin over hill and height
> And oft with his own hand at night
> He laid him on the bed. (2:361)

Sympathetic toward the widow's grief, Peter longs "to press her to
his heart" (line 1079), for now he is able, metaphorically at least, to
assume the role of the dead father. "Pale as death" (line 1031), he has
stuttered, with the same weak voice of the narrator who begins Peter's

story, his tale to the widow. But as Peter's rebirth into the legitimate word is completed, he loses his breathlessness: "Nature, through a world of death, / Breathes into him a second breath" (lines 1073–74). The mother has taught him his proper relationship to the omnipotent phallic signifier, his inevitable involvement with generation, and the need to wait until proper integration with the community to speak in phallic fullness.[8] We might be excused for assuming that the poet framing the story, or the narrator creating his fanciful prologue, is relieved to write himself into an acceptable family paradigm where the purchase of power leaves him with something of his own still left to say, for the prologue's puffery is the true conflict of *Peter Bell*: the contest between a self-achieved authority and a society that would have the poet speak its communal word. That the poem is not wholly successful, either in binding formally the two stories together or in engaging the reader in the fate of Peter Bell, reminds us of Wordsworth's unhappy intuition over the location—and price—of voicing desire, a tension whose irresolution nonetheless creates the context for his strongest poetry.

8. Michael Friedman also pursues the line of reasoning that Wordsworth internalized the father, but he arrives at very different conclusions from my own; see Friedman, 5 and 7, for example. Alan Bewell usefully connects Peter's entrance into human society with the role of narrative: "The interrelation of imagination, fear, memory, language, and punishment has been shown to be central to the development of the primitive mind" (342). Furthermore, it is helpful to connect Wordsworth's figure with his probable historical counterpart, Peter Bell, the "wild boy" of Hanover, whose lack of linguistic ability figured heavily in Daniel Defoe's fascinated eighteenth-century account (Bewell 330).

PART II

Shelley: The Frustrated Intercourse of Poetic Ecstasy

Every thought is also a prison.
—EMERSON, "The Poet"

Chapter 4

The Familial Subtext of Desire

The exciting dialogue being spoken today over Percy Bysshe Shelley's philosophical relationship with language, central to any understanding of the poet's linguistic engagements, locates ambivalence as Shelley's most consistent response to the contingencies of language.[1] While certainly refusing the idea of an enervating fatalism (one cannot accuse Shelley's verse of a lack of energy or variety), I wish to emphasize my own swerve from current discourse on this subject. I find Shelley's *frustration* at the bondage of language, rather than an ambivalence, both a more consistent and a more enabling part of his poetic motivation. Furthermore, I am willing to discuss his poetry in terms that at first glance suggest a naive conflation on my part of fictive (poetic) characters and authorial biography; but from a psychoanalytic perspective, I am instead tracing the textual contours shaped by a particular Shelleyan literary desire. Hegel's dialectic of power asserts that desire assumes its proper place only if the victory of master over slave is kept, to some degree, symbolic; a total ascendancy of desire, inattentive to biological imperatives, would result in a Pyrrhic victory, for the slave would be dead. Lacan accepted such limitations and made

1. See, for strong examples of the last decade's different renderings of linguistic pressure on Shelley's canon, Leslie Brisman, Richard Cronin, Jerrold E. Hogle, D. J. Hughes, and William Keach.

of them a claim to be our contemporary Romantic philosopher of the art of the incomplete, the longing for the infinite that consecrates what we term the Romantic. Shelley, however, refused a metaphorical tri- umph and instead wrote out his own discourse of desire to its logical if ontologically apocalyptic end.

I will now sketch the outlines of familiar questions of power, debt, and language in Shelley's companion pieces, "Hymn to Intellectual Beauty" and "Mont Blanc," wherein he sets up his representational strategies of self-advocacy versus systemic determination. These poems, because of their highly abstract semantic and syntactic level, have received extensive commentary through the years. I shall not attempt to adjudicate these exemplary, subtle, and detailed readings, for such is not to my point: I wish to use the poems (rather than explicate them, which, as I have suggested, is an end addressed else- where) as a ghost-tracked family paradigm informing my subsequent discussions of Shelley, even when I do not explicitly invoke these terms. In this rapid recovery of familial economies activating the philosophi- cal content of these poems (and, to some extent, in the discussion of *Prometheus Unbound,* which concludes this chapter), I will risk a more nearly allegorical mode than elsewhere, homologies set up between Lacan and Shelley, in a belief that what become heavily invested terms will serve more subtle and imminent heuristic purposes in the analyses that follow.[2]

Written in 1816, "Hymn to Intellectual Beauty," if read as invoca- tion to maternal voice, functions as a complex precursor to the confu- sions of paternal phallic power that inform "Mont Blanc." The "unseen Power" the speaker invokes in the first line is "Like memory of music fled / . . . dearer for its mystery" (lines 10, 12). As the mirror that will both reflect and idealize its onlooker in the paradisal mother/child dyad, the Spirit of Beauty "dost consecrate / With thine own hues all thou dost shine upon / Of human thought or form" (lines 13–15). But the child is betrayed by the mother's inability to ward off the inheri- tance of a fallen world:

2. Stuart M. Sperry mentions in passing the plausible connection between the pos- sibilities for prophetic change acted out in "Mont Blanc" and *Prometheus Unbound,* poems usually not considered together: "'Mont Blanc' . . . is in many ways a preliminary sketch for *Prometheus*" (*Shelley's Major Verse,* 68).

> where art thou gone?
> Why dost thou pass away and leave our state,
> This dim vast vale of tears, vacant and desolate? (Lines 15–17)

Freud, in his speculative essay "The Antithetical Nature of Primal Words," explores the nature of ancient Egyptian lexicons that combined in a single word opposite elements, so that "youngold" meant only "old" or "lovehate" meant only "hate." Thus he discloses the ancient intuition of what is now a linguistic commonplace: meaning resides in differential relations, not in similarity. Shelley too was aware of the conditions of meaning, and of deictic instabilities: in "On Life" he asserted that "the words *I*, and *you* and *they* are grammatical devices invented simply for arrangement and totally devoid of the intense and exclusive sense usually attached to them" (*Poetry and Prose*, 478). Or, further, "By the word *things* is to be understood any object of thought, that is, any thought upon which any other thought is employed with any apprehension of distinction" (*Poetry and Prose*, 478). It is precisely this understanding of the constitutive role of language in thought that energizes Shelley's most abstruse poetry as he explores the possibilities for an escape from a seemingly inescapable prior determination.[3]

Following the self-conscious stutterings toward recuperation of an organic whole in stanza 1, the poet locates the moment that language enters and dooms the subject to the truth of the never fully compensated Edenic fall from meaning predicated upon sameness, and to a new condition of iteration based on difference. Thus, coincident with the attempt to understand why the Spirit has suddenly withdrawn is the accompanying wisdom that refers at the same time to her replacement: we must ask

> Why fear and dream and death and birth
> Cast on the daylight of this earth
> Such gloom,—why man has such a scope
> For love and hate, despondency and hope? (Lines 21–24)

3. I here swerve from Keach's general position (esp. chap. 1) that Shelley was ambivalent toward more than convinced of the constitutive role of language in thought. Though his *Defence* shows such a vacillation, and, indeed, in many ways "On Life" undercuts its own linguistic insights by asserting that mind perceives, not creates, my reading of his poetry reveals a voice always seeking solutions against the first claim that language makes. Thus I would appropriate Keach's provocative discussion of speed in *Alastor* (chap. 5) to my own purpose of showing a poet frantic to break through a corrupt signifying system.

Since there is no speech outside the one thrust upon the infant, "No voice from some sublimer world hath ever / To sage or poet these responses given" (lines 25–26). Only as the Spirit becomes identified with poetic afflatus in stanza 3 is any deliverance from the "vale of tears" (line 17) possible. The Spirit gives "grace and truth to life's unquiet dream" (line 36), in a poetic condensation of opposite functions in one dream: the unquiet dream attendant upon a life-in-language, and the equally unsettling dream of an illusory paradise that the adult "remembers." If this Spirit would live forever within the human subject, such a subject would gain priority over those who want to preempt it: it would be "immortal, and omnipotent" (line 39). The maternal nourishment this Spirit could afford is "Like darkness to a dying flame" (line 45)—in yet another over-determined symbol, wherein the flame enacts the detumescent phallic signifier that is always fading, both in its inability to articulate need and in its indebtedness at every turn to signifiers that precede it. But the burning coals of poetic imagination, diminishing, according to Shelley's famous assertion in his *Defence*, before the real voice can speak itself, are illuminated to the degree that primal maternal darkness reclaims that indebted flame.

Stanza 5, with its Wordsworthian resonance of childhood anointment, is peculiarly un-Wordsworthian in its emphatic dissociation from prior authorities that inform the child's evolution into selfhood. "I was not heard—I saw them not" (line 54). It is poison to talk "with the departed dead" (line 52). But precisely when nature bids the earth awake to spring, the "shadow" (line 59) of an engendering power befalls the philosopher already "musing deeply on the lot / Of life" (lines 55–56), causing him to shriek and clasp his hands "in extacy" (line 60). Sexually charged when it bespeaks union with the narrator's primal soul mate, this erotically marked language translates elsewhere into his epipsyche. The passion accelerates in stanza 6:

> I vowed that I would dedicate my powers
>   To thee and thine—have I not kept the vow?
>   With beating heart and streaming eyes, even now
> I call the phantoms of a thousand hours
> Each from his voiceless grave. (Lines 61–65)

The speaker has been true to his first lover, making her the object of his powers, sending his thousand hopes to the grave unspoken rather than subject them to the defile of the signifier. The "dark slavery" (line 70) from which the poet hopes the "awful LOVELINESS" (line 71) will deliver him encodes the enslavement of language that creates in its gaps the speaker's desire. The Spirit is to "give whate'er these words cannot express" (line 72)—a thought in excess of its utterance.

Stanza 7 acknowledges the impossibility of sustaining life in the shadow's intensity. Although the blazing "noon" (line 74) of the Spirit's revelatory spring powers accedes to the adult belatedness of autumn, providing its own (solemn) harmony, the curious lines that follow encourage us to question the stability of this new acceptance. The Spirit's power is still invoked to supply "my onward life . . . / Its calm" (lines 80–81), even though the calm is ostensibly already present in the autumnal usurpation of noon. Furthermore, this peace-through-the-Spirit is analogous, the poet claims, to that which "nature on my passive youth / Descended" (lines 79–80). Yet what nature provided in stanza 5 was far from calm, but the ecstasy of reunion with that original image instead. Thus embedded in concluding language redolent of resolved conflict is the relentless drive of a desire that structures, psychologically and linguistically, the rest of Shelley's canon, and that creates the conflict of the companion to this poem, "Mont Blanc."[4]

In "Mont Blanc," composed only days after "Hymn," the narrator stands in awe before the appropriation of his world by the father. In deprecating his poem as "an undisciplined overflowing of the soul," Shelley also pointed to its subject as psychological truth.[5] Dynamics of desire that become a full-fledged dialectic in Shelley's later poetry are only hinted at here, but for a sense of the evolution of his heavily familial textual investments, we do well to sketch the tensions of "Mont Blanc" as we have its companion poem. For we will have to confront,

4. I mean to use the word "canon" somewhat polemically here, in that I am calling upon Stuart Curran's protest against an older tradition of taking Shelley's poetry as a grab bag of sorts, a number of separate, basically unrelated works. Instead, as Curran remarks, Shelley "had attached himself to the line of visionary poets who write a canon rather than an idle succession of individual flights of fancy" (xv).

5. "Mont Blanc" is replete with attempts to work one's way into—and then out of—a determining system of symbols. Particularly compelling in this poem is Shelley's collapse of the Freudian question of a mountain's gender into a brilliant bisexuality, so that Mont Blanc represents both pleasure and menace at the same time (Rapaport, 67–68). Herman Rapaport, however, defines Shelley's mountain as *only* maternal (67), although a "phallic mother" (70) when she becomes aligned with death. In contrast, I take as Shelley's most impressive achievement in this poem his alternation of male and female roles, a characteristic of what Rapaport acknowledges as "Shelley's fascination with images possessing a radical ambivalence with regard to the difference of life and death" (63).

everywhere we turn, Shelley's overwhelming realization of the determining powers of phallic discourse, be they linguistic or imagistic in nature.[6]

Shelley appears to valorize a power that pervades all life, a power suggested by the inaccessibility of the "piercing" mountain, "Mont Blanc." Yet there is a defensive sidestepping of the question of indebtedness, as Shelley would seem to invest in the equally typical Romantic program of subject/object delineation. The psychological undercurrents, however, already reveal a poet aware of what Ernest Jones would anxiously discover one hundred years later: the predominance of the phallus as emblem of life's determination. What Jones wanted to hide, in his horror over a phallocentric language, was the male textuality in which all social order comes inscribed (Gallop, *Daughter's Seduction*, 18). In 1816, Shelley already saw in nature the reminders of that phallic determination; but typical of the poet's resolution to create his own symbolism, he incorporates the usual symbolic use of mountain for breast into the role of phallic signifier, an inversion that evokes well the matrix of familial desire. Such a conflation of gender anticipates Jane Harrison's anthropological recasting of the "cultural meaning of mountains" into a "symbolic field in which the rival perspectives of male and female dominance struggled near the dawn of western culture," a field that creates a context of "social differentiation and conflict" (Randel, 515).[7]

In gazing upon the "Dizzy Ravine" (line 34), the narrator in "Mont Blanc" experiences a revery enabling him to achieve a sense of his "own separate phantasy" (line 36): his own mind, which becomes so passive that the universe can flow through it. He experiences in effect that oceanic feeling that Freud claims characterizes the infant's unbounded sense of life before the introduction of the Oedipus conflict. Emblematic of the fluid feminine symbol, the ravine will imply, by the end of the poem, "the breath and blood of distant lands" (line 124), words echoing birth itself. The paradisal glories of the maternal union will

6. Richard Payne Knight and Thomas Wright's 1788 book, *Sexual Symbolism: A History of Phallic Worship*, glosses Homer in such a way as to emphasize the uniting through fire of the three symbols of creator, destroyer, and preserver, with fire functioning as a supreme phallic emblem (147). If "Ode to the West Wind" most overtly enacts such a scheme, Shelley's other poems are clearly informed by its context as well.

7. Fred V. Randel's useful analysis of the Mont Blanc landscape as combining both "maternal and paternal qualitites" (525) in Mary Shelley's *Frankenstein* cites a synthesis of Wordsworth and Coleridge as her source, but it is also possible that she saw Mont Blanc through her husband's interpretation, which I present here.

visit the "still cave of the witch Poesy" (line 44); will, in fact, become the very object of the narrator's poetry.

But the father intrudes—as always, unannounced and unwelcomed—in lines that help illuminate Lacan's interest in the ancient ritual of lifting the veil off the universal phallus. The narrator abruptly interrupts his musing over the primal space of sleep and death in order to signal the entrance of Mont Blanc:

> —I look on high;
> Has some unknown omnipotence unfurled
> The veil of life and death? (Lines 52–54)

The mountain's preeminence overwhelms the narrator; his "spirit fails, / Driven like a homeless cloud from steep to steep" (lines 57–58). In a strong defensive reaction Shelley celebrates the silence of this mountain—"a silent snow" perhaps once enveloped by "a sea / Of fire" (lines 73–74). The psychic dynamic informing his poem becomes an identification with Mont Blanc: he incorporates it into himself and becomes the primal phallus that, even if once determined by the phallic fire of those who preceded him, has somehow escaped their enslaving words and reclaimed with his own "mysterious tongue" the original silence of the true poet. William Keach reminds us that "only in the paradoxical myth of an original 'infancy of society' when 'language itself is poetry' . . . is Shelley momentarily able to celebrate the power of words over thought," a myth that locates silence at the heart of poetry, since the "Latin *infans*, means 'unable to speak,' as Shelley certainly knew" (41).

In his bid for the ennobling nature of his reclaimed primal voice, Shelley assumes a Wordsworthian position opposite in its optimism to his fear in subsequent years of dispossessing others through his own bequeathed voice:

> Thou has a voice, great Mountain, to repeal
> Large codes of fraud and woe; not understood
> By all, but which the wise, and great, and good
> Interpret, or make felt, or deeply feel. (Lines 80–83)

But the last six lines of the poem suggest the conflicts already informing Shelley's search for an authentic voice. The silence of the originary

phallus that Mont Blanc symbolizes registers a paradox in that the
phallic signifier implies the sound of the father, the *absence* of silence.

> The secret strength of things
> Which governs thought, and to the infinite dome
> Of heaven is as a law, inhabits thee!
> And what were thou, and earth, and stars, and sea,
> If to the human mind's imaginings
> Silence and solitude were vacancy? (Lines 139–44)

If the silence of that law is a mere construction of poetic desire—if
it is an illusion of unmediated vision rather than truly originary—then
the entire paradigm for power relations in "Mont Blanc" reveals itself
as fantasy. The "secret strength" becomes transparent again as the inescapable Name-of-the-Father who desecrated forever the primal place of
silence the poet would inhabit. What Jerrold Hogle might call the
power of the displaced metaphor, we can extend by naming that psycholinguistic maneuver, language as the displacing sign of the father
("Shelley's Poetics," 166). For Torquato Tasso's dictum, four times
cited in Shelley's writings, to be true ("None deserves the name of
creator except God and the Poet"), the poet must lay claim to becoming himself the signifier par excellence. Shelley indeed, as current wisdom has it, rewrites Wordsworth. As early as "Mont Blanc," he exposes
his suspicion that divinity of any sort is always already enslaved in
(male) generation, an inherited subtext to language that in *Alastor*, for
instance, he will try to outrun; that in *Prometheus Unbound*, he will
determine to renounce; and that in *Epipsychidion* he will curve back in
on itself. The uncanny energy of "Mont Blanc" that has created a
critical history of extraordinarily voluminous explication underwrites
the economy of Shelley's other texts as well.

Shelley everywhere rails against the father's intrusion into his
paradise—to an extent that argues that he was compellingly aware of
the male, patriarchal tradition that asserted claims upon him. In his
personal life he strove to usurp determination by "real" fathers. During
a visit to Montanvert, for example, he gave legendary notice of his
commitment to escape a paternally inscribed Law by signing the guest
register at the inn as "democrat, philanthropist, and atheist" (White,
209). In this now-famous declaration, Shelley implies his nonallegi-

ance to the monarchical fathers of his own country; his disdain of those goods inherited from the father; and his denial of the priority of a divine father. All three denials of the father are inscribed repeatedly in his canon as well as in his life, whether he is (tacitly) encouraging the Irish to rebel, writing poems of revolution, giving away his inherited estate to all who ask—particularly to a God(winian) father who financially becomes Shelley's son—or denigrating a religion that enslaved rather than freed the soul.

Even in his fervent elevation of favorite literature Shelley trumpets his flight from an alienating Law. He writes James Hogg in 1811 of Antigone's morality: "Did she wrong, when she acted in direct, in noble violation of the laws of a prejudiced society?" (*Letters*, 68). But Antigone's obsession is to bury her brother properly, to elude the specter of an empty grave that too closely represents her father. Furthermore, entangled with this aim is her need to defy Lawgiver Creon's "prejudice"—his prejudgment through the social order of language—in her attempt to bury that very Name-of-the-Father Creon evokes. It is also felicitous, at the least, that Antigone is implicated in the oedipal conflict that Sophocles intuited long before Freud.[8]

8. I want to take this opportunity to juxtapose several important critical statements, hoping as I do so to pressure them into yielding a collocation of congruent but strongly individualist insights. Thomas Weiskel, in alluding to the Romantic poet's attempt to transcend heritage, cites the passage from *Paradise Lost* where Satan both ascribes his identity *to* the Father and yet reveals his need to wrest identity *from* him:

> Ah wherefore! He descried no such return
> From me, whom he created what I was
> In that bright eminence, and with his good
> Upbraided none; nor was his service hard.
> What could be less than to afford him praise,
> The easiest recompense, and pay him thanks,
> How due! Yet all his good proved ill in me,
> And wrought but malice; lifted up so high
> I deigned subjection, and though one step higher
> Would set me highest, and in a moment quit
> The debt immense of endless gratitude,
> So burdensome still paying, still to owe;
> Forgetful what from him I still received,
> And understood not that a grateful mind
> By owing owes not, but still pays, at once
> Indebted and discharged; what burden then?
>   (Milton, *Paradise Lost*, IV. 42–57)

As Weiskel claims, "Satan cannot really answer his own question, except by appealing to an inner necessity for which—the last irony—he has only his Father's terms" (9). It is this Satan that inhabits Shelley most, this Miltonic truth that structures the belated poet's desire. Harold Bloom leads us slightly astray when he asserts that "Shelley is captured by Milton"

Older criticism that faulted Shelley for his irreligious attitude toward the divine misses its own wisdom. Years ago Douglas Bush articulated a common complaint: "One looks in vain in a poet exempt from awe for any recognition of Christ's first and great commandment" (158). Yet it was precisely Shelley's awe at the overwhelming, oppressive truth implied in that commandment—at the positioning of a primal father who will determine all voice—that constituted his own poetic speech. Blake believed that he "must Create a System or be enslav'd by another Man's." But such a belief demands that would-be original poets blink at the burdens they will place on others. Perhaps because Shelley's poetic desire took shape as such bold relief against the claims of generation, even though he was keen at the same time to serve as a conduit to other vatic voices from the past, he refused for the most part to embrace the myth that an unenchained system is possible. Most poets who discover this truth can agree to live and write in illusion. Czelaw Milosz, for instance, who speaks from his own place of exile, acknowledges: "Alas, it is enough [for a poet] to publish his first volume of poems to find himself entrapped. For hardly has the print dried, when that work, which seemed to him the most personal, appears to be enmeshed in the style of another. The only way to counter an obscure remorse is to continue searching and to publish a new book, but then everything repeats itself, so there is no end to that chase" (11). Or poets such as Wordsworth intuit the wisdom of which Paul de Man speaks; and they write on in the hope that the need for constant new beginnings justifies them as writing in good faith: "The poet can only start his work because he is willing to forget that this presumed beginning is, in fact, the repetition of a previous failure, resulting precisely from an inability to begin anew. When we think that we are perceiving the assertion of a new origin, we are in fact witnessing the reassertion of a failure to originate."[9]

(*Poetry,* 98). It is not Milton who is the bogey but a language predicated on paternal terms, a language that qua language must consist of those terms. Thus, where Tilottama Rajan, for instance, claims as Shelley's position that "the external world is reducible to mental certitudes" (*Dark Interpreter,* 248n.), we might counter with Shelley's final knowledge that the external world is instead irreducible: It precedes him everywhere. This stance toward mind as being always already engendered by the system into which one is born is, of course, strikingly at home in contemporary linguistic theory. And, as Stuart Peterfreund remarks, "Whatever the notional and descriptive adequacy of Shelley's ideas may be, those ideas certainly place him far ahead of his poetic and linguistic contemporaries" (384).

9. De Man quoted in Brisman, *Romantic Origins,* 15.

Shelley's account of a way out of familial, linguistic entrapment is *Prometheus Unbound,* which stands as the poet's one dazzlingly optimistic account of an (evolutionary) escape from the patriarchal prison into which human beings are born. While it is as daring as its precursor *Paradise Lost,* it is also desperate in a way that Milton's epic is not. For while Milton could offer a paradise within—the God without no longer the only originator—Shelley wanted an Eden lacking any trace of God at all. Douglas Bush reminds us that in the opening of Aeschylus's *Prometheus Bound,* "the hero maintains a silence almost unendurable" as he is nailed to the rocks (145). We can hold, I think, that Shelley understood the truth of that heroism and wrote *Prometheus Unbound* across Aeschylus to see if there was any other response possible for the myth's modern-day heir. He took the position, however briefly he could sustain it, that precisely because the language he lived in had always been corrupt, had always been *stolen* through a Promethean theft from the gods, the restitution of that theft might cause an apocalyptic transformation of its object and a new language of humanity.

It is not surprising, although it is certainly rewarding to those interested in tracking the evolving shape of a poet's psychological and philosophical grammars, to find in what is generally regarded as Shelley's supreme achievement the paradigm that, without much exaggeration, we could insist underwrites the rest of his canon. *Prometheus Unbound* deals with the procreation of speech, the conditions of its debt, both before and after its present moment of utterance, and with its inherent master/slave configurations which, even in the pain of dispossession, therein offer a possible slippage from the oppressive repetition of a Jupiter that rapes or penetrates everything. In *Julian and Maddalo,* begun during the same period, the poet worries that dispossession is all there is; *Epipsychidion,* written over a year after *Prometheus* was finished, may well offer the most subtle negotiation of the problems mythologized in this prior poem, with Emilia Viviani providing the tool for Shelley to think through to an alterity that lets him have it both ways: to achieve saturated meaning even as he defers a deadening linguistic consummation.

From its opening moment, *Prometheus Unbound* announces that it means to break boundaries. Shelley will reconceptualize the Greek master through *not* imitating him: form is undone, "Unbound," as the subtitle ("A Lyrical Drama in Four Acts") prominently declares in its

generic contortion that undoes drama through its leaning upon the
lyric while at the same time, of course, dialogizing it. Nonetheless, in
the preface, Shelley takes pains to cast the principle of repetition (as
well as the inheritance of tradition) into form itself, whereby an *appearance* of mastery is available to lesser talents on the principle of imitation
alone; but the *strong* poet is described in terms redolent of the *Defence*
as well as emblematic of the Promethan fire-giver himself: "the spirit of
[great poets'] genius . . . must be the uncommunicated lightning of
their own mind" (134). Shelley's prefatory boldness that compares his
lineage with that of Homer, Aeschylus, Virgil, Dante, Shakespeare,
and their epochal counterparts (135) sets up the real point of this
situating of poet in society: a way of dealing with the contingency of
any would-be revolutionary voice. It is from such a literary and historical context, in fact, that a compromise (albeit an uneasy one) can be
effected: "Poets . . . are in one sense the creators and in another the
creations of their age" (135)—though surely with the implication already previously established that some poet may possess the "lightning" to illuminate the culture anew. In other words, the preface is an
extraordinary adumbration of the entire thesis worked out in the
poem, with the overt stationing of its writer envisioning the triumph
that was denied, as we will examine later, in the early attempt in *Alastor*
to frame a poet's vocation through a second poet's tale.

   While it would be difficult not to react to the dominant tone of
optimism in *Prometheus Unbound*, it is easy to miss the near-institution-
alizing of Shelley's utopian solution in his preface, wherein he suggests
a progressive dialectical rendering of history directly enacted by the
power of poets upon their age, a history whose teleology can be known
to the present only as a positive end, the terminus ad quem of strong
(Promethean) activity: "The great writers of our own age are, we have
reason to suppose, the companions and forerunners of some unim-
agined change in our social condition or the opinions which cement it.
The cloud of mind is discharging its collected lightning, and the equi-
librium between institutions and opinions is now restoring, or is about
to be restored" (134). And this poem implicitly vexes the linearly
understood movement of time, as it implies the irrelevance of ages that
are, in one sense, secondary in weight to the ability of language to
speak its own time, its own place. The "Three thousand years of sleep-
unsheltered hours" (I.12) are no more oppressive than the countless

"moments" that in their misery might as well each be a year instead (I.13). The opening of the poem establishes what will be the contrast to its conclusion: "No change, no pause, no hope!" (I. 24); the negation of these negations instantiates, at the end of act IV, the very possibility of earthly renovation that knows no end, that in its cyclical urgency forever undoes the stasis of Prometheus's curse, through which earth's potential champion had submitted, by reproducing his genealogical past, to a changeless view of the world.

The potency of speaking one's own poetic word offsets a dissatisfaction with the limitations of the ordinary ways of seeing, in the process articulating the excess that motivates art, which outspans a more ratiocinative mode. *Prometheus Unbound* translates such a dynamics into one of our most brilliant literary examples of a personal libidinal economy underwriting a social program of universal realization. In direct relation to what Shelley has set up in the preface, Prometheus hears the curse he originally uttered against Jupiter recounted by a Phantasm of the paternal God himself, but in a totally thoughtless— that is to say, formal—language, whereby that language is emptied of meaning at the hands of an odd conflation of the father voicing the son's own indictment of the progenitor: language thus disengaged from the curse and translated into a neutralized conduit for signification, a form waiting to be textualized by the one who hears. "Speak the words which I would hear," Prometheus tells the Phantasm of Jupiter, "Although no thought inform thine empty voice" (I.248–49). Furthermore, it has been established clearly that only a language of the dead can reinform Prometheus's wrongful attempt to usurp the tyrant through the medium that best serves humankind as an instrument of blessing that repeats progressively, rather than of curse that regressively figures itself in the image of that which it would undo. Freud tells us that we repeat because we cannot remember, a psychology necessary to the movement of this play. Prometheus reencounters the scene in order to be set free; through a narrative displacement that frees the hero even more than enactment through his own memory alone, Shelley makes pivotal the remembering, or rather, the re-membering, of the curse by Prometheus, but through Jupiter's phantasmic contaminated medium of discourse that begins the process of self-consumption: it eats itself up as it remembers in the name of the defiant son. It is precisely the repetition of the curse at the Other's tongue that allows "The Titan" to

be "unvanquished still" (I.315), to belong both to the past as a constitutive historical moment, and to be purified, to confront "thoughtless" form that awaits his self-gestation.

In Shelley's *Prometheus*, the fire-giver is importantly implicated in
the original enslavement of man, an identification close to Shelley's
honest concern for enchaining others through *his* legacy. In act II Asia
reveals that the one "law alone" that Prometheus gave to Jupiter when
he helped enthrone him was to "[l]et man be free (II.iv.45)." But
Prometheus was grievously shortsighted, for it is precisely the nature
of law to disavow man's freedom. Prometheus himself enchains humankind to law at the very time that he means to achieve the common
good: he gives the gift of speech and, "speech created thought / Which
is the measure of the universe" (II.iv.72–73). Thus Prometheus must
renounce his *own* speech in order to offer humanity true freedom.

At this point, it is well to rehearse Stuart Curran's genealogy of
Shelley's Prometheus myth. Originating in a *negative* prototype, the
conception seemed at an early stage to emphasize the enervating effects
of filial theft. As he found no way outside such a theft to claim a voice,
however, Shelley ameliorated his judgment of Prometheus. In the
notes to *Queen Mab*, Shelley created a Prometheus whose influence
upon mankind was pernicious; by stealing fire he had introduced the
cooking and consumption of flesh.[10] In Lacanian terms, Shelley revealed the curse of the Lawgiver, the inevitable incorporation of his
son that follows upon the father's "gift" to his offspring, because that
gift is always an illicit one.[11] But in *The Revolt of Islam*, as Curran
remarks, Laon signifies a Prometheus figure chained to a cave until a
Hermit rescues him and places him underground (36). Thus the thematic movement is toward the valorization of silence that always flits
around the edges of Shelley's poetry, with both the Hermit and the
cavern representing unnamed space. Such a poetic economy works in a

10. See esp. Curran, 36. And in 1819 when Shelley wrote his satire *Peter Bell the Third*,
his sense of the poem's inadequacy would reconfirm his suspicion that to appropriate another's voice, if only to mock it, always implicates the poet in the other's weakness (Curran,
150–52).

11. At the same time, the (Shelleyan) Promethean gift is brilliantly bifurcated into putative identity through the introjection of son into father *and* absolute difference, the impossibility of the phallus ever to stabilize generation and dissemination. Barbara Johnson's well-
known defense of Lacan's phallus against Derrida's charge of transcendental grounding
describes Shelley's phallic tectonics as well: "What Lacan means by saying that the letter
cannot be divided is thus not that the phallus must remain intact, but that the phallus, the
letter, and the signifier *are not substances*. The letter cannot be divided because it only
functions *as* a division" (495).

way similar to Lacan's appropriation of Saussure's famous paradigm: $\frac{S}{s}$ becomes the new system of meaning wherein the signifier, the phallic word carried off by the Promethean theft of fire, is barred from entrance (Laon enchained on a column) to the cave of womblike priority, the world of the signified where desire has not yet entered and established the gap. Or the column at the hilltop cave's entrance serves yet another linguistic function: as Lacan's $\mathcal{S}$, the subject barred forever from authenticity and from access to prior existence. It is precisely the silence that the column holds in abeyance that is the object of Shelley's poetic quest.

In *Prometheus Unbound*, however, Shelley achieves an extraordinary reversal of the death that silence usually marks. The extent to which Zoroastrian contexts inform *Prometheus Unbound* reinforces our hermeneutical use of the conflated fire/phallus:[12] "The basic ritual of Zoroastrianism, the worship of fire and, by extension, of the sun, establishes an immediate correspondence with the myth of Prometheus" (Curran 69). Zoroaster dwelt in flames at the summit of Mount Albordj until, "enveloped by that essential energy, [he] translated it into its earthly manifestation, the sacred laws of the ancient Persians." Thus Zoroaster is "representative lawgiver" (69). We might yoke the two Shelleyan images of poet as Promethean fire-bearer and poet as "legislator of the universe" in much the same way. The paternal phallus is the link between the two roles: it is both the fire of elemental procreation and the Law that speaks the universe. In the Promethean flame that simultaneously achieves the extinguishing of the old and the fiery birth of the new, Shelley solves the problem of passing on to those who follow him an antecedent fire; he will assert that the flame *must* come full circle and be reclaimed by the apocalypse anew.[13]

If we are tempted to doubt the radical responsibility Shelley was willing to assign his fellow beings, we need only to recall that he

12. For a useful psychological genealogy of the importance of "stealing fire," see Leon Waldoff ("Father-Son Conflict," 81–82). In general, Waldoff's study, *because* it tends (at times unfortunately) to allegorize familial configurations into Freudian niches, serves a student of this poem well as an initial and important mapping out of genetic father-son paradigmatic power struggles.

13. Carol Jacobs glosses elegantly the open-endedness of this poem's "conclusion" through the ontological slipperiness of "he who refuses to be named," Demogorgon, nonetheless assuming the burden of "Eternity" in answer to Jupiter's "what art thou?" For Jacobs, "Eternity . . . [functions] as the perpetual disruption of temporal and spatial stasis, a disruption already at play, in a sense, in Prometheus's first monologue. As in 'The Necessity of Atheism,' eternity (or necessity) is the questioning of the concept of origin; it is the pronounced incomprehensibility of first cause and, it goes without saying, then, of telos" (57).

composed *The Cenci*, that extraordinary account of paternal decadence and decay, between acts III and IV of *Prometheus Unbound*. It is as if, after the Spirit of the Hour unequivocally maps out in act III the new language, Shelley explores with Beatrice the vulnerability of individual will-to-good over the ageless accretion of paternal evils.[14] After completing this exploration into incest and parricide, Shelley then returns to his redemptive drama with the qualifying wisdom that Jupiter's phallic potency may penetrate the new world; but that with the power of the poet (any renovated being) as *legislator*, Jupiter himself can be castrated again. The last two acts of this poem locate the optimistic resolution of Shelley's desire in a joyful conclusion seen as fully only in his "Ode to the West Wind," "Hymn to Apollo," and his *Defence*.

Jupiter's speech to his assembled cohorts in heaven summarizes nicely the indebtedness of mortals to a preordained language and the polluting effects of that Law. Jupiter's inclusion of the assembled deities in his own omnipotence points precisely to the dilemma: these other powers are consequently derivative of the Greater God. All that troubles Jupiter now is the insurrection of that as yet "unextinguished fire" (III.i.5) with which the mortals below keep trying to penetrate his empire. Jupiter wishes to fill the gap in existence with his own voice; he will foreclose that space where biological being becomes human in language through his eternal fixing of a divine paternal sign. It will be "Heaven's wine" (III.i.25) that "fill[s] the daedal cups like fire" (III.i.26). But in a clever inversion of Shelley's own myth of the epipsyche, here Jupiter's recounting of his visionary maid's reception of her lover constitutes a paradigm for the loss of self that paternal penetration causes:

> "Insufferable might!
> God! spare me! I sustain not the quick flames,
> The penetrating presence; all my being,
> Like him whom the Numidian seps did thaw
> Into a dew with poison, is dissolved,
> Sinking through its foundation"— (III.i.37–42)

14. As Peter Thorslev has suggested, *The Cenci* especially impresses upon us "the sense of the past as being parasitic upon the future; of fathers, authorities, institutions, and traditions having outlived their usefulness, but being unwilling to grow old gracefully and wither away and even attempting grotesquely to renew their youth by devouring their young or by reproducing upon them" (47).

The emblem of the flame again marries the fire and phallus—the suggestion both of power and of suffocating antecedence. In a text well known to Shelley, Bishop Berkeley, seventy-five years earlier, had defined "pure invisible aether" in a way that incorporates well the phallic image: "So quick in its motions, so subtle and penetrating in its nature, so extensive in its effects, it seemeth no other than the vegetative soul or vital spirit of the world" (Curran, 107). Beatrice's description of Cenci's "penetrating presence"—"A clinging, black, contaminating mist / About me" (III.i.17–18)—also implies self-loss through the paternal fire.[15] Thus the fire that marks the Promethean myth as ennobler of human life likewise contains within itself a sign of alienated other.

Occasionally, as we have seen, Shelley worries that, in addition to lived experience, eternity itself may lay a claim to priority. When Demogorgon identifies himself to Jupiter as "Eternity—demand no direr name" (III.i.52), and then insists that the eternal alliance of indebtors—himself included—dwell "together / Henceforth in darkness" (III.i.55–56), he is clearing the stage for the unsaturated word. In conjunction with this ambivalence in Demogorgon's identification, Demogorgon asserts, "The tyranny of heaven none may retain, / Or reassume, or hold succeeding thee" (III.i.57–58). Yet in act IV he allows that it is precisely the possibility of tyranny's return to which man must be alert, in order to continue anew creating an innocent order that will keep the old one in suspension. Either Shelley's entr'acte writing of *The Cenci* tempered his assurance of our ability to overcome evil, or Demogorgon, by virtue of being implicated at this particular moment of the drama as Jupiter's kin, is temporarily shortsighted.

But in act III, scene iii, Shelley locates an important alternative to death-as-end *and* its heretofore dismal alternative—death-in-life. He has lifted the veil from life, and, as Lacan would say, has followed the ancient Greek tradition of seeing the phallus behind that veil. Through renouncing his curse on his father and thereby restoring his claim on that father, he has magically discovered his own world, his own fire unstolen, his own phallus. In effect, he has unbound his original debt

15. James Rieger's remark that "symbolic cannibalism and actual incest are Cenci's major sins" (117) serves as a condensed statement of Shelley's vendetta against all inheritance. The father eats the son or rapes the daughter, in both cases introjecting his progeny.

to the totem father. And Asia, as his epipsyche, shares in that rebirth.
When Asia asks Earth about death, Earth alludes to the difference
between voices now:

> It would avail not to reply:
> Thou art immortal, and this tongue is known
> But to the uncommunicating dead. (III.iii.110–12)

Then, in speaking of the "winged child" destined to guide the Promethean company to the forest, Earth claims:

> This is my torch bearer;
> Who let his lamp out in old time, with gazing
> On eyes from which he kindled it anew
> With love, which is as fire, sweet Daughter mine,
> For such is that within thine own. (III.iii.148–52)

It is a new language that Prometheus's apocalyptic love has generated. But it is in the final scene of this act, the act that originally closed
the play, that the heralding of that new language becomes loudest. The
Spirit of the Hour enters to tell the results of Jupiter's fall, and as she
recounts her newfound ability to see into the heart of things, she
prefaces her speech with reference to Jupiter's finally silent tongue:

> Soon as the sound had ceased whose thunder filled
> The abysses of the sky, and the wise earth,
> There was a change. . . .
> . . . .
> My vision grew clearer and I could see
> Into the mysteries of the Universe. (III.iv.98–100, 104–5)

The paternal flame has been extinguished; the father's phallus,
relinquished. No longer will a "tyrant's will" (III.iv.139), becoming
"the abject of his own" (III.iv.140), spur the prisoner "like an outspent
horse, to death" (III.iv.141). No one, in this Jupiter-free visionary
world, "wrought his lips in truth-entangling lines" (III.iv.142). Set in
contrast is the previously doomed dishonest wretch, who, having in his
inherited abject word sucked life's blood from others, becomes a "vam-
pire among men, / Infecting all with his own hideous ill" (III.iv.147–
48). This fear of the would-be poet, inheritor of others' words, that he

might infect others never left Shelley; it may in fact be *the* concern that marks Shelley's most extreme divergence from the Romantic tendency toward idealism. At the same time that Shelley valorizes the legacy of great art, he deeply fears—a fear enacted throughout his canon—an inevitable emasculation by that legacy. It is a brutal possibility for a poet to admit.

But in act III, scene iv, an extraordinary paean to the enfranchisement of speech, to the liberation of the signifier, locates Shelley's greatest moment of optimism. Now "None talked that common, false, cold, hollow talk / Which makes the heart deny the *yes* it breathes" (III.iv.149–50). "[T]he tools / And emblems" (III.iv.176–77) of the earth's captivity, "Which under many a name and many a form / . . . / Were Jupiter, the tyrant of the world" (III.iv.180–83), stand "unregarded now" (III.iv.179). The "painted veil" (III.iv.190) that enshackled men erroneously called life, "is torn aside" (III.iv.192) to reveal the originating word instead.

Act IV opens with a clear intention of eradicating the old orders. The voice of unseen spirits sings "Of the Father of many a cancelled year" and that "We bear Time to his tomb in eternity" (IV.11, 14). In the privileging of music typical of Shelley, the pine boughs are permitted to sing "Old songs" but "with new gladness" (IV.48–49). It will be singing, in fact, that "shall build / In the Void's loose field / A world for the Spirit of Wisdom to wield" (IV.153–55). Music, reference free, is ever innovative and unchained. Ione says: "Even whilst we speak / New notes arise" (IV.184–85). Panthea identifies these notes as "The deep music of the rolling world" (IV.186) created by the air's "Aeolian modulations" (IV.188). It is precisely this kind of music that the poet must produce within his words.

Soon there enters a winged infant whose chariot, as it passes over all earth, "wakes sounds, / Sweet as a singing rain of silver dew" (IV.234–35). The moon, in speaking of its own renovation, defines correctly its source: "Tis Love, all Love" (IV.369). The only positive alternative to death as authenticator, as we have seen in Shelley's previous poetry, is visionary love. But epipsychidion unions have, prior to this poem, never managed to thwart the father's intrusion. In *Prometheus Unbound* Shelley dethrones the father by giving him back his word, by renouncing the debt of a symbolic murder, even at the risk of silence. Prometheus thus overturns the paternal system and creates himself anew. Arriving at the maternal paradise—even as his epipsyche Asia stands in for the mother—he forecloses on the possibility of paternal entrance. In real life, such foreclosure may lead to madness; in myth, it leads to renewal. Suggesting the grammar of alienation in Lacan's mirror stage, Earth announces that hate and fear

> Leave Man, who was a many-sided mirror
> Which could distort to many a shape of error
> This true fair world of things. (IV.382–84)

Just as a child suddenly cured of leprosy "wanders home with rosy smile" (IV.391), so the individual cured of a defiled language is the vision that motivates the Romantic quest. In his *Defence,* Shelley asserts that poetry "purges from our inward sight the film of familiarity" (505) and here he claims that "Familiar acts are beautiful through love" (IV.403). Love penetrates and makes new those forms that bear the accretions of ages. And it is this poet—anyone renovated by earth-shattering love—who answers the question of evil Shelley explored in *The Cenci.* Only if Beatrice had been able to renounce the Law of her father and love apocalyptically—outside his cultural system—could she have emerged in true selfhood from such ravage of paternal evil.

Finally, the new language human beings can create for themselves suggests Shelley's mythic yet authentic alternative to silence. It is the poet as prophet, but the poet especially as legislator, in a meaning ignored by commentary on that famous conclusion to his *Defence*; that is, it is in the ancient sense of legislator as namer, fount of language as in Plato's *Cratylus*, that Shelley's most radical claim for language inheres. As Earth announces, the new man's

> "Language is a perpetual Orphic song
> Which rules with Daedal harmony a throng
> Of thoughts and forms, which else senseless and shapeless were."
>   (IV.415–17)

For new man, "Lightning is his slave" (IV.418); the fiery signifier of the Heavens is enchained at last by the son, so that through this new language of man "the abyss shouts from her depth laid bare / 'Heaven has thou secrets? Man unveils me; I have none'" (IV.422–423). As if in corroboration of these words, Demogorgon pours forth the truth; if the deep truth is imageless, it is language-less, prepaternal; and now that the father's reign is ended, Demogorgon can pronounce even the abyss. In reference to his approach that concludes act IV, Ione says, "There is a sense of words upon mine ear" (IV.517), to which Panthea answers, "A universal sound like words" (IV.518): the earth's new speech transcends language. Such transcendence is the aim of the extraordinary accumulation of different mythologies at home in this poem, as if by fusion an explosion would change their meaning forever. The poem thus works on its own level a kind of Promethean theft, sifting through cultural vestiges to turn that weight of ages back in upon itself. Roland Barthes speaks of would-be original voices: "There is no language site outside bourgeois ideology. . . . The only possible rejoinder is neither confrontation nor destruction, but only theft; fragment the old text of culture . . . and change its features according to formulas of disguise" (*Sade,* 10).

The theme of redeeming language from its writ-in capacity to be a Wordsworthian counterspirit motivates Shelley's major poetry—of that, at this point in critical history, we can be sure. Elsewhere, in a move reminiscent of Wordsworth's experiments with using women as markers of linguistic escape, he suggests that as poet he cannot free Emilia or Beatrice from their prisons of silence because in offering them liberation, he subordinates them, masters them, by removing the terrifying solitude of their secrets; for either woman he would "restore speech only the better to rob her of it" (Kofman, 48). Silence, in both *Epipsychidion* and *The Cenci,* solaces its female prisoners with their superiority, at least. But communal salvation means sullying one's hands—speaking, as the narrator in *Alastor* confronts. Shelley as poet plays out repeatedly the conflict between individual and communal redemption—a Wordsworth Redivivus again, but reconstructed in a vocabulary that swerves from its original, then recuperates that provenance in a circularity that elides the debt of linear time. In *Prometheus Unbound*, he boldly mythologizes the possibility of phallic return in the emblem of the serpent coiled around eternity, a compulsion to repeat that echoes structurally the cycle of suffering and regeneration signified originally by the vulture greedy for the hero's flesh. Certainly it is not surprising that a poetry close at so many points to the psychological discourse "of child-parent or the parent-child" should in *Prometheus Unbound* resolve itself in the cyclical time that psychoanalysis marks (Kristeva, *Desire in Language,* 275). Implicit in the phallic return is the chance that the new man becomes old too—and that the cyclical repetition of new Promethean acts alone will allow for a different world from the old. Contained in the conclusion to *Prometheus Unbound* is Shelley's recognition of the death drive informing all life; but it is a recognition that, for once, and with incomparable tact, Shelley has made the very salvation of a belated universe.

Chapter 5

Language, Freedom, and the Female

Is it possible to ground freedom from patriarchal determination in a sexual projection outside the self, therein constructing an anteriority wherein one feels the shock of self-recognition for the first time? Shelley's creation of the epipsyche explores this possibility. Here we do well to review Freud's essay "The Theme of Three Caskets," in which Freud addresses the question of why the traditional goddess of death, the third Moerae, covertly occupies in much literature the place of the goddess of love. He reminds us that "contraries are constantly represented by one and the same element in the modes of expression used by the unconscious" ("Theme," 75), signification similar to that of the antithetical words. Thus it becomes meaningful that every time a choice exists among three women (or symbols for them, such as the caskets in *Merchant of Venice*), that choice falls upon the third, in mythology the masked one, usually the emblem of silence/death—"that which no man chooses, to which by destiny alone man falls a victim" (75).

Such a choice actually allows the human being to rebel against the inexorability of death by seeming to reverse its terms, as the goddess of death, of necessity, is transformed into her antithesis, the goddess of love—the "fairest, best, most desirable and the most lovable among women" (76), the woman, that is, who represents Shelley's soulmate, *his* necessity. Within the goddess of death/love, the conflict in aims inhabiting the pleasure principle is mythically inscribed: an ancient ambivalence once totally identified the two goddesses (76). In the

Orient the great mother-goddesses "all seem to have been both faunts of being and destroyers; goddesses of life and fertility, and death-goddesses. Thus the replacement by the wish-opposite of which we have spoken . . . is built upon an ancient identity" (76). The illusion, at least, of choice among the women is important, for "Choice stands in the place of necessity, of destiny. Thus man overcomes death, which in thought he has acknowledged. . . . Just where in reality he obeys compulsion, he exercises choice; and that which he chooses is not a thing of horror, but the fairest and most desirable thing in life" (76).

Similarly, Shelley will always choose that double of the self, a kind of doppelgänger, which in classic psychoanalytic theory often functions as an emblem of death. Shelley locates his double, of course, in the epipsyche, which substitutes life-sustaining love for the claim of death inherent in the silencing of self that the double suggests. The poet, however, adds a twist to the Freudian choice of the third lady; he dutifully crowns her in place of death, but he admits to death imperiously reclaiming her throne.

In *Julian and Maddalo*, the madman's demise occurs at the hands of an epipsyche who betrays her male counterpart. Yet by the end, when the lovers embrace in death, Shelley suggests that it is the world, which is incapable of supporting an ideal love, that is at fault. It is the lovers' enslaving discourse—for which they are not culpable—versus the lover him or herself, that makes it impossible for two to become as one. But what of the conversation that precedes the "mad" discourse? Does it forward the dominant narrative line or comingle oddly with it? In fact, it is yet another variant of *Alastor*'s framing device, wherein the poet standing outside the authenticity of silence—or madness, that subversion of "normal" language—nonetheless possesses the voice, however belatedly, to tell the story. The entangled structure that too many readers have termed gratuitous serves an essential formal and thematic function instead.

Julian, in the opening description of his ride, paints a solitary landscape of "an uninhabitable sea-side" (line 7). He proclaims to

> love all waste
> And solitary places; where we taste
> The pleasure of believing what we see
> Is boundless, as we wish our souls to be. (Lines 14–17)

Here again is the psychic region of Freud's oceanic religious sense of infinitude ("And such was this wide ocean" [line 18]). In this poetic call to the sublime, however, the blurring of boundaries foreshadows that role Shelley wishes to ascribe to the ideal love, a place for perfect union. That is, his description of nature portends the crisis of the madman dying for lack of that lover. Thus from the beginning Julian sets up the conditions for the authentic life. The poem sings of freedom, the escape the ride brings, obliterating sad memories, "till we came / Homeward, which always makes the spirit tame" (lines 32–33). The following lines, however, imply just that sadness of coming home, of displacement from that part of the sublime that transcends existence. But Shelley defensively likens the two friends to those devils of hell that descanted on

> God, freewill and destiny;
> Of all that earth has been or yet may be,
> All that vain men imagine or believe. (Lines 42–44)

These are no mere inheritors of God's laws; these are challengers of tradition, indebted if at all to Milton's satanic hero: they will seek a break with a stagnant fatherhood. Such bravado soon exposes itself as a reaction-formation to Shelley's real fear: that he may lose his poetic voice, locate it where he will.

At first Julian claims to fear that his companion has taken "the darker side" (line 49):

> The sense that he was greater than his kind
> Had struck, methinks, his eagle spirit blind
> By gazing on its own exceeding light. (Lines 50–52)

Following this reflection, the sun pauses in its downward movement, while Julian catalogs nature's splendors surrounding him. Suddenly, as the sun sets, an apocalyptic transformation of nature occurs:

> And then—as if the Earth and Sea had been
> Dissolved into one lake of fire, were seen
> Those mountains towering as from waves of flame
> Around the vaporous sun, from which there came
> The inmost purple spirit of light, and made
> Their very peaks transparent. (Lines 80–85)

Immediately, however, his companion interferes with the sublime moment to say: "Ere it fade / . . . I will show you soon / A better station . . ." (lines 85–87). What Julian next sees, however, is the madhouse and its tower, with its bell signifying to Maddalo the emblem of "what should be eternal and divine" (line 122). Maddalo compares the human soul to the bell, "Hung in a heaven-illuminated tower" (line 124), yet tolling in its prisonhouse those unknown desires which an individual cannot define until

> the night of death,
> As sunset that strange vision, severeth
> Our memory from itself, and us from all
> We sought, and yet were baffled. (Lines 127–30)

Here the earlier apocalypse of sunset collapses into the promise of visionary death. The scene loses its physical distinctiveness until gray and gloom befall the area in a Wordsworthian obliteration of the light of senses—and Julian and Maddalo return home. Thus exactly when it appears that we are being prepared for vision proper, the accretions of meaning, paratactically realized, suggest that vision is deferred from this life.

The next day Julian opines that the mind itself is capable of locating the "love, beauty and truth we seek" (line 174). In response to Maddalo's derision of such Utopian vision, he claims that

> those who try may find
> How strong the chains are which our spirit bind;
> Brittle perchance as straw. (Lines 180–82)

Not only may Julian "never own such leaden laws" (line 163) as determine society, but he seeks a way to make the self all powerful and self-determining. There must be, he insists, "something nobler than to live and die" (line 187). Maddalo assures him that "As far as words go" (line 195) such an argument suffices, but therein, apparently, lies the problem: words do not suffice. Maddalo's friend who argued similarly months before has gone mad.

We now begin to comprehend how carefully Shelley has prepared the way for the madman's entrance and for his discourse to assume center stage. With madness, either in its schizoid avoidance of ordinary speech or in the silence of aphasia, one escapes the other release of life:

death. Therefore hope remains, however perverse it appears: madness may offer vision the authenticity that death alone keeps claiming for itself. Yet Shelley still posits fictionally in Julian's response that there is something other than the "living death" (line 210) of madness; one only needs "To love and be beloved with gentleness" (line 208). Nonetheless, the impossibility of meeting that need will prove the madman's entry into insanity.

The wild language that greets Julian and Maddalo at the madhouse yields to the "fragments of most touching melody," which the friends hear "on high" (lines 221, 220). Julian cannot locate the source, but he observes the music's ability to move the madmen into a happy silence. It is music alone that silences the Law gone out-of-control, the

> Fierce yells and howlings and lamenting keen,
> And laughter where complaint had merrier been,
> Moans, shrieks, and curses. (Lines 216–18)

It is, strangely, the music of the very madman whom they seek that preempts the insane language of those around him: it is this man— similar, as Maddalo has stressed repeatedly, to Julian in many ways— whose

> sweet strains . . . charm the weight
> From madmen's chains, and make this Hell appear
> A heaven of sacred silence. (Lines 259–61)

He too is one of those Miltonic devils of hell alluded to at the beginning of the poem, who will try to make or break his own prison. The madman actually creates, through music, a discourse outside the corruption of language that expiates the excesses of that language—he unchains the human slave. Thus, in a poem composed during the period of *Prometheus Unbound*, Shelley explores a topic not unrelated to his epic work: the heroics of rebellion against the father tongue.

The "madman" speaks articulately, even eloquently, about the source of his despair, and we discover that this madness is grief, not insanity.

> There is one road
> To peace, and that is truth, which follow ye!
> Love sometimes leads astray to misery. (Lines 347–49)

The status of a love that both leads the way to truth and ends up subverting it at the same time is problematic. There follows a tessellation of death and bride and desertion, a mosaic to which the madman will bear perverse witness as he watches the bridal bed from his winding sheet. A sense of betrayal abounds: the bride has taken the wrong groom, or death has bedded the wrong mate. The madman abruptly juxtaposes to this vision a direct address to the earlier cited lady from France, who deserted him, leaving him to wander the desert alone. The emotional apostrophes increase in intensity until it seems that Shelley, always in tenuous control of the personal material of this poem, turns almost full front to his own real domestic loss, as Mary Shelley's cycle of depressions turns to despair upon the death of their daughter Clara (White, 283–89). In Shelley's embarrassing analogy to his wife, he details the woman's responsibility for their initial liaison, then he chronicles his unceasing love even in the midst of her coldness. He anticipates the wearied lover's taunts of his sexual powers, but he assures her—strangely, since neither we nor, presumably, she, has reason to think otherwise—that he will never retaliate physically. In fact, he reminds her, he lives only "That thou mayst have less bitter cause to grieve" (line 495). He, for her sake, refrains "From that sweet sleep which medicines all pain" (line 499). The frenzy of this section reflects well the stakes implied in Shelley's binding with a soulmate: that desire of the Other is meant to "fill out his own ineluctable finitude, restoring the illusion of plenitude that was shattered by entrance into the symbolic order" (Richardson and Muller, 282). Thus the failure of such desire thrusts the poet back into madness, silence, or death:

> I do but hide
> Under these words like embers, every spark
> Of that which has consumed me—quick and dark
> . . . The grave is yawning as its roof shall cover
> My limbs . . .
> . . . .
> Let death upon despair! (Lines 503–510)

Julian and Maddalo reenter the poem, having been such mute audience to the monologue that they temporarily seem absent. Now they leave in earnest, so moved by this madman's tale that they forget their argument. They talk of the madman "And nothing else" (line 524). As they resume discussion between themselves, they resolve that some woman has betrayed him, forcing an innate purity into corrupt channels against truth. In the heaping of blame ("She had abandoned him" [line 533]), one hears the child's avowal of a mother's failure to love quite enough to prevent the world's intrusion, a precursor of that betrayal by the Shape All Light in *Triumph of Life*. It is in the context of this kind of nostalgia that one can allow Thomas Carlyle's pronouncement on Shelley: "Hear a Shelley filling the earth with inarticulate wail; like the infinite, inarticulable grief and weeping of forsaken infants" (White, 479).

If that mother has failed in keeping castration fully at bay, if the phallic order of the defining father intrudes against all her gestures, there is still hope in the retaliatory voice of madness that perverts the Law. And that madness, as we might now expect, comes to be called poetry. "For the wild language of his grief was high, / Such as in measure were called poetry" (lines 541–42). It is indeed in the antenatal desertion of the mother that the father, unbidden, enters:

> Most wretched men
> Are cradled into poetry by wrong,
> They learn in suffering what they teach in song. (Lines 544–46)

The conflict between poet as living-but-indentured singer and authentic poet out-of-this-world announces itself in the conclusion to the poem. After Julian and Maddalo discuss the madman's discourse, the poem somewhat abruptly shifts to Julian's justification for leaving the madman and returning to his affairs in the "rational" world of London. He asserts, on the one hand, the power to claim the poet back from madness—a task to which he is tempted—but at the same time, he suggests a solid sense of the need to escape the madman's lure: "the deep tenderness that maniac wrought / Within me" (lines 566–67).

When Julian returns to Venice many years later and inquires after the madman's health, he learns that the madman has died—as well as his lady: both lie in mute marble. The emphasis on silence suggests its ability to avenge the madman's claim against life, as the girl who relates their story insists upon keeping her own quiet and asks instead that the "silent years / Be closed and ceared over their memory" (lines 613–14). Finally she unveils the truth to Julian, but he turns abruptly on his audience, and declares "she told me how / All happened—but the cold world shall not know" (lines 616–17). Thus the speaker framing the story, the voice *left*, as in *Alastor*, refuses to speak; and a poem that begins by rapturously elevating the opportunity for rational discourse ends in the valorization of a madman and in a resolution to remain silent. In one sense, then, this ending is more somber than that of *Alastor*, for there, at least, the "inauthentic" poet was willing to speak. Julian, in contrast, refuses to share a story his audience will not understand.[1] Perhaps, as Newman Ivey White suggested years ago, Shelley at heart resented singing to a world he could not love and yet could not escape.

Though composed almost two years earlier, this poem begs to be read in continuum with *Epipsychidion*, which again negotiates the potential salvation through a love-ideal. Nonetheless, of greater significance in *Julian and Maddalo* is the structural shift from the poem's initial promise of a dialectic of reason to its centering upon "mad" discourse instead. Such discourse emphasizes Shelley's consuming desire to intervene in linguistic contingencies until he mythologizes his own speech, a speech capable of locating itself this side of death. The object of *Julian and Maddalo* is, yet once more, the granting of priority to an authentic voice over the traditional, patrilineal corrupt echoes. But again, in *Epipsychidion*, Shelley would find his optatives to be already hopelessly indebted to the contexts he would undo. We can read Shelley's poetry as an exploration of what it means to deny the oedipal complex, with the subsequent answer supplied by both Lacan and Shelley: denial of the phallus, in society propped up by the gender power constructs as we know them, results in silence.

It should be clear at this point that my interpretation of Shelley's canon insists upon his strong investment in the linguistic analogues or enactments of phallic power, a puissance that, instead of female body derivations, came mythologically to represent the renewing powers of nature. If we assume that (in particular, artistic) males might graft their wish for a womb onto the presence of that which they already

1. In a recent essay that came to my attention as this manuscript was being typed, William Brewer says much the same thing: "'The cold world shall not know' is a statement uttered by a disillusioned poet who withholds information as a protest against an audience which will, presumably, misunderstand or perhaps mock the story Julian has heard. Like the Maniac himself, Julian will not 'give a human voice to [his] despair' . . . he chooses silence" (137).

possess, we see the ubiquity of the phallic symbol that so alarmed Ernest Jones as a reaction-formation to the absence of what men really wanted—the power to give birth, to be that most indisputable sign of God-like power, the mother-creator. Shelley seeks to fulfill this wish for the female by projecting an ideal other for himself in the epipsyche. But precisely because this other is created out of male terms—both from Shelley's own image and from male-encoded linguistic tools of imagery—it cannot fulfill the role he defines for it. He seeks an epipsyche that embraces a fiery silence that escapes language, yet he creates her out of language, a language he feels is earth-male-bound.[2]

The motto to *Epipsychidion,* which Shelley attributes to Emilia Viviani, describes perfectly (in tandem with his Augustinian quote in *Alastor*) Shelley's conception of the role love fulfills. That Freudian excess of self-love which must find its object outside the self or destroy the self underwrites the project of this poem: "The loving soul launches beyond creation, and creates for itself in the infinite a world all its own, far different from this dark and terrifying gulf" (motto). Emilia is physically situated in a prison, just as her soul-outside-her-soul is imprisoned if separated from her. "Poor captive bird! who, from thy narrow cage, / Pourest such music" (lines 5–6). The pure sounds of this soulmate, however, cannot be comprehended by the coarse language of the world's denizens, who are "deaf to all sweet melody" (line 8). In a reference that helps us understand Lacan's explanation of a soul's earliest illusion of wholeness, the poet addresses Emilia:

> Thou Mirror
> In whom, as in the splendor of the Sun,
> All shapes look glorious which thou gazest on! (Lines 30–32)

Though the shadow of language always falls between this primal image and perception of it, "even the dim words which obscure thee now / Flash, lightning-like, with unaccustomed glow" (lines 33–34). Herein occurs the poem's first hint that union with an epipsyche can ward off the polluting effects of a learned language.

The speaker's idea of union is a total dissolution of ego boundaries: "I am not thine: I am a part of *thee*" (line 52). Implied is the hope that

2. See my essay "The Bifurcated Female Space of Desire," in Claridge and Langland, *Out of Bounds.*

such a young soul as Emilia—in real life nineteen years old—can influence the speaker against the inheritance of the ages: "Young Love should teach Time . . . / All that thou art" (lines 55–56). Such a soul is "void of guile" (line 56), "vanquishing dissonance" (line 60). From lines 69–129, Shelley suggests both the lure of the epipsyche and his covert knowledge that life disallows such a union:

> I measure
> The world of fancies, seeking one like thee,
> And find—alas! mine own infirmity. (Lines 69–71)

There follows an account reminiscent of the visionary maid in *Alastor*—when desire descends full force on the speaker, with its accompanying seduction of death: "She met me, Stranger, upon life's rough way, / And lured me towards sweet Death" (lines 72–73). By gazing upon such a vision, the speaker intermingles with love—eternity—itself:

> See where she stands! a mortal shape indued
> With love and life and light and deity,
> And motion which may change but cannot die;
> An image of some bright Eternity;
> A shadow of some golden dream; a Splendor
> Leaving the third sphere pilotless. (Lines 112–17)

It is almost as if Shelley, in his secular revision of Christian theology, appends Saint Paul to Lacan's mirror of identity. Paul assigns to love the apocalyptic powers that all other virtues merely hint at: even prophecy can see in a mirror but darkly, whereas with love, one looks in the mirror and "knows as we are known"—fully (I Cor. 12–13).[3] A psychoanalytic commentary on love would add that we know ourselves through the love object we choose.[4] But like the mystic forced to

3. Leslie Brisman spells out the Pauline influences on Shelley's poetry, especially the Pauline understanding of love ("Mysterious Tongue," 392–93).

4. Lacan would qualify Freud's explanation of love-object so that any self-knowledge obtaining from love is illusory to the degree that the self upon which it is modeled is an alienated ego from its outset. Shelley himself came close to Freud's definition in his famous assertion in the *Defence*: "The great secret of morals is love; or a going out of our own nature and an identification of ourselves with the beautiful which exists in . . . persons not our own." Freud would no doubt point out that upon reflection the person's beauty "not our own" bears a startling closeness to our favorite conception of ourselves.

descend the mountaintop, the person privileged by such a vision of love faces the trauma of death-in-life after the vision flees. In *Alastor*, the only answer lay in pursuing the truth of death. In *Epipsychidion*, the answer is close at times to the optimistic response to similar questions in "Ode to the West Wind." *Epipsychidion*'s lover cries:

> Ah, woe is me!
> What have I dared? where am I lifted? how
> Shall I descend, and perish not? (Lines 123–25)

The speaker in "Ode to the West Wind" pleads with the wind: "Oh! lift me as a wave, a leaf, a cloud!" (line 53)—and then immediately provides the famous contrapuntal image of traumatic descent instead: "I fall upon the thorns of life! I bleed!" (line 54). The juxtaposition in both poems of these vertical opposites implies an interstice where something happens. That something is the speaker's recognition that, unless he choose death, he is earthbound; he bleeds because he has known the ecstasy of being "lifted up"—but the scission in such freedom effected by the "weight of hours" (line 55) in "Ode to the West Wind" and the "chains of lead" (line 590) in *Epipsychidion* vex his sense of escape. Through his willingness to abnegate self and assume a plastic receptivity to the universe, he renders nugatory the master/slave economy. It is an answer akin to Prometheus's abrogation of a word that enslaved as it empowered—so this suspension of willful self in favor of allowing the wind to play *through* him. And the concluding theme in "Ode to the West Wind" of a cyclical regeneration that will not brook tyranny evokes the myth of the phoenix rising out of the ashes after its consumption by fire. It is more than convenient coincidence that such an emblem recalls the revivified phallus (Freud, *Acquisition of Power*, 298). For however brief a moment, Shelley allows himself the doughty comfort that his "trumpet of a prophecy" will sound through a new kind of word.

Epipsychidion rescues Shelley's ontological carapace of "thorns" by privileging love's ability to make "all things equal" (line 126), unlike Byron's validation faute de mieux; thus by loving Love, as he sought in *Alastor*, he becomes Love. The prototype of Love is his mother, the "Being whom my spirit oft / Met . . . / In the clear golden prime of my youth's dawn" (lines 190–92). James Rieger's allusion to Virgil is psychologically acute and quite to the point: *"Epipsychidion* asks Emilia Viviani the question Aeneas blurted out when he failed to recognize his mother, Venus: *quam te memorem, virgo?"* (185). When the speaker recalls, "She met me, robed in such exceeding glory, / That I beheld her not" (lines 199–200), we enter the fullness of Shelley's desire, wherein he is one with that mother, unable in this primordial union of souls to see her because he *is* her, as he spoke of his epipsyche earlier ("I am not thine: I am a part of *thee"* [line 52]). Her voice alone averts the storm "which with the shattered present chokes the past" (line 212); that is, she intervenes in the present fragmentation of life and restores the innocence of a presymbolic world.

In an extraordinary poetic inscription of what Lacan would calibrate as the struggle for social versus isolate identity, this speaker springs "from the caverns of my dreamy youth / . . . as one sandalled with plumes of fire" (lines 217–18); he is rewriting his history as a wish fulfillment, becoming in this dream the phallus for his mother, becoming, as Lacan would say, her desire. "And towards the lodestar of my one desire, / I flitted": he flits, that is, toward "A radiant death, a fiery sepulchre, / As if it were a lamp of earthly flame" (lines 223–24). In this Hegelian minuet where the dance may be to the death, the speaker seeks to preempt the father by becoming the all-engendering phallus himself—the "lamp of earthly flame"—which will foreclose on the need for any other symbolic intruders. Paul H. Fry's description of Shelley's "dialectic of love" helps explain how Shelley sought a way out of language through love. "Love," Fry maintains, "is the perception of similitude in dissimilitude of which the emblem and vehicle is metaphor" (*Reach of Criticism,* 162). If we understand Shelley's linguistic modus operandi to be based on something akin, at least, to our own principle of difference, then love becomes for him the way to circumvent the production of meaning and to predicate a new meaning based, impossibly, on similarity.

But even in Shelley's metaphysics, language always overcomes love. The speaker incurs castration; he is not strong enough for the father who names: "She, whom prayers or tears then could not tame, / Past . . . / Into the dreary cone of our life's shade" (lines 225–28). It is not really she, but the speaker, who passes into the shadow of the Father Language, exacting stupendous grief for the lover:

> And as a man with mighty loss dismayed,
> I would have followed, though the grave between
> Yawned like a gulph whose spectres are unseen. (Lines 229–31)

That grave is precisely the gap unapproachable, that space where the needs of the child, assumed by him to be known intuitively by the mother, are now translated into an unsatisfactory language of demand—with something always lost in between. The subsequent lines show a desperate youth seeking everywhere "this soul out of my soul" (line 238):

> But neither prayer nor verse could dissipate
> The night which closed on her; nor uncreate
> That world within this Chaos, mine and me,
> Of which she was the veiled Divinity,
> The world I say of thoughts that worshipped her. (Lines 241–45)

The speaker stumbles through the world, trying among all these "new forms" (line 252) in which he is irrevocably entangled to find "one form resembling hers" (line 254)—but such a search is doomed: once experience is mediated through language, there is no recapture of innocence. The false solution here is analogous to that which betrays the madman in *Julian and Maddalo*; the speaker encounters "In many mortal forms" (line 267) the appearance of the original, but they always fail him. At one point of possible "Deliverance," the poet removes to a womblike cave, where he seeks a symbiosis with his vision. He is "laid asleep, spirit and limb" (line 295), as if awaiting birth: "I then was nor alive nor dead" (line 300). The music of the speaker's "soul within the soul" (line 455) seems, after all, "Like echoes of an antenatal dream" (line 456).

Of the possible biographical implications of the "one abandoned mother" (line 304), we might recall not only the image of Mary Shelley abandoned through the death of her children, but also of Shelley abandoned by the same mother-wife, the epipsyche who was meant to fill that *beance* which compels Shelley's poetry. "Love," Rimbaud sagely reminds us, "has to be reinvented." That maternal paradise must reestablish itself, since, as Newman White notes, "for Shelley's nature complete sympathy was almost a vital necessity" (149), and thus the hopeful flow throughout his life of Harriet Westbrook, Elizabeth Hitchener, Cornelia Turner, Mary Shelley, Emilia Viviani, and Jane Williams. On 18 June 1822, Shelley alluded to his misplaced optimism in a letter to John Gisborne less than a week before the poet's death: "I confess it is not easy for spirits cased in flesh and blood to avoid [the error of] seeking in a mortal image the likeness of what is perhaps eternal" (*Letters* 2:434). In the myth of a woman outside the law, Shelley hoped to locate his word in a signifier that skirted the phallocentrism of his own language.[5]

The lover in *Epipsychidion* will not give up; he asserts he has found the vision he seeks—and that this time it is true. The poem becomes all the more poignant when we recognize the time sequence in Shelley's real life: he met Emilia Viviani in December of 1820 and wrote this tribute to her salvific powers within the two months following. The desperation of the poet's search imitates Shelley's own willingness to base an Ideal upon his very short acquaintance with a nineteen-year-old naif. In addition, Shelley was soon to be disabused of his faith in Emilia; even she would reveal herself to be all too mortal. But temporarily at least, Shelley the man and the speaker in *Epipsychidion*

> felt the dawn of my long night
> Was penetrating me with living light:
> I knew it was the Vision veiled from me
> So many years—that it was Emily. (Lines 341–44)

She shall escape the convent, leaving behind "a vacant prison" (line 395); he, "Like lightning, with invisible violence / Piercing its continents" (lines 399–400) (or Mont Blanc "piercing the sky" [line 60])

---

5. Carol Jacobs suggests, in her discussion of Prometheus's attempt to recall his curse, the Shelleyan allegory of self-identity articulated through the simultaneous negotiation of form and image, a strategy that obtains only through death: "Thus the attempt to unite power and name, to give speech to a shape, or authority to an image, is a violent and unsuccessful ventriloquism. The figure who speaks the curse will experience that voice as total alterity, as the invasion of an other that rends him from within" (29). In one sense, the narrator's falling upon the thorns of life in *Epipsychidion* represents just such a moment, wherein he is almost successful, through his epipsyche, of naming or voicing himself, but that voicing of the Lacanian ego, a mirrored (impossible) moment in which the narrator is seeing into his own inevitably inauthentic, authentic formation, is piercing—and will not sustain his vision.

shall escape the precedence of the word—he shall become *greater* than death. Love shall impel him, like heaven—but "liker death" (line 401) who "makes his way" (line 402) through all of the phallic emblems of a father-ridden past: "Through temple, tower, and palace" (line 403). But "more strength has Love" (line 404) than even death, as Shelley proffers his daring claim for the epipsychidion union over the power of death:

> For it can burst his charnel, and make free
> The limbs in chains, the heart in agony,
> The soul in dust and chaos. (Lines 405–7)

Triumph over death is rare in Shelley. His dynamics of desire enact a constant struggle between his perceived apocalypse of two souls and the compelling drive toward resolution, with its ultimate consummation of desire. The problem always implicit in the epipsychidion solution, however, is that love is still mediated with words of the past. Shelley himself valorizes the purity of silence:

> And we will talk, until thought's melody
> Become too sweet for utterance, and it die
> In words, to live again in looks, which dart
> With thrilling tone into the voiceless heart,
> Harmonizing silence without a sound. (Lines 560–64)

> our lips
> With other eloquence than words, [will] eclipse
> The soul that burns between them. (Lines 566–68)

A difficult ideal for a poet—to inscribe his own silence within his text—but Shelley temporarily resolves the paradox by creating an eternally flaming desire that will never burn out—a fire that transcends the ages in its very inextinguishability:

> [We] like two meteors of expanding flame,
> . . . .
> Touch, mingle, are transfigured; ever still
> Burning, yet ever inconsumable. (Lines 576–79)

In such a solution Shelley conscientiously seeks, as he consistently does, to avoid creating his own enchaining poetic legacy.[6] This eternal union of souls is "Like flames too pure and light and unimbued / To nourish their bright lives with baser prey" (lines 581–82). Yet immediately after this claim of immortality, of one-upping death, the poet calls out "one immortality, / And one annihilation. Woe is me!" (lines 586–87). This apparent contradiction becomes clear when we realize Shelley's own truthful recognition that the fulfillment of desire he describes necessarily preempts the need for poetic voice. He has written within his poem his own poetic annihilation, and thus, at the end of the next four lines, he dies to the ecstasy of silence, giving it up and resuming the burden of death-in-life, where language both imprisons and constitutes him as a poet:

> The winged words on which my soul would pierce
> Into the height of love's rare Universe,
> Are chains of lead around its flight of fire—
> I pant, I sink, I tremble, I expire! (Lines 588–91)

Thus the "Weak Verses" (line 592) yield to life—to the need to speak, to be alive and therefore indebted—and kneel at life's ("your Sovereign's" [line 592]) feet. A recent commentator on another visionary poem, *The Pearl*, offers an insight that must have occurred to Shelley at his most optimistic. "If the highest poetic words say they cannot say, then what cannot be expressed must exist, must ever maintain a reality outside these verbal and imaginative constructions that say they cannot say" (Watts, 26). But such happy absence would assuage Shelley's fears a short time; as his last line proclaims, he is love's "guest" (line 604)—but as poet he can never truly be her mate.

---

6. For what I take to be the best formal analysis of Shelley's maneuvering out of the self-engendered system that will inevitably enslave others, see Hogle, "Shelley's Poetics," 190–91. I still would maintain, however, that Shelley's desire for an original language was too intense to allow him any real resting place in poetry's regeneration by readers or future poets, for the new "encompassing shape" (191) still must use what precedes it as a first term.

Chapter 6

Death and Artistic Authenticity

Death inhabits the heart of Shelley's poetry, a critical perspective articulated if largely ignored long ago.[1] Certainly one can hold this position without its suggesting a fatalism that compromised the whole of Shelley's vision: "If life excites you, its opposite, like a shadow, death, must excite you, too" (Francis Bacon, painter).

Freud's insistence on the privileged place of death in psychic drives reminds us of the romanticism subtending psychoanalytic ways of seeing. According to Freud, there exists a category of destructive instincts that compel the living being back to the inorganic state from which it perceives itself as having arisen, a regressive urge toward stasis. "If we are to take it as a truth that knows no exception that everything living does for *internal* reasons—becomes inorganic once again—then we shall be compelled to say that the *'aim of all life is death'* and, looking backwards, that *'inanimate things existed before livings ones'*" (*Beyond the Pleasure Principle*, 38).

But in order to negotiate the tasks of everyday life, the subject must allow the secondary process to substitute the realist principle, with its insistence upon *deferring* that reduction of excitement to an inorganic state. It is here that Shelley's allegiance to the death instincts becomes clearest, for he chafes at the impotence of language that disallows him

---

1. See, for only one extreme example, Kurtz, *Pursuit of Death*.

the presence of union through words. Shelley's stronger-than-usual reliance on the primary process may be typical of artists in general, yet the degree to which he accepts the logical but explosive yoking implicit in the pleasure and death instincts is striking even in a literary period well in touch with destruction. I shall, therefore, pause to situate several heavily invested concepts that philosophically complement the discourse of Eros and Thanatos writ into Shelley's poetry.

Lacan amplifies Freud's analysis of death by applying a Heideggerian perspective that in many ways reflects Freud's own valorization of Schopenhauer's belief: death is "the true result and to that extent the purpose of life" (*Beyond the Pleasure Principle*, 50).[2] For Lacan, "the death instinct essentially expresses the limit of the historical function of the subject" (*Ecrits*, 103). Heidegger, of course, famously postulates that death represents the ultimate boundary of existence; hence, it is the perfect emblem of human finitude, and every Being is necessarily a Being-unto-Death. In many ways, we could read Heidegger's ontology as an attempted happy gloss on an otherwise dark acknowledgment of a retrograde moment in the flurry of human activity that arrests the historical, that emphasizes the aloneness of human subjects even as part of their otherwise social constitution. Lacan enlists Freud's *fort/da* game in his explanation of language's proximity to death: it was through words that the child mastered the absence of his mother, through a primitive speech that marked "the birth of the symbol" in the child. The child knows limit—ultimately the Heideggerian limit of death—through loss of an illusory symbolic union henceforth to be recreated only in words, but words whose own limits soon appear. Combining Freud and Lacan, we can say that the father's insistence upon cultural conformity occludes any hopes of the calm "inorganic" state of the mother/child dyad and dooms the social being to search henceforth, through the signifier, for that stasis again and again, until resolution is final.

2. Perhaps unnecessarily, but at the same time inscribing what will become for future readers of this book a mark of its local conditions, I acknowledge the ethical difficulty facing any critic who wishes to enlist the insights of Martin Heidegger at this moment in history. I note here that I am using his "psychology" in a very limited fashion, primarily to the extent that it allows for a mythologizing of death that proves functional to any poet trying to write his way outside of the limitations of life. How such mythologizing can cooperate with nationalistic deracination is, of course, a separate issue, though the possibility of a connection between the aesthetic and the political realization of such a myth deserves, from an ethical perspective, special attention. See Eagleton, *Ideology of the Aesthetic*, 288–315.

Thus "the replacement of the mother by a symbol" assumes the equivalence of her death; "the symbol manifests itself first of all as the murder to the thing" (Lacan, *Ecrits,* 104). Henceforth, the child will impose death on things "by substituting for them the symbols of speech." It is no wonder that death appears everywhere part of the "humanizing process" (Richardson and Muller, 94).[3]

Certainly there appears to be a natural affinity between Romantic writers and an appreciation of death, whether its presence is betrayed by the flagrant expressions of the Gothic novels or the subtle suggestions of death's lure in Wordsworth's poems of absence and memory. The goal of freedom, so much a part of Romantic ideology, appears at its uttermost possibility in death. Heidegger develops the difficult position that anticipating one's own death frees the self from an inauthentic existence wherein the subject feels determined by all "factical possibilities" that capriciously pave one's path.

> Anticipation [of death] discloses to existence that its uttermost possibility lies in giving up, and thus it shatters all one's tenaciousness to whatever existence one has reached. . . . Free for its ownmost possibilities, which are determined by the end and so are understood as finite, Dasein dispels the danger that it may, by its own finite understanding of existence, fail to recognize that it is getting outstripped by the existence possibilities of Others, or rather that it may explain these possibilities wrongly and force them back upon its own, so that it may divest itself of its ownmost factical existence. (Heidegger, 309)

As a Being-unto-Death, the poet can claim himself *for* himself, unaligned to the determination of the Other. But it is the *noncontingent* status of death in particular that confers authenticity upon the poet. The ability to "mean" outside the system of differential relations to which Shelley alluded in his "Essay on Life" and "Speculations on Morals" offers liberation from the inheritance of linguistic mediation. As Lacan insists, upon the advent of speech the child enters the social order to already-governed relationships that his father symbolizes as the Law.[4] But self, by proleptically knowing death, experiences free-

3. Richardson and Muller have clarified my own reading of Heidegger and have made Lacan's co-opting of the philosopher easier to follow.

4. For a particularly acute account of this by now commonplace poststructuralist position, see the Sartre of the early 1960s in *Search for a Method*, esp. 101, 105.

dom. "The entity which anticipates its non-relational possibility is thus forced by that very anticipation into the possibility of taking over from itself its ownmost Being, and doing so of its own accord" (Heidegger, 308).

If Being can stare at its own death and accept its own fullest potentiality-for-Being, it undoes all indebtedness of relations to other Beings. "This ownmost non-relational possibility is at the same time the uttermost" (Heidegger, 294). Yet the hard truth remains that for the poet in good faith to escape the "relational" word—to refuse Wordsworth's path of filiative generation—is to abnegate poetic voice.

Alastor is the quintessential Romantic poem of death and desire. It is also the text that puts most clearly into relief the dilemma of the poet who must relinquish the claim to a social voice in order to remain true to himself. It enacts the Shelleyan question of how the artist or the art can insert itself into historical realities contingent upon familial, sexual economies of power. In *Alastor*, Shelley alerts us, as early as 1815, that he is willing to embrace Hegel's Pyrrhic victory of mastery over the slave by killing that slave—language. Yet the death the poet seeks is not an entanglement of treachery and despair, as some critics would have it, but a final location of *jouissance.*[5]

Shelley's Augustinian epigraph to *Alastor*—"Not yet did I love, yet I was in love with loving; . . . I sought what I might love, loving to love"—maps out the coordinates of the necessary projection of self onto objects—vis-à-vis other selves—but in a way that enacts the ultimate tease. When Shelley translates the drive to fulfill yearning into successfully consummating his desire of the definitive Law of the Other, he reaches the silence of death, which is the end of *Alastor.* The putative conflict between Shelley's acceptance of the title Peacock provided, with its sense of "evil genius," and the valorization of the solitary poet in Shelley's preface disappears then, when this text is engaged from a Lacanian perspective.

For Shelley entertained both anxiety and self-admiration over daring not only to desire the Other but also to plot the conflagration and hence obliteration of that passion. It is worth quoting at length from

5. See, for instance, Barbara A. Schapiro's interpretation of *Alastor* as gloomily nihilistic (xiii).

the preface wherein he reveals his dialectic of desire that moves from the child stage of object relations to the human desire born when the infant enters the symbolic world of father. "So long as it is possible for his desires to point towards objects thus infinite and un-measured, he is joyous, and tranquil, and self-possessed. But the period arrives when these objects cease to suffice. His mind is at length suddenly awakened and thirsts for intercourse with an intelligence similar to itself. He images to himself the Being whom he loves. . . . He seeks in vain for a proto-type of his conception. Blasted by his disappointment, he descends to an untimely grave."

But next to this portrait Shelley paints those people whose desire fixates in the object stage; in spite of language, their vocabulary of the heart never becomes human. The "morally dead" are those "who love not their fellow-beings" and "live unfruitful lives, and prepare for their old age a miserable grave" (69–70). Both the poet-hero of the poem and his implied foes in the preface die, but the distinction between those deaths is the crux of *Alastor*. Shelley's sonnet lamenting Wordsworth's surrender of the quest for truth was published with *Alastor*, an event that explains further Shelley's opening and concluding quotes from the older poet. Wordsworth represents at best the poet-framer of *Alastor* who can look at truth only from the outside, a poetic position spatially echoed by the position of the indebted quotes, and temporally indicated by their content: the woe "too deep for tears" (line 713) is, in Shelley's conclusion, the inability of the "cold powers" (line 710) of feeble art to touch death, a death only those real poets of Shelley's epigraph can experience.

Harold Bloom, noting the omission of fire in Shelley's cataloging of the elements as he invokes Mother Nature, concludes that Shelley as poet was assuming the identity of the fire; he is brother to the other elements (*Poetry and Repression,* 105). Fire becomes for Shelley an emblem of maleness, a phallic giver of life. As I have noted elsewhere, the conflation of fire and phallus is an easy one, with the waxing and waning of both objects, with their penetration of darkness. Since the Mother does not possess the phallus, it is Shelley's potential gift to her. Still, there is always the suggestion of indebtedness that clings to fire and phallus; the Promethean son stole it from the gods. The Law continues to step in and police the "lover's" offering. Thus, the poet-hero at the end of the poem will flee society in an attempt to travel

back into the recesses of Mother Earth to that origin which is un-
effaced.[6]

But it is the living poet, the framer of *Alastor*, who speaks to this
Mother of desire, for this invocation takes place while the narrator sets
up his story. He will, in fact, relate the fiction of a poet-son who
achieves the big bang of death, who gives his mother the fiery phallus
and therefore antedates the father. The language is erotic:

> Mother of this unfathomable world!
> Favor my solemn song, for I have loved
> Thee ever, and thee only; I have watched
> Thy shadow, and the darkness of thy steps,
> And my heart ever gazes on the depth
> Of thy deep mysteries. (Lines 18–23)

The narrator tells of strange encounters with the vagaries of death,
all calculated to give answers to primal questions "of what we are" (line
29). His search for knowledge has been mixed

> With my most innocent love, until strange tears
> Uniting with those breathless kisses, made
> Such magic as compels the charmed night
> To render up the charge. (Lines 34–37)

The erotic language points to the typical Shelleyan psychological linkage of sex and death; in death, one transcends linguistic contingency
and achieves instant union of subject and object. Thus sexual union
(the collapse of ego boundaries in the orgasm of love) assumes its
metaphorical function for outsmarting language and creating unmediated discourse.

Though his mother never yields her secrets, the poet's fantasies and
dreams allow him the sense of inhabiting an Aeolian harp, that musical
emblem of precedence over the symbolic order of words. In order for
the melody the poet/harp plays to be universal, however, he awaits the

6. It is true too that a certain anxiety attaches to the narrator's homage to this mother.
For while on one level the symbolic world of a poet answers to paternal governance, paternity itself is an imaginary effect, with the mother after all attaching, through her naming
alone, the phallus/baby to a particular father. Thus for a poet who appreciated the power of
carving up the world through calling it—the legislator of *Cratylus*—the mother's word is a
peculiar (and vexed) cite of potency.

breath of his "Great Parent" (line 45), that he may be born a poet. His desire for this "Great Parent" counterpoints two dynamics: the dominant thrust of the poem at this point asks the mother to grant him the primacy of authentic voice untouched as yet by the paternal. At the same time, however, the narrative covertly implies that the advent of that other great parent is exactly what is required to transform the poet's blissful silence into language that will impose poetic vision upon the universe.

What Shelley achieves in *Alastor* is the presentation of those alternatives: the dead poet's quest for reunion with an earlier and unalienated self that in its refusal to be overruled by the father will conflagrate in death; or the narrator's borrowed existence as a poet, framing another's story in a language inherited—but at least alive. For in *Alastor*, the "true" poet never writes.[7] The narrator laments the poet whose death occasioned no "frame" of monuments. Shelley will expand this theme in *Adonais*, where he himself will mark Keats's monument, a poet inscribing another poet. The true poet—the definition of which is the narrator's real purpose—"sung, in solitude" (line 60). Herein lies the central conflict of the poem: the priority of silence over the claim of life, for now "Silence, too enamoured of that voice, / Locks its mute music in her rugged cell" (lines 65–66). How can one name oneself without the tools of language?

> When early youth had past, he left
> His cold fireside and alienated home
> To seek strange truths in undiscovered lands. (Lines 75–77)

That alienated home paradoxically becomes aligned with the "rugged cell" (line 66) of silence cited in the previous stanza: exiting the father's home ensures a muting of the poet's tongue. In a choice between the indebted silence of the paternal hearth and the personal teleology of a self-consummated desire, the true poet must pick the second. Now, as the young poet leaves that alienated home, he will see "truths in undiscovered lands" (line 77) not already settled by his forebears. But the

7. Frederick Kirchoff is one of several critics who have, in the past few decades, explored this point. I would simply add that what Kirchoff sees as the poet's failure—his death that results from his inability "to accept alienation of the field of the self" (122)—I see as the "truth" Shelley despairs of overcoming throughout the rest of his canon.

visit to the past offers up ambiguous wisdom: the poet properly appreciates the ancient achievement of Athens and Jerusalem, but he intuits among the "ruins of the days of old" (line 108) their castrating priority to the would-be poet. In the art on the walls of ruined temples, the poet learns where "dead men / Hang their mute thoughts on the mute walls around," believing that he views "memorials / Of the world's youth" (lines 119–22). After a vacant, transfixed gazing, during which his mind becomes a passive instrument, he sees "The thrilling secrets of the birth of time" (line 128).

Significantly, the emphasis throughout this encounter with ancient language is on silence: the dead men's thoughts are "mute," hung on "mute" walls; the poet gazes on "speechless shapes" (line 123). It is as if the two possibilities of authentic birth present themselves again: temporal precedence over others, or the silence of self-constituted voice. Tilottama Rajan underestimates the degree to which Shelley deviates from the Romantic program of valorizing art's ability to stave off the artist's own temporality (*Dark Interpreter*, 20). It is, after all, no mere lesson from the history on the walls that is revealed to the poet; rather, it is the "birth of time" (line 128) itself that becomes his visionary knowledge, the very knowledge he must escape in order to create his own discontinuous and unindebted existence.

Indeed, immediately following this extended reference to the fathers, an Arab maid's approaches to the poet are rebuffed; the maid brings him food, but it is "her daily portion, from her father's tent" (line 130), and it is to her "cold home" (line 138) that she must return. In contrast, the maid whom the poet will finally accept betrays no provenance other than her own; she must pretend, at least, to origin itself. The poet sees clearly the need to throw off the chains of an inherited medium in order to create his art; every time his needs meet a merely human response, the response is inadequate for him. In the fragmentary novel *The Assassins* on which he worked during this period, Shelley depicted an "isolated sect practicing a purer form of religion than the rest of the world could understand or accept" (White, 167). And in 1817, before he moved to Marlow, the poet informed his future neighbors that he and his family planned to associate with none of them (White, 237). Shelley's impulse to exist outside community, then, appears in the poet's life outside his poem. And, in *Alastor*, the poet wastes away into less than human form, almost skeletal as well as

wild; cottagers who see him minister "with human charity / His human wants" (lines 255–56), but such care cannot halt his drive toward
self-annihilation. The youthful maidens whom he encounters will "call
him with false names / Brother, and friend" and will watch with tears
his departure from their imprisoning "father's door" (lines 268–69,
271). Even the Spirit who communes with the poet must be beholden
to nothing prior: "Clothed in no bright robes / . . . / Borrowed from
aught the visible world affords / Of grace, or majesty, or mystery," this
Spirit "Held commune with him, as if he and it / Were all that was"
(lines 480–83, 487–88).

Thus the poet in *Alastor* locates truth within his own originality,
and only there. His moment of revelation comes in his sleep when,
through his imaginary union with the visionary maid, he finally feels
himself outside the phallocentrism of the tradition that formed him.[8]
We recognize immediately the double of the poet: "Her voice was like
the voice of his own soul / Heard in the calm of thought" (lines 153–
54). Harold Bloom helps here with a concise condensation of Freud's
theory of love: "We fall in love, according to Freud, as a defense against
a narcissistic cathexis or self-investment when our passion-for-
ourselves threatens to go too far [and result in our sickening of excess
and dying]. But in such falling, we continue to love what represents
ourself, whether we were, or what we would like to have been" (*Poetry
and Repression,* 164). Shelley's love object, his epipsyche, is predicated
on such a polished mirror of the self that he experiences, even *through*
love, the excess of self that leads to death. "His strong heart sunk and
sickened with excess / Of love" (lines 181–82). In *Alastor*, the maiden's
themes of "knowledge and truth" (line 158) combine with "hopes of
divine liberty" (line 159), a liberty wherein the poet will find his own
truth. Implicated in the same Shelleyan epipsyche, then, that we explored in the previous chapter, is a drive toward death that rents difference and burns through language in a union with an Other that reveals, paradoxically, only the lover himself.

Anxiety hovers, however, around any claim of originality. The poet
sees his reflection in the fountain

8. For an interesting treatment of Keats's similarly explicit erotic representations—the
only other Romantic poet to figure sexual moments so graphically as Shelley in the erotic
dream—see Leon Waldoff's discussion of "Keats's reliance on the idea of a quest as a defense
of desire" (*Keats,* 45).

> as the human heart,
> Gazing in dreams over the gloomy grave,
> Sees its own treacherous likeness there. (Lines 472–74)

This reflection is scored by tension over its object: the singular self that one hopes finally to encounter in the grave, or the always already preemptive cultural ego that has determined even the context of death. This anxiety of predetermination continues throughout the next stanza where, "Obedient to the light / That shone within his soul" (lines 493–94), the poet explores the rivulet that winds through life. Before the ego forms itself on its mirror Other, there is the "hollow harmony / Dark and profound" (lines 497–98). Next the rivulet dances "like childhood laughing" (line 499) in its illusory wholeness of maternal union. Finally it creeps "in tranquil wanderings," with the symbolic function of "Reflecting" all that "overhung its quietness" (lines 501–2). It is at this point that the poet apostrophizes the stream, asking where its waters tend, waters "whose source is inaccessibly profound"; for this stream "imagest my life" (lines 503–5). The water, of course, leads back to an illusory, prephallic maternal order, now forever barred by the nature of subjectivity. Swiftly the bold assertion follows that upon the poet's death, his thoughts will become sourceless too.

It is clear from the moment of the poet's imaginary sexual union with the veiled maid that death must be his goal.[9] "He eagerly pursues / Beyond the realms of dream that fleeting shade; / He overleaps the bounds" (lines 205–7)—the boundaries of language. He will seek authenticity in the one place that it exists. As he accepts the terrible insight that death alone is the place where desire finds its lack, he accepts also the reversal of ordinary values: life is the real vault, and death its reversal. "The insatiate hope which it awakened, stung / His brain even like despair" (lines 221–22). The boat moves forward in a frenzy toward its appointment with desire: "A whirlwind swept it on" (line 320). Absence in death marks, however oddly, the only "pure" presence one can achieve, because the nature of the signifying chain has changed from Being to No-Longer-Being.

Thus the paradox: real presence inheres only in the absence that constitutes death. As Heidegger claims, "The *end* of the entity qua

---

9. As Georges Bataille says: "There is no better way to know death than to link it with some licentious image" (24).

Dasein is the *beginning* of the same entity qua something present-at-hand" (281).[10] Shelley prophesies instead that death locates the originality that life denies. The poet in *Alastor* arrives at originary silence, a space where his step, "One step / One human step alone, has ever broken / The stillness of its solitude" (lines 588–90), and finally he dies, so that his voice, "a bright stream / Once fed with many-voiced waves" becomes part of the "voiceless earth and vacant air" (lines 668–69, 662).

It is in this paradoxical juncture of unmediated voice and its eternal silencing by death, the agent of its authenticity, that the tension of this poem inheres. Lacan worries about the classic adage, "the letter killeth while the spirit giveth life," for "we should also like to know how the spirit could live without the letter" (*Ecrits,* 158). The narrator's survival against the poet's demise in *Alastor* is a grimmer recasting of Wordsworth's anxiety over voice: Wordsworth often placed the true poets, those mute inglorious Miltons, in the grave, with their secondary storytellers apologetic for their inability to speak poetry as pure as the dead. Shelley worries that such apologies merely further indict those who would be true poets of unbelated vision. Still, death's offer to be the real authenticator presents the obvious problem of allowing silence as the poet's only hegemony over truth.

Alastor concludes with a return to the "bad Faith" that the narrator must assume in order to continue speech. We hear his own vision, which in the context of the preceding "poem" assumes the dreary theme of deathless life. He prays, inauthentic man that he is, for the gift of a restorative drug that will resurrect the dead poet for "this so lovely world" (line 686). Yet his putative view of this world is immediately undercut by his allusion to that which the poet has escaped through death:

> Heartless things
> Are done and said i' the world, and many worms
> And beasts and men live on . . .
> . . . .
> . . . but thou art fled. (Lines 690–95)

10. Again, Bataille glosses well the poetic investment in death: as adults, "we achieve the power to look death in the face and to perceive in death the pathway into unknowable and incomprehensible continuity—that path is the secret of eroticism and eroticism alone can reveal it" (24).

The narrator again undervalues the release the poet has finally achieved as he laments that the poet is no longer alive to

> love the shapes
> Of this phantasmal scene, who have to thee
> Been purest ministers. (Lines 696–98)

If the dead poet escapes language, however, those ministering shapes nonetheless still live on "Now thou art not" (line 699). But any potential claim of the potency of language over the priority of death is vitiated by the narrator's insistence that no art is strong enough to "weep a loss" "too deep for tears" (lines 711–12). And the true poet, in his insistence upon filling the gap, may have freed even legacy from its conservative nature: "Nature's vast frame, the web of human things, / Birth and the grave, that are not as they were" (lines 719–20).

By juxtaposing a study of *Adonais* with that of *Alastor*—thereby marking roughly the temporal perimeter of Shelley's mature corpus— we futher insist upon Shelley's fidelity to death as the strongest situation of "truth." What we discover in *Adonais* is *Alastor*'s muted optimism (as it suggests the poet's liberating influence) evolved into a disavowal of the poet's ability to leave his world unindebted through his art. By the end of *Adonais*, Shelley specifically denies that art can hold onto the moment of Revelation; and he embraces, instead, the presence in death. To that extent, *Adonais* is a far darker, more daring poem than most readings have allowed.

The power of poetry to transcend death is suspect from the start. Adonais's poetic "quick Dreams" (line 73) "ne'er will gather strength, or find a home again" (line 81). Echo, though feeding "her grief with his remembered lay" (line 128), can speak herself no more, as if allegiance to the poet suffocates her own voice. Upon the poet's death, she loses, not strengthens, her powers of mimicry so that the art that survives the poet has no ennobling influence. Again, as in *Alastor*, a narrator tells the story of a real poet, with the narrative inauthentic voice merely repeating, perhaps compulsively, the authentic tale he can construct only through words, which efface their truth in translating a speechless thought into an imprisoned language.

In stanza 20, the narrator asks if "that alone which knows" (line

177) "Be as a sword consumed before the sheath / By sightless light-ning?" (lines 178–79); his fear is that the center of Truth is as "th' intense atom [which] glows / A moment, then is quenched in a most cold response" (lines 179–80). At this point death does not yet offer repose for this atom's eternal flame; and the narrator, his syntax echo-ing Shelley's "On Life," bespeaks the problem of existence, which becomes the compelling object of his quest:

> Whence are we, and why are we? of what scene
> The actors or spectators? Great and mean
> Meet massed in death, who lends what life must borrow. (Lines 184–86)

Hence even death holds no promise of exclusivity as a place where only the authentic poets meet. Nonetheless, death is accorded respect to the extent that it limits, in the Heideggerian sense, all that can come before it.

But from this point on the subtext leads, working at times against its dominant narrative, toward the conclusion in stanza 38 that Adonais's peace is that of "the enduring dead" (line 336). Urania meets with her "son," a liaison that is the conflation of death and Adonais, and the concomitant sexual caresses between that union and Urania suggest the interrelatedness of birth, death, and love. Earl R. Wasser-man notes the strangeness of translating Urania, usually a lover, into a mother symbol, but in fact it is a perfect coalescence of parts that fulfills a compelling psychic drive (350). When, in stanza 26, Urania laments that she cannot join her son permanently, it is because she is "chained to Time, and cannot thence depart!" (line 234). That is, she is chained to Father Time, who claims the primal mother for his own.

Allusions follow to the struggle on earth between the Lawgiver and his progeny: the "frail Form" (line 271), or depleted word that repre-sents Shelley as well as the true poet of all time, wanders the world's wilderness, akin to the poet of *Alastor,* while "his own thoughts, along that rugged way, / Pursued, like raging hounds, their father and their prey" (lines 278–79). The syntax here is richly ambiguous: are the poet's thoughts out to kill that which generated them, the language in which the poet couched them? Shelley acknowledges, even in his high-ly defensive *Defence of Poetry,* the problematic relationship between conception and expression. In his famous analogy of the mind in cre-

ation to the fading coal, he alludes "to the fracturing of the sign that
occurs in the transition from inspiration to composition."[11] Some of
the most exciting recent commentary on Shelley's sophisticated linguistic theory emphasizes his ambivalence toward the priority of language over thought (Keach) or his engendering replacement of a linguistic first term with a "will to meaning," or metaphoric displacement, instead (Hogle, "Shelley's Poetics," 179). Yet Shelley's poetry
can also sustain a reading of his rarely mitigated despair at words
preceding the synthetic work of the poem.[12] Certainly the world in
Adonais that surrounds the narrator's ill-communicated thoughts is too
leaden for this poet's powers, which "can scarce uplift / The weight of
the superincumbent hour" (lines 282–83). If Prometheus finds a way
to throw off that weight, the alternative to his voice of cyclic engenderment is this movement toward the strange land where Adonais lives.
The tension in the phrase "both father and their prey" (line 279)
repeats itself in the narrator's description of the brow of the poet/Shel-
ley being branded like "Cain's or Christ's" (line 306): Cain's totemic
killing of his brother asserts his priority over Abel's God, while Christ's
unique historical claim was to have transcended and achieved priority
over death. Such religious figures are most fully understood "in terms
of the worthiness of offerings to the dead" (Schneidermann, *Jacques
Lacan*, 55). In Shelley's attraction to martyrdom (Rieger, 13), he
seems to emphasize his own poetic offerings as embraceable only by
the dead. White remarks that he "enjoyed acting as if he were mount-
ing the scaffold." During the publication of *The Revolt of Islam*, for
example, Shelley excitedly wrote Byron, "I can but die; I can but be
torn to pieces" (line 256). In the narrator's address to the worst of the
indebted, those who use language to excoriate poets who "write" it, we
hear *Alastor*'s quandary restated as well as the gleam of a possible
solution to the historical nature of death. The good will die first and
travel to a place those dry as dust cannot follow: "Thou canst not soar

11. Tilottama Rajan discusses Shelley's theory of the sign at some length in *The Supplement of Reading*, a condensation of which she also delivered at the 1983 Modern Language
Association convention. For a first-rate analysis of the distance between word and authenticity that Shelley explores in his *Defence*, see William Keach, chap. 1. Still, I find Shelley more
defensive, less reconciled to the limits of language than does Keach.

12. Though I would certainly agree with G. K. Blank that "the limitations that he
enumerated and struggled with in his poetry likewise only serve to draw attention to those
limitations, so much so that his poems often tend to become inspired statements of limitations"(42).

where he is sitting now. / Dust to the dust!" (lines 337–38). Thus, the earlier equitable death in stanza 20 at this point assumes elite proportions. Death becomes inseparable from oceanic origin, in Shelley's oft-quoted lines:

> the pure spirit shall flow
> Back to the burning fountain whence it came,
> A portion of the Eternal, which must glow
> Through time and change, unquenchably the same,
> Whilst thy cold embers choke the sordid hearth of shame. (Lines 338–42)

The "burning fountain" contains the phallus of the eternal flame, the sword of lightning that in its self-consummation and self-engenderment owes a debt to no one. At his most optimistic, Shelley posits that the ashes the flame leaves behind assume the prophetic power of always regenerating truth, similar to those scattered ashes in "Ode to the West Wind." He is careful to couch that truth in metaphors of nature's cycles, so the chains of language seem magically unentangled in his bequest to others. Shelley, in fact, here takes the path we have seen Wordsworth try: the use of nature to subvert the real danger of binding others to the father language. Thus, the "cold embers" of a nonpoet will choke; the lightning-hot embers of the poet will, however, burn through the "dream of life" (line 344). Shelley replays the dialectic of *Alastor*: by dying young, before he is tempted to write beyond the authenticity of silence, the poet avoids the fate of "A heart grown cold, a head grown grey in vain" (line 358), a Wordsworth who, "when the spirit's self has ceased to burn / With sparkless ashes load an unlamented urn" (lines 359–60). It is as if the allusion to Wordsworthian poets subconsciously directs Shelley to the displaced truth of the early Wordsworth, a truth whose dark revelation caused the older poet to lose heart and turn elsewhere: one becomes unified with nature only when one dies, as did Lucy, now "rolled round in earth's diurnal course." It is a unity for which Wordsworth yearned: "He is made one with Nature: there is heard / His voice in all her music" (lines 370–71); but such a union necessarily implies an end Wordsworth could not embrace.

In death the artist assumes priority over art, in fulfillment of Shelley's suspicion that art that outlasts its creator loses its objective innocence. The poet in death becomes the mover now, not the moved: he becomes the originary wind that sweeps through the Aeolian harp, inflecting its song with his movement, not the instrument on which it is played.

> He is a portion of the loveliness
> Which once he made more lovely: he doth bear
> His part, while the one Spirit's plastic stress
> Sweeps through the dull dense world, compelling there,
> All new successions to the forms they wear;
> Torturing th' unwilling dross that checks its flight
> To its own likeness. (Lines 379–85)

In the objectification of death, one preempts life's claim to priority. Thus the unsung poets escape the world's ignominy as they rise "from their thrones, built beyond mortal thought, / Far in the Unapparent" (lines 398–99). It is they, and all poets "robed in dazzling immortality" (line 409), who live, paradoxically, in death whereas they died during life. Their priority continues as long "as fire outlives the parent spark" (line 408); that is, as long as the poetic phallus as ultimate signifier consumes itself in its indebtedness to no one, becoming the sword of lightning that will burn through the parental scabbard that would contain it. In death the poet *achieves* the eternality available only to poets, not even to the songs they bequeath:

> And he is gathered to the kings of thought
> Who waged contention with their time's decay,
> And of the past are all that cannot pass away. (Lines 430–32)

As a recent study of Shelley's "rhetoric of silence" suggestively pursues, his "complaints about the arbitrary nature of language" argue that "the significance of language lies more in its potentiality in 'the invisible nature of man' than in its articulation in art" (Pierce, 126).

In contrast with the true immortality of a poet's death is the illusion on which history feeds of having escaped time. The phallic "flame transformed to marble" (line 447) of Gaius Cestus's pyramidal tomb becomes the signifier prematurely fixed, protected from slippage. Such immobilization aligns itself with the "grey walls" (line 442) of Rome that "dull Time / Feeds, like slow fire upon a hoary brand" (lines 442–

43) as if "hoary" time threatens to immobilize and thus castrate the fiery phallus of youth. Of use here is Earl Wasserman's explanation of the false etymology of "pyramid" (line 444) that obtained in Shelley's day. "Pyramid" came from π—fire—and thus the shape of a pyramid was held to imitate that of a flame. The Egyptians invoked the pyramid as a symbol of human life, "the symbol of immortality" (350). Shelley interweaves the paradigm fire/pyramid/phallus throughout *Adonais* to explore the false promises of procreation versus the true immortality of an unfathered flame.

From stanza 51 on, in direct contrast with the dual vision at the end of *Alastor*, the narrator explicitly aligns his quest with the fate of Adonais. It is as if the narrator in *Alastor*, six years earlier, has revised his tale of an anonymous poet so that now the only honest life is located with that poet in death.

> From the world's bitter wind
> Seek shelter in the shadow of the tomb.
> What Adonais is, why fear we to become? (Lines 457–59)

And most overt is a call, in stanza 52, to

> Die,
> If thou wouldst be with that which thou dost seek!
> Follow where all is fled! (Lines 464–66)

All earthly claims to beauty are mediated truths:

> Rome's azure sky,
> Flowers, ruins, statues, music, words, are weak
> The glory they transfuse with fitting truth to speak. (Lines 466–68)

In his paean to death, the narrator pauses just once, whereby he implies the Shelleyan alternative to dying—the epipsyche. His heart, however, cannot "turn back" (line 469) from death because, as in Shelley's own domestic life at this time, "what still is dear / Attracts to crush, repels to make thee wither" (lines 473–74). Thus, the narrator must thrust forward to consummation of meaning: "No more let Life divide what Death can join together" (line 477).

The dazzling pyrotechnics of Stanza 54 locate that ultimate phallic fire as originary Logos, as that which kindles the universe, and which allows true poets to join in its eternal desire. All "are mirrors of / The fire for which all thirst" (lines 484–85); and now the narrator embraces the flame, allowing it to consume "the last clouds of cold mortality" (line 486). In the concluding stanza, the narrator, allowing the world to tear itself apart in birth that seems, paradoxically, to lead inward back to the womb, points to an apocalyptic new birth outside the temporality of language and into the bode of death: "The massy earth and sphered skies are riven! / I am borne darkly, fearfully, afar" (lines 491–92).

Most significant in this late poem in Shelley's canon is the direction it takes at the end—away from the two alternatives of the early *Alastor* and toward an unyielding locus of truth: the narrator overtly claims the privilege of the dead poet as that place to which he too must aspire. And thus, toward the end of Shelley's short career, the narrative mediating voice threatens to collapse into the silence of authentic poetry, a collapse reinacted in *The Triumph of Life*. As D. J. Hughes notes, "No English poet is more notorious than Shelley for poems which yearn beyond what is and which are best understood as 'desperate leaps' out of their own forms" (260). The inevitable question bears repeating: what would Shelley have finally done with the poetic vision occurring throughout his poetry and culminating, however fortuitously, in his last major poem? What direction would the necessary swerve have taken?

It may well be—though never a popular position to hold among Romantic readers, at any rate—that poetry such as Shelley's with its Nietzschean subtext is necessarily predicated on a short life span. If Nietzsche's allegiance to authenticity logically fulfilled itself in madness, Shelley's may have led inescapably to the "music" of John Cage's 4' 33". Cage's belief in "art by subtraction," though in execution at odds with Shelley's method of accreted symbols, translates into the same concern. How does the artist avoid definition by the entrenched standard he wishes to escape, and against which he defines himself? Cage explores the conditions of meaning, calling for "tacet music," a paradox only if the musician operates within traditional temporal confines. Cage as silent artist will wave his hands three times during a four-minute "performance," thus framing his own meaning by using time as a found object, creating an aesthetics that sets perimeters around the ticking of minutes until the artist baptizes time as art. It is yet another version of the poet as legislator of the universe, achieving vision, if not outside of time, then by becoming time's ruler. Enchained by the literary dictates of his own historical era, Shelley nevertheless points the way to a modern "wordless" poetics. It may in fact be a supreme irony that in the privileged iconoclasm of modern literature's claim upon minimalism and white space reverberates the linguistic virtuoso Shelley, who, fearful of influencing others, nonetheless staked out that territory of silence first.

The Triumph of Life is "about" failed artistic redemption and bewilderment, a shock that so much good can come to nought, can come to a silence that is empty after all. Accidentally, of course, the text serves as Shelley's literary last will and testament, even if its assessments were surely preliminary in the draft version bequeathed us. In Shelley's last poem he returns to the darker vision reminiscent of Heinrich Heine's "Questions," where the sea is to answer "the riddle primeval and painful." Heine's poem echoes startlingly the questions in *The Triumph of Life*: "Tell me, what signifies man? From whence doth he come? And where doth he go?" It is Heine's last line, however, that captures the final grim wisdom Shelley allowed his poetry: "And a fool is awaiting the answer."[13] Shelley's Truth Unveiled in *The Triumph of Life* is so unyielding that one is tempted to align his oft-cited "willful obscurity" with Lacan's defense of his own "impenetrable prose style": "If they knew what I was saying," Lacan claimed, "they would never have let me say it." Yet its tensile strength grows out of its own textual ambivalence; as Balachandra Rajan reminds us, the poem's "double abstention" over the question of what part of life is to be found in the pageant is not "prevaricating" but "creatively uncertain" instead (line 187).

The easy rebuttal to any teleological renderings of Shelley's last

13. In addition to reading Shelley's strong Romantic voice against the relative proximity of a Heine, I suggest a modern Romanticism quite at home with the conclusions of *Triumph of Life*: "A scarecrow prophet from a boulder foresees our judgement, / Their oppressors howling; / And the bitter psalm is caught by the gale from the rocks: / 'How long shall they flourish?'" (W. H. Auden, "Which Side Am I Supposed to Be On?")

major work depends, of course, upon accusing the reader of confusing the fortuitous with the deliberateness of a coda. Nonetheless, against current tendencies that would deny the fatalism in his last major poem, an analysis built on this book's conclusions would insist that *The Triumph of Life* exposes Shelley's deepest fears come to fruition: even in death desire cannot sustain an authentic voice. The worst suspicions are confirmed: death does not destroy life, but life destroys even death. Life appropriates the purity of that courageous and desperate last frontier. It is not the poem those who love Shelley would choose as his final legacy, for we are left necessarily wondering what way out existed for a poet who had boldly destroyed, in his unwavering commitment to truth, any illusion of redemption for the inauthentic, belated human being. Silence is a difficult act to follow without seeming noisily redundant.

Even the invocation of voices that Shelley earlier praised is in this poem subversive. The references to Dante and Rousseau provide contrapuntal harmony to their appearances in Shelley's *Defence*. There these two true poets are celebrants of love as life force. "The poetry of Dante may be considered as the bridge thrown over the stream of time, which unites the modern and antient world" (*Poetry and Prose*, 498) could be cast into psychoanalytic terms so that "The poetry of Love may be considered as the bridge . . . which unites the adult and infant worlds." This was Shelley's hope, his chance outside death to ascribe a redemptive meaning to life in this world. But now, through his use of Dante's terza rima and in his evocations of Dante's *Purgatorio*, he recalls the Poet of Love only to assert the truth of Purgatory: neither life nor death, heaven nor hell, awaits the human being, but a horrifying Pinteresque no-man's land whose exit is unclear. Dante's own status as an exile from Florence furthers his role in this poem as voice for the dispossessed participant in life.

Shelley's use of Rousseau as a major figure relies on a sense of the naivete informing Rousseau's rejection of society, as if he could escape contamination by it. It is also possible that Shelley was quite aware of Rousseau's "selective interpretation" of Plato, wherein Rousseau creates a false Socratic emphasis on the deleterious effect of the arts upon mankind (Rousseau, 8n.). Perhaps Rousseau's own dishonest implication in interpretive chains of language suggests a paradigm for the inescapable human condition dramatized in *The Triumph of Life*. The shade of Rousseau laments that

> Figures ever new
> Rise on the bubble, paint them how you may;
> We have but thrown, as those before us threw,
>
> Our shadows on it as it past away. (Lines 248–51)

Any suggestion that such linguistic displacements free the poet from enslaving others disappears when we recognize that Shelley is responding textually to Rousseau's own inescapable legacy.

The poem opens with the false promise of the sun, that emblem of the Apollo who, in Shelley's triumphal "Hymn of Apollo," uses his sunbeams to "kill deceit" (lines 13–14) and to whom "Victory and praise in its own right belong" (line 36). The *Triumph of Life* also presents the sun in its primal potency, felling the "mask / Of darkness . . . from the awakened Earth" (lines 3–4). But there is suspicion on the speaker's part early on, aroused perhaps by the surrounding signs of indebtedness and burden:

> [All that] wear
> The form and character of mortal mould
> Rise as the Sun their father rose, to bear
>
> Their portion of the toil, which he of old
> Took as his own, and then imposed on them. (Lines 16–20)

Immediately the speaker, somewhat in discordance with the putative fullness of the preceding portrait ("But I, whom thoughts which must remain untold / Had kept as wakeful as the stars" [lines 21–22]), surrenders his wakefulness of the night to a trancelike state now that this sun has birthed the day. If there is any chance of authentic vision, one must block out the sun, just as Wordsworth's light of senses must disappear—and create one's own vision out of darkness. But in doing so, one necessarily leaves behind those Apollonian sunbeams that presage the very goal the dark poet would achieve.

In the particular vision granted here, the narrator finally sees into the heart of things. At approximately age twenty-seven in "On Life,"

Shelley had spoken at length of the concern later to permeate his last poem:

> What is life? Thoughts and feelings arise, with or without our will, and we employ words to express them. We are born, and our birth is unremembered and our infancy remembered but in fragments. We live on, and in living we lose the apprehension of life. How vain is it to think that words can penetrate the mystery of our being. Rightly used they may make evident our ignorance to ourselves, and this is much. For what are we? Whence do we come, and whither do we go? Is birth the commencement, is death the conclusion of our being? What is birth and death? (475–76)

In *The Triumph of Life*, the speaker answers that

> none seemed to know
> Whither he went, or whence he came, or why
> He made one of the multitude. (Lines 47–49)

The "Janus-visaged" (line 94) shadow that accompanies the chariot evokes the claims in Shelley's *Defence of Poetry* that all religions have the Janus-like feature of both the falseness and truth of allegory—and that poetry exposes this truth. But the subsequent implication of the four-faced charioteer makes the context of poetry's ability to reveal the truth more suspect. As Harold Bloom notes, the charioteer "is derived from the Ezekiel-Revelation-Dante-Milton tradition of a divine chariot made up of four-faced cherubim." The implication of that chariot is the visionary nature of the charioteer's sight: the "plethora of eyes" is the emphasis of the religious tradition (*Visionary Company*, 372). That Shelley invalidates those eyes—"All the four faces of that charioteer / Had their eyes banded" (lines 99–100)—suggests that even the power of poetry to extrapolate the visionary true part of allegorical religions is nugatory.

Soon the speaker alludes to the terror of seeing frenzied crowds join the chariot's flight. It is as "When Freedom left those who upon the free / Had bound a yoke which soon they stooped to bear" (lines 115–16). That freedom so quickly looks like the Law again not only articulates the horror of this particular passage, but it suggests the motivation for the bleak vision throughout the poem. All joined in this claim of the Chariot's—of Life's claim—"All but the sacred few who could not tame / Their spirits to the Conqueror" (lines 128–29)—that is, those sun/son/Apollonian poets whose phallic insistence upon new potency allows them to touch "the world with living flame" (line 130), though they too will end up with their signatures effaced. As the wild Dionysian frenzy quickens, its participants "dance round" (line 148) that Life which "dims the sun" (line 148). The sexual metaphor that follows alludes, as usual, to the consummation of death, but Life that overshadows the sun of poetry even preempts death, forcing it into cold anonymity. For the end of the sexual union unfolds not into postcoital bliss but into consummate despair:

> the fiery band which held

> Their natures, snaps . . .
> One falls and then another in the path
> Senseless, nor is the desolation single,

> Yet ere I can say *where* the chariot hath
> Past over them; nor other trace I find
> But as of foam after the Ocean's wrath

> Is spent upon the desert shore. (Lines 157–64)

This vitiation of death's potency contrasts with the textual suggestion, though incomplete, that precedes it. Fifteen lines earlier the speaker allows those from "Athens and Jerusalem" (line 134) to escape the triumph. If this allusion is to Socrates or Christ, Shelley suggests that the pursuit of truth that propelled them toward a death assumed for others is one possible liberation from life still left. Just as important, Socrates and Christ are not writers.[14] Their textuality is thus open to endless interpretation, and if such openness invokes misprision, it thereby ensures the innocence of the hero's intent, at least, and the infinite possibility that their unwritten legacy will escape the system they sought to undo. That this particular section goes unexplored in

14. Susan Hawk Brisman makes this point, "Unsaying his High Language," 70n., though she actually takes an opposite stance from my own in that she believes Shelley laments that "without voice . . . language is subject to misinterpretation" (70).

his unfinished manuscript suggests Shelley's difficulty in allowing or integrating even this moot optimism.

Shelley's fear that life destroys even death informs the "ghastly shadows" of life that "fulfill / Their work" so that the spent men and women in "the dust whence they arose / Sink and corruption veils them as they lie—" (lines 171–74). Both origin and end are dust; all else is illusion. When Rousseau enters, it is in a myth of reversing belatedness, a context evoked as well by Rousseau's emblem in the poem as that valorizer of origins. He will "relate / The progress of the pageant since the morn" (lines 192–93), he tells his listener. But though he exhorts the other to follow his thirst for knowledge "even to the night" (line 195)—the time of poetic vision when the world's lights are out—Rousseau himself says he is weary, "like one who with the weight / Of his own words is staggered" (lines 196–97). Rousseau, who believed in the possibility of a pure language, has been disabused of his vision. The "spark with which Heaven lit my spirit" needed to be "with purer nutriment supplied" (lines 201–202). Here we encounter a poetic model for the Melanie Klein/Dorothy Dinnerstein explorations of the mother withdrawing the nurturing breast, with the child's interpretation that the maternal object is now partial and thus inadequate to its task. Indeed, the bad object for Rousseau becomes the metonymic part for the mother who stood between him and the Law; had "purer nutriment" (line 202) been supplied, "Corruption would not now thus much inherit / Of what was once Rousseau" (lines 203–4): Rousseau in the illusory wholeness and originary state of his maternal Eden.

Coincident with Rousseau's corruption by the father is the terrible possibility—and an agonizing if covert fear of Shelley's—that the poet's own words may serve to enchain others in the future: "If I have been extinguished, yet there rise / A thousand beacons from the spark I bore" (lines 206–7). But this ostensibly generative legacy helped fire the French Revolution; and Shelley had lived to see the fallacy of systemic rather than personal revolution. Thus the stanzas that follow on Napolean's corruption point to the danger of *any* inherited discourse, however well meant. It is Shelley's grief as a poet that "God made irreconcilable / Good and the means of good" (lines 230–31). The universe is condemned to a repetition that in the end may doom all Promethean poetry, as the world's "false and fragile glass" (the mir-

ror?) is sentenced to "New figures" "As the old faded" (lines 247, 248).
And

> Figures ever new
> Rise on the bubble, paint them how you may;
> We have but thrown, as those before us threw,
>
> Our shadows on it as it past away. (Lines 248–51)

There is no escape for anyone from a doomed ontological inheritance. Caesar's and Constantine's crimes bred "many a sceptre bearing line / And spread the plague of blood and gold abroad" (lines 286–87); but in addition, men of moral intention such as Saint John also corrupt the "true Sun" (line 292) they would illumine. Their mediation creates not access but "shadows between Man and god" (line 289), and the mediator, the language itself, becomes worshiped instead of its—inexpressible—desire: "Their power was given / But to destroy" (lines 292–93).

There follows a myth of antenatal innocence—an "April prime" (line 308) spent "Under a mountain" (line 312), time "yawned into a cavern" (line 313) from which issues a gentle stream. It is a nepenthe time of prelife, which now reveals the proleptic allusion in the failed object of the mother: here, in this wombful bliss, "A sleeping mother then would dream not of / The only child who died upon her breast / At eventide" (lines 321–23). In this same enchanted bower of prelife, the king-father will not grieve over his inevitable dispossession by his progeny; he will

> mourn no more
> The crown of which his brow was dispossest
> When the sun lingered o'er the Ocean floor
> To gild his rival's new prosperity. (Lines 323–26)

But the shape all light intervenes. In many ways this shape is Shelley's darkest symbol, because conflated in her is life—always a constraint—but also the mother of infancy and the Ideal of love itself. She betrays her captive by erasing all memory of innocence from his mind. The ultimate torture, however, may be those Wordsworthian "saving" gleams of a prior day, for the speaker is doomed, in the light's severe excess, to sense dimly

A light from Heaven whose half extinguished beam
Through the sick day in which we wake to weep
Glimmers, forever sought, forever lost. (Lines 429–31)

It is as if here Shelley reveals that his earlier denigrations of the apostate Wordsworth served largely as a psychic defense; better to decry his politics and his waning poetry than to face the larger more desolate truth that Wordsworth's early untainted hope was wrong.

In spite of an individual's strongest resistance, he is born into a chain of signifiers that define his life, and that chain relates one link to another; wherever one fits in that rusty system, even if she begins pure, she will take on the neighboring corrosion. Everyone will end as captives of the Car, with "all like bubbles on an eddying flood" falling "into the same track at last" (lines 458–59). When, in lines 475–77, Rousseau evokes Dante's claim for the eternal power of love—"all things are transfigured, except Love"—he unwittingly parodies, in word and in inherited terza rima form, the false belief of yet another belated Romantic, since the preceding stanzas have just desecrated that hopeful claim. Even love has no privilege. Shelley's earlier vision of the cyclic nature of a renovated world becomes transformed here into a cycle that will consist of "old anatomies" (line 500) who laugh "from their dead eyes / To reassume the delegated power" (lines 502–3). Human beings are doomed to repeat the system that bears them, the system that allows for no metalanguage to escape determination by it. It is worth quoting at length from the conclusion that serves as an epitaph for the poet who refused in the end to flinch from the truth: the medium of his art was also his prison.

I became aware

Of whence those forms proceeded which thus stained
The track in which we moved. . . .
. . . .
. . . and in the eyes where once hope shone,
Desire, like a lioness bereft

Of its last cub, glared ere it died; each one
Of that great crowd sent forth incessantly
These shadows, numerous as the dead leaves blown

In Autumn evening from a poplar tree—
  Each, like himself and like each other were,
At first, but some distorted, seemed to be

  Obscure clouds moulded by the casual air;
And of this stuff the car's creative ray
  Wrought all the busy phantoms that were there. (Lines 516–34)

These autumnal dead leaves give way to no seed of spring, and the obscure clouds crush the earlier hope implicit in the conclusion to Shelley's poem "The Cloud": "Like a child from the womb, like a ghost from the tomb / I arise, and unbuild it again" (lines 83–84). For life's final "triumph" may be its unending procession of insistent voices crying out that desire after all dies with a whimper, not a bang.

When Wordsworth acceded to the realism of a paternal order that acknowledges only mediation as the source of meaning, a particularly enabling myth of self-constructed or at least mother-constructed desire that motivates his greatest poetry was necessarily lost to him, even as this paternal law allowed for the illusion, at least, of the male-encoded generation of meaning. For, as Shelley negotiated throughout his canon, the Logos, to retain primacy, must consume itself, must assent to the power, as Paul tells the Corinthians, of the il-logos, the existential absurdity of the Word's crucifixion as a means of enabling the world to come, a position that we will see Byron articulate in order to exploit in texts as diverse as *Marino Faliero, Cain,* and *Don Juan.* The radical demands of the Western, Judeo-Christian Word for conflagration—a word without beginning or end—are too severe for any poetic voice, unless it mystify itself—or celebrate itself in the very act of its demystification.

Byron: Art of the Perpetual Tease

Our hulking confrere scraping the wall,
piling the dust over the motionless face:
in the abyss of time how he is close,
his art an act of faith, his grave
an act of art: for all,
for all, a celebration and a burial.
                    —JOSEPHINE JACOBSON, "In the Crevice of Time"

Chapter 7

Underwriting Death, Overwriting a Theme

The confusion over where to locate voice and the inevitable drive toward death that this impulse engenders in Wordsworth and Shelley both inform Byron as well. Nonetheless, there remains the task of reconciling the oddness of Byron—the recurrent note among critics that Byron stands apart from the major Romantic impulse—to the hegemony of Lacanian desire compelling Wordsworth and Shelley.[1] Byron actually rounds out the Romantic urge toward an escape from the prison house of language as he establishes a myth wherein language holds death in abeyance rather than leading to it; linguistically self-conscious, he articulates most clearly the intersection of language and the familiar Romantic trope of insatiable desire. Because in many ways Byronic *textuality* is seriously underinterpreted in the canons of Romantic criticism, I shall depend extensively in the following chapters upon "straight" poetic explication, though I will invest heavily in establishing Byron's intuition of the psychological dynamic later limned

---

1. As recently as eight years ago, Peter J. Manning maintained that "of the six major English romantic poets, Byron remains the odd man out" ("Review," 401). In an earlier attempt to reconcile Byron to what he sees as the Romantic project, George M. Ridenour makes a claim nicely congruent with my own position: "Byron's refusal to be 'vatic' while embodying many of the values of the vatic pose tends to support that pose, and this may prove to be one of his important functions as Romantic visionary" ("*Don Juan* and the Romantics," 571).

by Freud in *Beyond the Pleasure Principle* as a particularly compelling paradox of life and death.[2]

Most dramatically present in *Manfred*, a preoccupation with the inability to die to a suffocating world subtends much that is either exoteric or heroic in Byron's poetry. Yet the textual pressure creasing even the happy narrative line is better understood as the wish to die a *proper* death. The Freudian wisdom that "the aim of all life is death" (*Beyond the Pleasure Principle*, 38) complicates much of Byron's poetry.[3] Freud tells us that the organism wants only to die in its own fashion; not short-circuited by external stimuli, it follows its life to an appropriate, innate extinction. Byron's discourse enacts this quest for an apposite conclusion, one undetermined by the law, and one whose location (even if in mobility) confers meaning retrospectively upon life. It is, of course, an odd thing to speak of Byron as if he were so self-consciously considering a course of accommodation with linguistic determination: after all, he asserted often in his letters and personal comments that he was uninterested in systematic explanations of his acts of writing. Still, without engaging the questions of intentionality, or second-guessing motivation, we can nonetheless pursue the course his literary workings-out took, the textual trajectories of Byronic energies by which his verse speaks to us. We can, that is, as another critic suggests of Blake, retain "Byron" as an "operational fiction" (Ault, 5). For such a poetry, an "organic" death into the prephallic stage of Wordsworth's great ode forecloses upon a labile desire whose fragmentariness functions, it turns out, much as Wordsworth's valorization of unity. In "Darkness," for instance, Byron elaborates on the theme of the Last Man by opposing the remaining two survivors, bared, soul to

2. For an interesting collection of essays that does much to remedy the paucity of textual, formal engagement extending beyond the suavities of Byronic meaning, see Beatty and Newey. Particularly suggestive in this volume is the trenchant analysis of a kind of existential freedom realized at the level of form by Drummond J. Bone. Bone's essay *"Beppo,"* while in no direct way engaging with the issues I pursue here, nonetheless suggests the kinds of freedom from a particular Romantic (and, of course, modern) ideology available when a poet (and the critic) refuses the operative equation of depth versus surface. In *Beppo*, Bone locates a peculiar textual freedom at the level of form that would seem, paradoxically, to depend upon the materiality of language to efface its claims upon construction of a teleological, content-full end.

3. Denis de Rougement remains one of our strongest commentators on the inevitable linkage of death and love as subject matters for Western authors. Byron is, of course, mythologized as the poet of love; I wish in the following chapters to emphasize how love serves as a handmaiden to his drive toward a self-determined death.

soul, who finally die—into darkness, not light—at the revealed Otherness from whence they came. Byron finally decides that the word *is* the correct death, a death to presence that paradoxically ensures a never-silenced meaning as the word points always to that which cannot quite be captured in a name. The proper death, Byron jubilantly concludes, is known only to a living language.

"What operates in the text through repetition is the death instinct, the drive toward the end," Peter Brooks reminds us (102); and repetition constructs the master rhetoric of Byron's poetry. Language may kill as it names, but it confers a life-giving death upon its purveyors. Harold Bloom laments ("I am afraid that Freud implies . . .") that for Freud, "what desire desires is desire, which means that desire never can be satisfied," and "In Freud's view, the unconscious component in desire dooms all erotic quests to the worst kind of repetition" (*Poetry and Repression*, 147). But for the poet, this is good, not lamentable news. Precisely because desire can never be satisfied except that it finds solace in the compulsion to repeat, the life of poetry is ensured. The proper death, for Byron, depends upon a promised infinite life for the word that names him.

Byron's uncanny celebration of the very medium not "fit" enough to resolve tension ironically depends upon his attempts to accept language at its word, as the paternal trope of a legitimizing origin. In fact, the traditionally odd dual critical emphases on Byron as emulator of a neoclassical order and Byron as modern existential writer reconcile neatly if we locate his need to define proper authority in the first impulse and the drive to "legitimate" the meaning of the present in the second. Byron weds these tendencies in his celebration of the word as the structure of the Law, a Law he believes in if the fathers forming it can be of his own "original" mettle. As much as Wordsworth and Shelley, Byron yearned initially to help define the very Law against which he seemed to rebel. Even his last action, his mission to Missolonghi, aimed to reestablish what he understood as the rightful social order by restoring Greece to its proper inhabitants and inheritors.

Paradoxically, given his flamboyancy in the role of pariah, Byron may by nature have been far less the paternal slayer than Shelley. He was willing to locate his mandate as a poet in a proper first Word, but as he lifted the veil from culture, he found the punitive sons of *Marino Faliero* always already having inscribed the pure source. Byron came to recognize that desire too is structured against our wills, or better yet, determines our will.[4] Authority comes not from the "pure source" (48) of "Prometheus," but from the fetters of words themselves. Language, if it does not incarnate our deepest thoughts, if it does *not* prove a fit medium of desire, could become a counterspirit, Byron would surely concede to Wordsworth. But that very counterspirit finally transcends origin as it embraces both beginning and end of one's own story. And, most important, the counterspirit will prove to have a life of its own, a life that will threaten, as in *Don Juan*, to go on forever.

Byron ends *Childe Harold's Pilgrimage* by affirming the role that language plays in perpetuating life, its superiority as a tool of engenderment over the actual penis that proves, as the framing filiation of canto III poignantly confirms, impotent in staving off the claims of others over one's own progeny. In the interim he nonetheless entertains Shelley's anxiety over its life-sapping potential. Byron's tension surfaces as he displaces his mistrust of language onto women, who, he fears, might absorb his voice. An ecstatic absorption, however, effects at least a death proper to the organism: his passion for Augusta Leigh ("Augusta! C' etait un refrain perpetuel") as Teresa Guiccioli sighs [Lovell, 252]) points to the annihilation Byron sensed as present in the perfect sexual union.[5] Death in its proper sequence—a death self-willed as the culmination of its organic aim—is a resolution unavailable to imitations of the real thing, the real passion (incestuous); and thus the embrace of women *inside* the social order merely threatens to domesticate the poet's voice that would speak as if from beyond that inadequate system. "Ordinary" sexual relationships might short-circuit life into a premature death through an insistence of a signifying chain that, to Byron, keeps meaning limited, unlike the satiated, meaning-ful word of an incestuous union.

Childe Harold emphasizes the importance of Harold's resistance to

4. Though using a different vocabulary, Kim Ian Michasiw speaks elegantly to this point: "Separating the essential from the acquired within a metaphorical structure of inside/outside or form/deformation is not an option Byron considers open." I cannot agree, however, that such formation is canted upon an essentialist plane that makes prior being equally valid in Byron's ontogeny: "[His heroes'] esssential beings are deformed by a social or legal force" (31). Byron's poetry increasingly comes to insist upon the underwriting of any psychological signature by an anterior linguistic (thereby social and material) fund.

5. Peter Manning argues convincingly that while talk is "sexualized" for Byron, "consummating the desire for women must be resisted, deferred, because it would annihilate the poet's voice" (*Don Juan*, 218–19).

a woman's beauty, woman as she defines for others "Their hope, their doom, their punishment, their law" (II.32). In order for the narrator and Harold to tread the mountain-paths and sail the "varied shore[s]" (II.36), they must keep their goals open-ended, refusing, Don Juan-like, to allow for fulfillment. It is the "base pursuit" (II.33) of woman that has deflected the quest from defining the truthful life; honesty with women leaves the man empty-handed so that he must learn to "Disguise ev'n tenderness," for "What careth she for hearts when once possess'd?" (II.34). Otherwise, the prize for the winner annihilates (too soon, in a premature climax) the animating desire:

> When all is won that all desire to woo,
> The paltry prize is hardly worth the cost:
> Youth wasted, minds degraded, honour lost,
> These are thy fruits, successful Passion! (II.35)

Although *Childe Harold* relies thematically and rhetorically on epitaphic inscriptions, the poem's narrative drive depends upon closure imposed only at the proper moment.[6] Woman, with the ambivalent exception of the all-too-perfect incestuous partner, represents a foreclosure.

And timing—historical, sexual, textual—is everything in this poem. With the narrator scornfully casting his eye upon the dusty remains of past glories, canto II opens by exposing the "dreams of things that were." "Is this the whole? / A school-boy's tale, the wonder of an hour!" (II.2). Neither homage to the past nor anticipation of the future conveys wisdom, as human strivings for a life after death reflect a stunted appreciation of life on earth:

> Is't not enough, unhappy thing! to know
> Thou art? Is this a boon so kindly given,
> That being, thou wouldst be again . . . ? (II.4)

If the human being wishes to locate sense in repetition—an impulse that I am seeking to establish as a recurrent theme throughout *Childe Harold*—that meaning cannot rely upon a teleology that promises to

---

6. To the extent that the Wordsworthian epitaphic mode of language as incarnation infuses *Childe Harold*, G. Wilson Knight and, more recently, Paul Fry are surely justified in claiming the image of a massive graveyard as the poem's dominant motif (Fry, "Absent Dead," 413).

confer significance retrospectively. The position that "All that we know is, nothing can be known" (II.7) underwrites more poems than this one, as it motivates most of Byron's major works, including the oriental tales in their doubling motifs, *Cain, Manfred*, and finally, most strikingly, *Don Juan*. Byron insists that if repetition is inherent in life, it has meaning in and of itself.

This position is most fully, personally realized, however, in canto III, a seminal (in both senses of that word) text in Byron's canon. The extraordinary mosaic of history, literary tradition, and familial claims enacted in canto III—*Childe Harold* being reconceived at this point after the scandalous 1816 marital separation and exile—richly complicates what previously appeared a self-contained trajectory of desire. I think it worthwhile, therefore, given the canonical significance accorded to both canto III and canto IV in the critical reception of Byron, to reflect upon the personal dynamics of his life at this time.

Reading the infamous separation letters from Byron to Annabella—or "Bell"—and to Sir Ralph Noel in the first months of 1816, one cannot help being struck by the obvious pain Byron feels at the betrayal of a relationship he would seem to have constructed, legally, with every intention of honoring. One senses him *constructing*, in fact, his love for Annabella, as she and his daughter become configured as parts of his legal body and identity—"am I not the husband and father"—"my wife and not your daughter"—"the signs of affection, Bell, that have passed between us daily": these letters from February 1816 are among the most difficult to read precisely because he *means* to love, to love well. And it seems fair to say that he does love both wife and child, if we must admit what may seem to us the curious state of having to "will himself to love"—paradoxical, of course, only in light of patterns of romantic, versus older patterns of contractual (as well as aristocratic) love. Being robbed of his opportunity to perform properly his legal, his lawful responsibility to love and care for Annabella and their child effaces him, as he is barred from the duty he would perform. Thus, Byron's exile not from England alone but from the legality of England, from *marriage*, a law he had chosen to speak from within, and the "second" layer of that legitimation, its production of a legal heir, charts his way out of a previously cast luxurious solitude in cantos I and II of *Childe Harold*—a false solitude to the extent that his "alienation" after all provided the terminus a quo for social indulgence and worldwide celebrity status—and a move *into* the life of poetry, word irrevocably inflected, infected by world, world *possibly* redeemed by word.

I would argue that partly as a result of his confrontation with the law of conjugal possession and dispossession, Byron effects a new cohabitation with words, words that *are* things, reified, though often into markers of temporal and spatial near hits, always slightly, necessarily, missing their mark. These are words which both reflect and offer the *liberation of incomplete contemplation to the reader*—as important an identification of a "Byronic" text as is the currency granted the "fragment" for the rest of the normative Romantic canon—and a source of power that goes far to explain our sense of a critical potency in Byron's works still underexplored, in spite of the masses of secondary criticism. Byron spends 1816 finishing what began his career—a poetics of self-absorption, answering questions about beginnings, middle, and endings; now he begins—ironic as it is, given that the Byron myth to this point fed precisely on the refusal to separate artist from tale—to write out of a poetics subtended by his own personal drama. Byron dramatically loses control over the rules of interpretation of his private constructions as soon as he enters, as man, the larger world of random signification. And this experience sees itself constructed back into the new fictions. Incest is a metaphor, marriage its legitimation, for the means by which one purchases self-authenticity, paradoxically, through engagement with others.

Byron uses the literal silencing of his own voice through his wife's storytelling in England as a paradigm, in the verses on the Brussels ball preceding the Battle of Quatre-Bras, for the yoke that marriage imposes, the short-circuited desire that creates a premature end. Through rhyme, he juxtaposes the putative opposites of marriage and death— "all went merry as a marriage bell; / But hush! hark! a deep sound strikes like a rising knell!" (III.21)—as a segue into the carnage that follows the dance. To oppose the castrating powers of the normative social order, Byron describes the good "marriage" in terms of illicit relationships, particularly with his sister. Alluding to this subversion of the Law as a particular strength that incest offers, he claims as an antidote to his servitude, the "one soft breast" (III.55)

> Which unto his was bound by stronger ties
> Than the church links withal; and, though unwed,
> *That* love was pure, and, far above disguise,

Had stood the test of mortal enmities
Still undivided, and cemented more
By peril, dreaded most in female eyes. (III.55)

What confuses readers in their attempts to understand Byronic
desire is the simultaneous existence of the poet's flailing of social order,
of the law of everyday existence, with his elevation (more than any of
the other Romantics) of a proper source in which to situate authority.
For Byron is willing even to conceptualize the possibility of a God, and
if the laws that claim to inscribe God are inane representations, Byron
himself attempts an alignment with a functional space of a proper
father, at any rate, who has the right to name. It is in part this impulse
that allows him such easy admiration of the Popean generation of
adherents to classical form, writers who paid homage to the notion of a
hierarchy of being. "Let me quit man's works, again to read / His
Maker's," the narrator tells us, (III.109) as he prepares to "pierce" the
clouds covering the highest Alps surrounding him, in the process rein-
vigorating his song "which from my reveries I feed / Until it seems
prolonging without end." At this point in Byron's engagement with
questions about the constituency of thought, words are *not* things, as
he laments in canto III, stanza 114, and thus the poet's authority comes
from outside the determination of language and from a natural order
whose "things" precede the writer's act of interpretation.

If Byron can stake his claim to proper voice in the vatic power of a
first, real Maker, however, his song will rightfully seem "prolonging
without end" (III.109). Just as he strives, at this point in the poem, to
distance himself from those who are mere imitators of primal Law,
those who cry "aloud / In worship of an echo" (III.113), so Byron's
quest includes a need to name himself as a *real* proper father as well as
in lineage with a name-conferring symbolic father. His daughter, Ada,
thus opens and closes canto III in Byron's use of his unfulfilled relationship with her as a metaphor of stumbling toward a paternal blessing that will sanction his right to write. He is threatened, however, by a
social order determined to vitiate his iconoclastic powers of speech.
But there is liberation in lack, in finding the social order both too little
and too much: no father can be good enough.

The last two cantos of *Childe Harold,* but especially canto III, discover that the patrilineal claim to originate subjectivity does not be-

long to the father after all; instead, such claims contextualize the question of filiation that others determine, including all those literary
figures the icons of which fill the often explicitly historical narrative of
this canto. Art and history, self-situation and material constituency—
one speaks to the other in Byron's poetry of this period, questioning
the wisdom of fidelity to categorical thinking. The urgent, real ways in
which it was impressed upon the poet that inner and outer cannot be
clearly delineated, the fault line quite faultily invaginated instead—that
the way in which the legal definition wrought through the marriage
contract had curled back on itself and reached into the most private
parts of this man and author and had created identities, reflections,
parts, and pieces beyond his control of interpretation—surely this new
experience of the violation of privacy shifts his position toward writing
as a profession—in both senses of that word—and enlarges his perspective on the relationship between a poem and its interpreters. Thus
those vexed problems of self and object, of possession versus being
owned, become the bookends for the quest in canto III of *Childe
Harold* for representational strategies of self-advocacy and legitimation.
Byron as progenitor of his real child, a father who, risking a particular
kind of vulgarity out of keeping with the aristocratic delicacy in evidence elsewhere, uses his infant's real name to frame his text, both to
serve as imprimateur over all those other real literary voices he invokes
within the canto and to arrest the historical pulverulence therein. At
the same time, he confronts the emptiness of his particular procreation,
the truth that this writing—in spite of his intentions otherwise—
served merely, as Matthew Arnold would put it, to relieve himself, a
volcanic eruption that stays the earthquake, in his oft-quoted 1813
letter to Annabella—but which does not, in the end, ensure the self-
identity that appears the mainstay of the major canonical male Romantic project.[7]

The problem of ownership and authorship, of control over and
authorization of interpretation, of who and what one is perceived to

7. For Byron, the loss of a mythical united self is recompensed by virtue of the subject
constructing its meaning through what we might call a Heideggerian program of "throwing"
into the future. Heidegger's concern that subjectivity has become a totally self-conceived
entity disallowing formation in relationship to an outside resembles the progress of Byron's
thought as well, however unlikely the match first appears. We might also invoke Adorno's
privileging of the position of the object in a way that again rehearses Byron, as a kind of check
upon the imperialism of the desiring and all-consuming (all-naming) self instead.

be—and therein, to some extent, what one is—plays then as high drama through Byron's begetting himself as a legal father. He owns his issue—Ada is, literally, of him, by him—but if the process of filiation were so clear, why the adjunct of affiliation, why the legal filaments? For in fact, fathering the child is not a natural identification; society appropriates even this most personal moment of subjectivity by doling out rights and responsibilities, by naming vis-à-vis patrilineage (though only the mother can know for sure), by redefining the father as soon as he produces the commodity, the goods; and, of course, that same social law enables the conditions of meaning, the field into which that coin of the realm, that human artwork, can come into being. It is, in a way, becoming a father when he does, in the emotional morass—the debacle turned crucible—that helps impress upon Byron the impossibility of self-identity, the necessary objectification of subjecthood.

Thus it is that canto III of *Childe Harold* plangently affirms its importance in Byron's self-engenderment-through-others as it frames Byron's voice and person; no equivocation here, since he invokes at beginning and end of this canto his identity as father, and his desire to be a proper one at that. This paternal inscription of course frames another voice, the Harold who takes the rest of the canto through what would appear to be its very different paces: the historical, the political, the literary invocations of Wordsworth and Rousseau. Both author and persona ask to be taken as a generation principle—the insistence upon fatherhood; regardless of what anyone might want to deny, Byron has established that genealogy. He is, both man and poet, fathering figures of mind and flesh. To write, to procreate: in his new legal status as historical father, he can, as a poet, homologously stake out the paternal claim unequivocally by writing in (and of) his fertility at the beginning and end of canto III. Through boldly conflating in a way unmatched at any other moment in his poetry, the real and the imaginary, he points to the fictional, invented nature of text and history, its generational slippage that makes no death quite final, no son or daughter ever enough to tell the whole story.

And so the material of the body fails in its bid for reproduction, and Byron's fictional progenitors will have to succeed on other grounds. If not physical filiation, then lexical affiliation. Consequently, when Harold learns that "life's enchanted cup but sparkles near the brim" (III. 8), he is on the track of revaluing language versus the body, as the medium to stave off a premature end. Language enchants; the stability the innocent hope to discover beneath linguistic representation—the God who would name once and for all—turns out never to be there. As Harold thinks he drinks from a deeper source whose "spring [is] perpetual" (III.9), he finds instead that corruption inhabits even this holier ground. For while the conclusion of canto IV already points to the freedom that Byron will eventually celebrate in this endless play of signification, he still despairs in canto III over the linguistic enervation in which he must travel. It is a social law with too much meaning, and its codifications seem, at this point, to enslave him:

> Still round him clung invisibly a chain
> Which gall'd for ever, fettering though unseen,
> And heavy though it clank'd not; worn with pain,
> Which pined although it spoke not, and grew keen,
> Entering with every step, he took, through many scene. (III.9)

Byron appears to invest as heavily as his Romantic peers in the possibility that an original mind exists prior to the language in which it is realized, but he is ambivalent toward this privileged position. "The beings of the mind are not of clay" but are "essentially immortal" (IV.5); they lack the materiality of words, and words themselves lack the plasticity of "pure" form. The narrator laments that the truths of fantasies fill his "mind with many a form" (IV.7), which in the cold light of reason—of language—seem unsound, or phantasmagoric. We can juxtapose here the famous passage from the *Defence* wherein Shelley speaks of the relationship of words to original image: "Poetry is not like reasoning. . . . A man cannot say, 'I will compose poetry'. . . . For the mind in creation is as a fading coal. . . . When composition begins, inspiration is already on the decline" (503–4). That learning "other tongues" (IV.8) fails to affect the mind that initiates the poet's phrases both points to the mind's provenance outside language and the inability to escape one's debt to an inadequate medium of desire *whatever* strange tongue the poet might try.

The much-touted loneliness or solitude of the Byronic hero exists, for the most part, as an assault upon a cultural standard that disallows the poet to speak what he believes to be his true self. We can read Byron's insistence that the social order threatens to rob him of identity through the Lacanian position that the human being forms an ego only by modeling on the gestalt of another, so that the inability to speak oneself is built into the process of becoming fully human. The problem of self-authenticity is only exaggerated by the onset of language, where the very medium by which one must express desire is, to some degree, responsible in its inadequacy for that to which it gives rise. Thus as the narrator attempts his Wordsworthian flight into nature, he claims as motivation the need to regain a sanctioned voice, for the Law keeps his spirit repressed. He seeks the restorative silence of Lake Leman, though its echoes of prior human intrusions as well as the vestiges of societal intercourse that cling to him attenuate its potential renewal.

> There is too much of man here, to look through
> With a fit mind the might which I behold;
> But soon in me shall Loneliness renew
> Thoughts hid, but not less cherish'd than of old,
> Ere mingling with the herd had penn'd me in their fold. (III.68)

If nature fails us, it is by virtue of its absolute insistence upon mortality, its reminder of the binding materiality that language as well as nature imposes on its inhabitant, "a link reluctant in a fleshly chain" (III.72); while the soul, the self that would claim priority to such anterior determination, spurns "the clay-cold bonds which round our being cling" (III.73). In the subsequent digression the narrator's solution to alienation stands at odds with the poem's dominant impulse: in death the spirit will comingle happily with the immortal wisdom that even now submergence in nature suggests. Such salvific faith in the future, however, is distinctly un-Byronic, and as the narrator asserts, "This is not my theme; and I return / To that which is immediate" (III.76). Byron courageously moves in *Childe Harold* toward locating meaning in the "now," while he puzzles over the Romantic dilemma of wresting authenticity from a system imposed on him from outside. Even the linguistic powers possessed by a liberator such as Rousseau seem, in the end, to subvert their own intention, as "good with ill" is overthrown in the pursuit of freedom (III.77–82).

In the extraordinary stanza 97 of canto III, the narrator voices his frustrations at a language inadequate, finally, to the divine ends of poetry.

Could I embody and unbosom now
That which is most within me,—could I wreak
My thoughts upon expression, and thus throw
Soul, heart, mind, passions, feelings, strong or weak,
All that I would have sought, and all I seek,
Bear, know, feel, and yet breathe—into *one* word,
And that one word were Lightning, I would speak;
But as it is, I live and die unheard,
With a most voiceless thought, sheathing it as a sword.

Byron, unable to loose his tongue of fire, could not claim the confidence of Shelley's *Defence*: "Poetry is a sword of lightning, ever unsheathed, which consumes the scabbard that would contain it" (491). Yet if stanza 97 is Byron's strongest statement of the paucity of words, it also points the way to his solution: repetition (poetry itself as alliteration, assonance, rhyme [Brooks, 99]; all the defining tropes of the genre) as an infinite stumbling toward the meaning that finally *will* unsheathe the sword. For the visionary spark exists in tandem with the confines of the law into which one is born: this is Byron's wisdom. The problem becomes how to create a suppleness from a determining chain that too often occludes human potential:

from our birth the faculty divine
Is chain'd and tortured—cabin'd, cribb'd, confined,
And bred in darkness. (IV.127)

The famous opening lines of this last canto, "I stood in Venice, on the Bridge of Sighs; / A palace and a prison on each hand," suggest the inevitable encroachment of a stifling system that threatens any attempt to signify outside itself, an enslavement ever present in the sliding of signifiers toward a goal of full meaning.

As Byron tries to wend his way creatively through a labyrinth of linguistic determination, he implies an opposition between history as event and the history of the word (a tension that will structure *Marino Faliero*), with the first offering only the illusion of progress, and with the chance of real renovation residing in the latter. Napolean may have pierced the law, but now he nonetheless "wears the shattered links of the world's broken chain" (III.18). Yet if the ordinary human being can make nothing constructive of vestigial chains, a poet, through the infinite reverberations of his echo, can rebuild a new world. Byron translates the echo into emblem of power in four significant places: in his insistence upon separation from the imitation that echoes can imply (III.113); in his use of the cannon's echo to portend the death knell of old orders (III.22); in his privileging of his own echoes over the records of history (IV.142); and, finally, in the triumphal open-endedness of poetry itself, as canto IV concludes with the poet's voice transformed into an echo that assumes prophetic powers, always imaging (for those with ears to hear) a future they can shape, by heeding the poet's call.

History as a procession of triumph and decay implies the question motivating *Cain*—what, then, is the purpose of life? For in the repetition of events, there is no meaning even as

> men bled
> In imitation of the things they fear'd
> And fought and conquer'd, and the same course steer'd,
> At apish distance. (IV.89)

People act as mere "puppets of a scene" (IV.87). Historical filiation seems not to proceed from a divine Maker, but from effete fathers who bear their children into an always oppressive legacy:

> And thus they plod in sluggish misery,
> Rotting from sire to son, and age to age,
> Proud of their trampled nature, and so die,
> Bequeathing their hereditary rage
> To the new race of inborn slaves, who wage
> War for their chains, and rather than be free,
> Bleed gladiator-like, and still engage
> Within the same arena where they see
> Their fellows fall before, like leaves of the same tree. (IV.94)

If "the moral of all human tales" reduces to the end of death—with life "but the same rehearsal of the past" (IV.108)—where can one locate freedom? In a stanza following yet another account of the debacle of history, the narrator alludes to the disruption of voice, the detour that his very poem itself provides on the path to extinction. As he visits the Roman colisseum where he recalls that death and life were "the playthings of a crowd," he becomes aware, among the ruins of "seats crush'd" and "walls bow'd" (IV.142), of the weight of his own poetic presence: "My voice sounds much / . . . / my steps seem echoes strangely loud" (IV.142). This sequence recalls both *Alastor's* interest in the history on ancient walls and the potential of art, at least, to outstay history. The power of the word to hold death at bay until the appropriate discharge of tension will result in ecstasy; as the living word glides along a signifying chain toward a conclusion, it detours textually until the right/ripe time.

Prophetically, in light of Byron's exclusion from burial in Westminster Abbey until 1969, the narrator in canto IV predicts that his name will be omitted from the temple where the nation's dead are honored. Imbedded in his suggestion of the humble epitaph appropriate for his burial ("Sparta hath many a worthier son than he") is an anxiety again over his right to claim the vatic voice of the proper, enabling father. The narrator laments his own inadequate lineage: "I should have known what fruit would spring from such a seed" (IV.10). Indeed, the very next lines invoke the "spouseless Adriatric" (IV.11) and the non-renewal of "annual marriage," as if the question of voice and paternal rights occurs at a juncture with Byron's biographical alienation from wife and child. As the narrator chastises Venice for her failure to recognize her real history in Tasso, we witness a displaced reprimand to an England turning its back on a prophetic tongue that, if rightly acknowledged, would serve a proper procreative phallic role. If the poet can take any comfort from his exile, it occurs in the linguistic mystification and mythology that situates an outcast narrator as marginal to the community Law, hence escaping its limitations; just as the Logos lives only outside the law of the Pharisees, so

> the tide of generations shall roll on,
> And not the whole combin'd and countless throng
> Compose a mind (IV.34)

like the true poet's. If the poet in *Childe Harold* escapes language, it is because he cannot be understood.

But at the same time, linkage with the proper or primal father offers itself as replacement for a meaningless cyclical history. Filiation, at least in theory, bears a life-giving impulse as it enables generation. In canto

IV, the narrator gazes into a dark dungeon until a sight forms (fantasy or real?) that invokes the poem's earlier dictum that "in creating [we live] / A being more intense" (III.6). In canto IV, stanzas 150–51, the vision of a daughter offering to nurture her father with her breast defines for the narrator a way out of the prison of life, through a union so intense that "Heaven's realm holds no such tide" (IV.150). Now the imitative, socially imposed inferior laws have been subverted, as an oedipal desire integral to identity finds generous satisfaction when it explodes the limited medium thus far available for its expression. The meaningless recurrence of history is at least temporarily undone:

> And sacred Nature triumphs more in this
> Reverse of her decree, than in the abyss
> Where sparkle distant worlds. (IV.151)

In Byron's myth of a perfect daughter-father reciprocity, the child gives of her "clear stream," a life-giving milk and honey of the promised land, repaying old age with "the milk of his own gift," water from the "pure source" that locates the divinity inhabiting man in Byron's "Prometheus." As the daughter replenishes her proper father's life by "render[ing] back the debt of blood / Born with her birth," the use of Ada as the frame for canto III retrospectively serves even better as reminder of Byron's truncated paternal function.

By now we can argue that the most important questions informing *Childe Harold's Pilgrimage* are these: what meaning does one make of the present, and how can that interpretation be rendered significant? Byron pressures the past and projects a future all in the service of a quest to rescue life's inherent drive toward extinction—to justify what a later existentialist would term our being and nothingness. In canto III Harold "wanders forth again" [with] "the very knowledge that he lived in vain" (III.16), for the drive toward immortality which seeks "to break the link / That keeps us from yon heaven which woos us to the brink" (III.14) is thwarted by the clay binding us to earth. Finally, only desire itself serves as a raison d'être: we love to love, and if in the lack constituting that love Shelley finds the compulsion toward consummation, Byron celebrates in its tendency to curve back upon itself the very justification for life and language and writing.

In the conventional anthologizing of cantos III and IV—the common choice to omit the first two cantos totally—the history of Byron criticism has shown itself sensitive to the disjuncture between the two halves, a rupture, however, far more significant than traditional analysis of compositional dates would allow. For the most important shift of sensibility that occurs between the first two cantos and canto III is the translation of the *vagueness* undergirding Harold's dissatisfaction and ennui into the narrator's frame of paternal *lack* that I have emphasized above through his invocation of Ada.[8] As desire becomes further humanized, particularized—desire of and for the Other wherein identity is founded—the poem commits itself to the unifying structural trope of the repetition of desire that has haunted, as we have seen, the entire poem. Even though in its lack, desire implicates the temporality of past and future, becoming, in fact, the very metonymy of time, it collapses those absences into a concentration upon *what one lacks in the present*. Stanza 2 of canto III sets up the metonymy of desire as it describes the recursive rhythms of the narrator's journey:

> Once more upon the waters! yet once more!
> . . . .
> Still must I on; for I am as a weed,
> Flung from the rock, on Ocean's foam, to sail
> Where'er the surge may sweep, or tempest's breath prevail.

As the narrator doubles back to pick up the same Harold of his previous song, he finds the theme mitigated by the "wandering outlaw['s]" (III.3) own muted passions, a new mellowness that therefore needs more than ever the power of the word. In the famous stanza describing the motivation for writing, or

> why thought seeks refuge in lone caves, yet rife
> With airy images, and shapes which dwell
> Still unimpair'd, though old, in the soul's haunted cell (III.5)

we discover both life's purpose as Harold locates it, and the famous fictional displacement of the justification for writing itself as Byron experiences the activity.

8. Vincent Newey, though in terms different from those guiding my own discussion, writes of the importance of fathering to this canto (Beatty and Newey, 148–90).

'Tis to create, and in creating live
A being more intense, that we endow
With form our fancy, gaining as we give
The life we image, even as I do now. (III.6)

Good writing binds textual energies until the right moment for
their proper discharge. But there is a distinction between the fantasy of
writing and the real temporality of the act. The fiction, or fantasy, of
the poem allows for consummation, for the very explosion that writing
instead keeps always in abeyance through repetition as it suggests (as in
Don Juan) that something else must happen next: that life still needs to
be lived. Thus stanza 7 of canto III recounts the dangers of pursuing in
reality what should be a fictive conflagration instead.

Yet must I think less wildly:—I *have* thought
Too long and darkly, till my brain became,
In its own eddy boiling and o'erwrought,
A whirling gulf of phantasy and flame:
And thus, untaught in youth my heart to tame,
My springs of life were poison'd.

It is, after all, the invisible "chain / Which gall'd for ever, fettering
though unseen" that gives him signifiying powers; the narrator,
Harold/Byron, must learn a way to exploit the powers of the chain that
seems present "with every step, he took, through many a scene" (III.9).

If too often the demands of systemic signification serve only to
weigh down the spirit, imposed constraints can, paradoxically, also
activate freedom. Failure of the pleasure principle, or as Freud first
called it, the *un*pleasure principle, allows such excessive stimulation to
excite the organism that it is overwhelmed, unable to bind its energies
enough to effect communication with the "subdued" world in which it
resides. "Protection against stimuli is an almost more important function for the living organism than reception of stimuli" (Freud, *Beyond
the Pleasure Principle*, 27). Uncontrolled desire necessarily becomes so
solitary that it drives toward premature self-annihilation:

Even as a flame unfed, which runs to waste
With its own flickering, or a sword laid by
Which eats into itself, and rusts ingloriously. (III.44)

And what does the poet do with the "fire / And motion of the soul which will not dwell / In its own narrow being, but aspire / Beyond the fitting medium of desire" (III.42)?

The potential liberation is implicated in the problem itself. Even as language oppresses as prior determination against which the independent spirit struggles, it also contains within itself the possibility of effecting an escape from total loss of power. Artists can control and orchestrate their need for originality by creating formal boundaries that, in the case of a *Don Juan*, will leave desire boundary-free. The writing of canto III in the spring of 1816 (as well as *Manfred* in the autumn of that year) paves the way for poetry as artifacts, poems as words that are things, that could be said to work as deictics—those words of orientation such as "I," "you," "here," "there"—a kind of spatial and temporal stabilizing of an otherwise uncontrollable motility. This marking of place and time points, on the one hand, to the subjectivity of the artist crafting the object (therein, however, inhabiting the same lack out of which any subjectivity issues as it forms itself on reflected images of that which is outside itself). At the same time, it suggests that poetry can achieve an object status, words that *are* things (whether a daughter or Ada as text), but words nonetheless that again reflect loss, the specificity that a deictic achieves good only for its brief, contextual moment in time—an illusion of singularity. The subject is always object for someone or something else. The freedom Byron points toward in 1816 in *Childe Harold,* canto III, and in *Manfred* through his procreations and deaths of daughter and self, and the pun imbedded in dying to oneself—that in the ecstasy of dying one can create new life—speak of a working out of a poetics and philosophy that engender *Beppo* and *Don Juan*, from the sociability of system, of being in the world and of it.

Hence even as Byron elevates the Byronic madmen who aspire to a status beyond the merely mortal, he rescues himself from paying the price for that land of freedom by inscribing their stories within his own self-controlled textuality. The solution to language as prison house is language as written text, whereby Byron reverses the Western priority of speech over writing that has earned Derrida's wrath and posits writing as a subversion of its own medium. The present tense *as it is created* by art becomes the detour of the continuum birth-death; the poem enacts the appropriate middle narration between the passage

from past to future. Art, rememoration, representation, all allow us to
create our own conclusions. Art is the detour, the necessary deferral
that engenders meaning.

> We gaze and turn away, and know not where,
> Dazzled and drunk with beauty, till the heart
> Reels with its fulness. . . . (IV.50)

> The gods become as mortals, and man's fate
> Has moments like their brightest. . . .
> . . . .
> We can recal such visions, and create,
> From what has been, or might be, things which grow
> Into thy statue's form, and look like gods below. (IV.52)

It is disquieting that desire at its most human is born out of the
imposition of language, and ultimately out of language's inability to
speak one's need. At the moment of symbolic intervention, the Edenic
lived illusion of unity and fullness recedes, with words never quite
adequate as a medium of their translation:

> Where are the forms the sculptor's soul hath seized?
> In him alone. . . .
> Where are the charms and virtues which we dare
> Conceive in boyhood and pursue as men,
> The unreach'd Paradise of our despair,
> Which o'er-informs the pencil and the pen,
> And overpowers the page where it would bloom again? (IV.122)

Unquenchable longing blesses the writer in its mandate to write
on. Byron makes of the emptiness in language its salvation, as such lack
works against "The dull satiety which all destroys" (IV.119). Poetic
words, through generations of readings, will defer absolute closure.
This fissured linguistic texture constitutes the divinity of poetry, something uncanny that will surely reincarnate the creator, that which lives
in Byron's literal progeny Ada of canto III, and that even outlives her.
Byron fathers words that father him, words he carves from worlds that,
in the Shelleyan mode, could prove propaedeutic to an as yet unvoiced
age:

> But there is that within me which shall tire
> Torture and Time, and breathe when I expire;
> Something unearthly, which they deem not of,
> Like the remembered tone of a mute lyre. (IV.137)

"Harold" is "himself as nothing"; it is only if he "could be class'd /
With forms which live and suffer" that he can become meaningful
(IV.164). Happily, Byron the writer will finally locate those "words
which are things" (to the extent that he decides that things are words)
which, in canto III, he despairs of ever finding.

Thus out of the myth that language enslaves, Byron elicits an opposite paradigm: language liberates. Even as the narrator recounts
another near-incestuous passion between father and daughter (III.66),
he suggests that biological filiation can only instantiate a final coming-
gling as "one dust." Since "these are deeds which should not pass away,
/ And names that must not wither" (III.67), it is writing that confers
significance, just as writing Ada's presence into the opening and end of
this canto allows her father his self-determining definition of paternity
even as it is articulated and enacted through social codes previous to
his own existence—codes that fathered him. The compulsion to repeat, the death drive as much a structuring trope in language as in life,
becomes a *life*-giving force as it reverses order: death is recorded by
virtue of the act that names absence, thereby engendering life, since
writing makes even death available as presence to the reader. In theory,
any reader can hope for this resurrection from the dead, as she at least
has her epitaph to anticipate.[9]

In writing, then, one masters life: writers create both beginning
and ending; they decide the appropriate length of being. Byron does
not struggle here with the primacy of language; rather, he asserts a
linguistic authority over the claims of biological life itself. Writing
overwhelms life: "Though a dreary strain, . . . / . . . it shall seem / To
me, . . . a not ungrateful theme" (III.4). These words preface his justi-

---

9. Of course, desire for death is merely the obverse of a nostalgia for origin, a moment
outside of language. As Lacan says, "When we wish to attain in the subject what was before
the serial articulations of the Word, and what is primordial to the birth of symbols, we find it
in death, from which his existence takes on all the meaning it has" (Lacan, *Speech and
Language*, 85).

fication for writing, that "in creating" we gain "as we give / The life we image" (III.6). "Real life" is too often lived without purpose. Stanzas 31–35 describe the uselessness of revolutions that create dead heroes and "vain longing"; the narrator recounts the meaningless repetition at the heart of history, as men "mourn, but smile at length; and smiling, mourn" (III.32). More significant is Byron's presentation of the "middle text" of life as an effete form hiding the real presence of death inside:

> the heart will break, yet brokenly live on
> ....
> The same, and still the more, the more it breaks
> ....
> Living in shattered guise, and still, and cold,
> And bloodless, with its sleepless sorrow aches,
> Yet withers on till all without is old,
> Showing no visible sign, for such things are untold. (III.32, 33)

Still, acquiescence to the detour itself may be heroic:

> There is a very life in our despair,
> Vitality of poison,—a quick root
> Which feeds these deadly branches; for it were
> As nothing did we die; but Life will suit
> Itself to Sorrow's most detested fruit. (III.34)

Finally, the degree to which language, always the tease, keeps absent the final articulation of full desire ensures the pilgrimage of this poem. Loss, or the linguistic recurrence of that original trauma over which Freud puzzled, means life as well as death. And writing always records that loss, as in a self-aggrandizing fashion it calls attention both to its own status as the displacement of desire and its co-incidence with language as originary premise for that desire to exist. Writing also allows authors to bind, structurally, their libidinal energies through fictional displacements, so that the id's arrant impulses that threaten to annihilate a Byron are brought under the control of the text: "my soul wanders; I demand it back" (IV.25).

As *Childe Harold* comes to an end, the narrator tells us that the song "has died into an echo" (IV.185), a repetition that both subtracts from and adds to him. He is less ("I am not now / That which I have been" [IV.185]), for language has written him, has assumed its own life in part by extracting it from the writer. Yet this echo will be the cause of "recollection" (IV.186) and will allow the collapsed narrator/creator the stature of a prophetic poet whose "moral of his strain" persuades others. The narrator has earlier denied the efficacy of echoes, contemning their production (III.113), but he now implies that in their status as always having preceded him, they provide the only venue to immortality. Words, in their metonymic existence as emblems of lack, subvert in their very acts of deathlike repetition the actual end of death itself. Where Byron criticism has shortchanged its subject most dramatically is in neglecting the extent to which such subversion underwrites the movement of the poet's entire canon, providing its particular tensile strength. By supplementing the critical tradition with strategically interjected "l's"—Law, legality, lack, loss, Lacan: word into wor(l)d—we begin to appreciate a more complicated Byron whose healthy appetite for his own fictions of total divestiture has too often seduced us into celebrating as "constitutionally Byronic" tonal suavities of meaning, instead of a poetry bent on gainsaying the Romantic myth of a subjectivity that allowed itself to make the truth call on that which it would master.

Chapter 8

Patriarchal Dramas
and Social Reproduction

The renewed interest in British Romantic drama, a genre until recently more often considered for what it was not than on its own terms, well serves students of Byron's considerable dramatic output.[1] My own mining of three texts in this chapter, *Manfred*, *Marino Faliero*, and *Cain*, attempts to calibrate the representational strategies more self-consciously, less condescendingly, than could be allowed by an older tradition that was by and large blind to the peculiar virtues of Romantic drama. At the same time, I do not mean to adjudicate past positions that would delimit *Manfred* and *Cain* as "closet dramas" and *Marino Faliero* as a neoclassical pretender; rather, I would prefer to pressure our categorical understanding of these plays by suggesting that they act out, somewhat sequentially, familial tensions that force the grid out of which the subject declares him or herself.[2] *Manfred*

1. In addition to the past decade's impressive array of critical essays engaged in study of the plays, for example, we experienced the excitement in the spring of 1990 of seeing an entire symposium on *Sardanapalus* sponsored by Yale University. Alan Richardson's *Mental Theatre* thoughtfully attends to the topic of Romantic drama; and Daniel P. Watkins and Terence Allan Hoagwood are compiling a collection of previously unpublished essays on the subject for a forthcoming volume.

2. Jerome Christensen's bold juxtaposition of *Marino Faliero* and *Don Juan*, in part on the grounds that "*Faliero* represents, with all its faults, a poetics of Byron's satire" ("*Marino Faliero*," 313) leads me to suggest that, pursuing the genealogy Christensen establishes, this chapter could be read as the dramatic trajectory culminating in *Don Juan*, as *Manfred*, *Marino Faliero*, and *Cain* all trace the "faults" that "bring satire into being, and satire punishes the faults that make it possible" (314).

enacts an experiment that would, as an autotelic text, fence us out as readers and beget itself as poem through a self-spoken world; the tentacular *Marino Faliero* contests that possibility of solitary construction, insisting in the end upon the inevitable inscription of the political upon the personal and vice versa; and *Cain*, intoxicating the reader with its scandalous courage, invites the reader to become part of a cyclical movement of interpretation, already implicit in the vexed questions of public/private in *Marino Faliero*. By reading these dramas thus, I suggest that the relentless hypotaxis of *Don Juan*—Byron's endless troping on a trope, his dialectical pressing of time into nonstop rhetoricity—seems well and hard won, an expensiveness we must heed. As *Don Juan* exfoliates, revealing its quarry to be the ways in which self and society play off each other and how such an interplay creates, feeds, and denies desire, it becomes clear that this odd epic is far from being at odds with its textual predecessors.

Through its suicide, *Manfred* clears space for us to father—self-consciously, not naturally—our own regeneration. I invoke here a male-gendered procreative mode deliberately, relying upon the Lacanian sense of the phallic as social, as a self-contesting lawful representation of the ways culture interdicts and intervenes in the very act of ego formation. *Manfred* explores the same Freudian insight—late, troubled, hideous to most of Freud's disciples then and now—that we have seen underwrites *Childe Harold* as well: the organism seeks a self-authenticated return to the zero degree of a static Nirvana. *Manfred* experiments with what it might mean to achieve authenticity on one's own solitary terms, whereas Byron in *Childe Harold,* canto III, fathered a social commodity over which he failed to retain authority. *Childe Harold,* canto III, and *Manfred* were written within six months of each other, and to the extent that they have both long been acknowledged as poetic aftermaths to the marriage exile, I'm conflating them as plotted poetic moments on a canonical graph. These two texts enact between them the costs of isolation and social entanglement, in the process granting to us a chance to reconceive of the well-worn Romantic subject/object ideology; the antinomy of self and society in Byron is worked out rather more dramatically, more textually, than at the level of thematics in the period's other major poetic maneuvers. Byron tracks individual versus and through group, refusing in his supple segue from one to the other to foreclose on system in the name of an anodyne idealism that only apparently voices poetic authenticity, but that, in refusing the random and instead grounding itself on "pure" reason, disavows the real self-achievement of death in the proper fashion. The idea of the Law, of legality, and love (in alphabetic shorthand again, the L's of Lacan and, as we will now see, Laura's Petrarchan insistence upon the truth of lack and loss) coalesce in a way distinctive of Byron's mature work.

Byron's ability to play to the lack and the loss encoded within the familial configurations constitutive of identity, the cleft nature of the subject from the start, provides the odd, contrapuntal strength to his more easily appreciated adroit, clear, writerly sense of statement. And if *Childe Harold*, canto III, used the idea of father to undermine our smug conventions of socially stabilizing discourses, what better representation of the inevitable near miss of identity than Manfred's incest with a half-sister—another near miss. Byron's 1813–14 reading of Italian authors motivated him to imitate Petrarch's sonnets, several of which were entitled "To Genevra" and first published in the second edition of *The Corsair* (Vasallo, 2–3). Peter Vasallo persuasively links these Byronic Petrarchan sonnets—however disgusted Byron professed himself to be at the result—to his difficult feelings for Augusta at a crucial time in the development of their intimacy.

But while Vasallo reasons that Byron's ultimate dissatisfaction with the sonnets stemmed from his frustration over not finding the form adequate for his complex feelings, I instead would suggest the *exact* fit: Byron's unhappiness as a proper Petrarchan response to the form itself, the ideological pressure of the Petrarchan promise. The point of Petrarch's sonnets is that Laura can only prove absent; the resolution is always deferred, the quest and its object never achieve self-identity, thus allowing the artifact, the work of art, a privileged place in the world, paradoxically, an arrested moment subject to time and place yet pushing beyond it.

In a wonderful twinning of the impulse promoted by the Petrarchan psychology of inadequacy, Byron himself laments his inability as a poet to pull off the getting of the goods—sonnets à la mode are "the most puling, petrifying stupidly platonic compositions. I detest the Petrarch so much that I would not have been the man, even to have obtained his Laura, which the metaphysical whining dotard never could" (2). It is, again, writing as blood line, textual genealogy that gainsays the guarantee of achieved meaning. The ideology of absence that underwrites the Petrarchan sequence is quite to Byron's point. Thus the common narrative myth that privileges living (and dying) *naturally*—with Manfred's incest its strongest Byronic manifestation—allows Byron little repose; the cataloging of nature in *Childe Harold,* canto III, will yield quite honestly, through the textual working out of anxious other possibilities in *Manfred,* to the stronger emphasis on text, on writing, on art that suffuses canto IV of *Childe Harold* in 1817.

By positing incest as a signification that escapes the prevailing system, *Manfred* obviously would seem to explore the Romantic quest(ion) recurring in *Childe Harold* of how to elude the chains of language. But Byron becomes too aware of the other side of escape: the Shelleyan silence whose authenticity and lawlessness would be poor compensation for a lost poetic vocation. He therefore opposes the glorious zero-degree ground of incest to linguistic generation and hints, at least, that he prefers enslavement within the system, a conclusion that points to the regenerative power of the "need to interpret" that haunts his other major metaphysical drama, *Cain.* The odd appeal of *Manfred* has too easily been tied to its biographical status regarding Byron's incestuous relationship with his sister or to its position as a "period piece," heavily Goethean in its excessive sensibility; but a more subtle reading suggests that the psychodrama of *Manfred* unsettles the reader because it is unsettled itself. The poem is a textual working out of the pros and cons of liberation from the word.[3]

Certainly the poem's emphasis on defying social conventions constitutes a drive toward a self-defined existence. Manfred insists upon dying in his own way, at his own time. "We seek in fictions the knowledge of death, which in our own lives is denied to us," in Peter Brooks's redaction of Walter Benjamin (Brooks, 284). Death's silence that Manfred cannot effect at the opening of act I suggests the overwhelming materiality of the signifier, the oppressive force of thoughts that will not allow for rest. We tend, as a result of the past decade's

---

3. It is true that incest as a Byronic theme has justly received critical attention for some years, although its implicit parallel with a self-consummating language deserves much greater treatment in Byron's canon. Incest's transformation into an engendering structural trope has gone largely unremarked. Though not to my purposes herein, I believe a particularly exciting potential lies in a subtle working out of the two poles of psycholinguistic or sexual/textual fulfillment: on one end, incest as the silent collapse of discrete signifiers, and on the other, bisexuality as a confusion of signifiers into indeterminacy. Both positions represent oversensation, overspilling the medium of language.

criticism, to read Byron as a celebrant of the material world, a position surely at most points accurate. But there is also the Byron who instead worries that "clay, / . . . clogs the ethereal essence" (II.iv.56–57). Such concern consorts fruitfully with the

> sorrow [that] is knowledge: they who know the most
> Must mourn the deepest o'er the fatal truth,
> The Tree of Knowledge is not that of Life. (I.i.10–12)

Life, "that all-nameless hour" (I.i.24) of incestuous passion that the later appearance of Astarte marks, opposes knowledge, which is, instead, mere representation of life, a play of shadow that tortures those who have known its eidos. When the witch asks Manfred "what could be the quest" (II.ii.44), Manfred's answer suggests that he wishes above all else to escape the signification of others and to collapse into a non-contingent, authentic self. "Though I wore the form," he laments, "I had no sympathy with breathing flesh" (II.ii.56–57); instead, he made his "eyes familiar with Eternity"(II.ii.90). He finds life in his soul mate, the woman so like himself that he inadvertently though inevitably destroys her (II.ii.118).

Knowledge, not life, leads to a fruitless repetition of history. As one of the voices sings about the "Captive Usurper":

> I broke through his slumbers,
> I shivered his chain, / I leagued him with numbers—
> He's Tyrant again! (II.iii.16, 20–23)

The world according to *Manfred* is the cycle that Shelley's Demogorgon predicts, but without the Promethean recurring apocalypse. Nemesis recounts the inevitable end of any daring attempts to think outside of the prevailing system: she has been

> Marrying fools, restoring dynasties,
> . . . .
> Shaping out oracles to rule the world
> Afresh, for they were waxing out of date,
> And mortals dared to ponder for themselves,
> To weigh kings in the balance, and to speak
> Of freedom, the forbidden fruit. (II.iii.63–71)

But even as Nemesis swears allegiance to Arimanes, Manfred refuses the ruler's claims, refuses, that is, to accept as authoritative the emanations that flow out of another's mind, for neither they nor Arimanes are one with "the overruling Infinite—the Maker" (II.iv.47). The struggle lies between the claims of the material and those of an outside order that escapes such a realm; one of the conjured spirits claims in admiration: "No other Spirit in this region hath / a soul like his—or power upon his soul" (II.iv.71–72). Of course, a problem remains if Manfred's dream is in his mind; if indeed he conjures up these forms, the forms must therefore still exist inside the language bequeathed him, unless he can prove that the mind is its own place *outside* of the words that name it thus. He does not offer such a proof, of course: he is no closer to the Infinite than they.

Knowledge, or philosophy as ontological revelation, is, then, in Manfred's view, bereft of any wisdom. As Manfred asserts this position the abbot enters, wooing him with compliments over the "noble name" he has inherited from his fathers. But for Manfred to accede to the role of proper father, he will have to accept governance by the Law. "I shall not choose a mortal / To be my mediator" (III.i.54–55), he tells the priest. The abbot misapprehends Manfred's nature and rushes to assure him that

> Our institutions and our strong belief
> Have given me power to smooth the path from sin
> To higher hope and better thoughts. (III.i.60–62)

Manfred denies the old man's power over a mind he would believe is its own hell or heaven, and to the abbot's offer of absolution he responds that such loyalty is too late. In contrast to the strong theoretical or philosophical emphases of Wordsworth and Shelley, Byron engages the problem of the Law's oppression on a personal level, a maneuver that we will see most obviously at work in *Marino Faliero*. At times, especially given his easy admiration of his neoclassical predecessors, he seems willing to accept a hierarchical ordering dictated by the Law—if only that law were capacious enough to include him. Both Byron's and Manfred's "nature [are] averse from life" (III.i.125), but society's continual loyal embrace would have allowed both creator and his fiction to signify within the Law.

Manfred's unspoken narrative center, the incest that defines the antihero in opposition to the rest of the signifying system, achieves its centrality as an act that creates meaning as it differs from the norm. Thus in theory, at least, incest functions as one way out of the synchronic chains of Manfred's/Byron's culturally narrow world. Peter Brooks finds that "throughout the Romantic tradition, it is perhaps most notably the image of incest (of the fraternal-sororal variety) which hovers as the sign of a passion interdicted because its fulfillment would be too perfect, a discharge indistinguishable from death, the very cessation of narrative movement" (297). Always hovering around the edges of Byronic heroes, madness as well as death are offshoots of such "interdicted passion"; to the point is the reality that "madness is the supreme testimony that the individual pays an intolerable price for his initiation into culture" (Morse, 21).

Byron depends upon incest as the grounds of ego sustenance: he uses as his mirror the gestalt of someone so close to himself that he can deny the alienation nonetheless still present because, in Lacanian terms, his ego originally formed itself on an unlike Other. Manfred tells the witch that Astarte

> was like me in lineaments—her eyes,
> Her hair, her features, all, to the very tone
> Even of her voice, they said were like to mine;
> . . . .
> She had the same lone thoughts and wanderings,
> The quest of hidden knowledge, and a mind
> To comprehend the universe. (II.ii.105–11)

To some extent, at least, incest compensates for the passionless world that seems the human being's only modern-day inheritance. "Half dust, half deity" (I.ii.40), humankind is a poor match for the splendors of the surrounding heavens. In nature's sublime, "the patriarchal days are not / A pastoral fable" (I.ii.49–50), so when nature opposes culture, the inadequacy of the latter reveals itself. These lines also suggest the attenuated paternity infusing contemporary life; in Manfred's world "patriarchal days" are corrupt and always indebted, with the phallic power of speech assumed only through the murder of the father who first possessed it. The blood that Manfred sees in the wine cup that the Chamois Hunter offers (II.i.17) becomes an over-

determined symbol: the slaying of the father and the illicit appropriation of his wife/word; the eucharistic blood of the slain Logos of the
father; the purity (and violation) of the first sexual encounter between
two forbidden (therein virginal) lovers; and finally the kiss of death
Manfred's passion confers. The end of act III, scene iii, connects the
blood motif with paternal power, as the scene is described in distinctly
phallic terms—the red cloud resting on "Eigher's pinnacle," Count
Manfred mysteriously "occupied" in his tall tower, his sole companion
"the only thing he seem'd to love,— / As he, indeed, by blood was
bound to do" (III.iii.41–6).

Incest functions, then, as a quest for identity: Who am I? From
whence do I get my particular authority to speak? In his own life
Byron often explicitly endorsed self-love as the only truth of love; and
incest most clearly fulfills the necessary emotional investment of the
self-in-love (Rapf, 642–43). In addition, incest serves equally as an
emblem of the self-chosen death, the defiant death defined outside the
social law and appropriate only to the one choosing. Hence the *potential* triumph of *Manfred* is, in one sense, the triumph over death, as
Manfred claims his own terms for it. If death improves upon life, that
improvement may issue from the collapse of meaning, of differentiation, which incest suggests: the sameness after death will be a relief.

Incest, Manfred believes, may mark the silence he at first seeks. As
incest blurs distinction it obliterates memory as well, the boon Manfred claims to want most of all. The two lovers' passion is strong
enough to break the grave, as Nemesis remarks, so Astarte is able to
rise from the dead (II.iv). But Manfred misinterprets Astarte's silence;
he begs her speak to him, but her silence subverts ordinary meaning.
Manfred again worries aloud that immortality will consist of repetition
only—"A future like the past" (II.iv.131). His obsessive fear of repetition will finally reveal itself as a reaction-formation, however, to his
real fear of *not* repeating, of death silencing him forever. When Astarte
finally answers him, it is only to announce his name and his death: she
speaks his name as a gift of love, for by naming him she confers his end
upon him. She promises to give him the eternal silence of death, a
silence Manfred thinks he desires until it is offered. Manfred at least
intuits her power, for he announces "I now depart a debtor"
(II.iv.168)—in debt this time to the power of the word to kill as it
names.

In spite of the overt drive of this poem toward a freedom outside of human boundaries, we now can perceive the contradiction that complicates our reading and in fact, when teased out, strengthens the integrity of the poem. For *Manfred* also exhibits an ambivalence toward escaping language: both Byron and Manfred signify in their "oddness" *only* from within a system. Only the system makes their difference possible. Thus Manfred displays a reluctance at the end of the poem to merge with one so like himself. Implicit is Byron's larger desire to signify: the poet wants to write.

Even as act I opens we witness to what extent language and its inherited forms shape Manfred's quest. It is, after all, through the "thought which is within me and around me" (I.i.48) that Manfred can compel the spirits to his will. He creates them through invocation, through voice, and so finally it is language that gives him power. If Manfred prefers creating a hell to a heaven, it may be because of the greater heterogeneity of devils than of saints; he seeks difference far more than a transcendental good that absorbs all into union. For all of Manfred's putative privileging of life above knowledge, knowledge gets the edge, because it ensures self-reproduction. Life as a sudden presence to self, as illusory as the early Edenic attachment of mother and child that aped wholeness, is awareness so intense that the signifying chain of knowledge cannot sustain it—cannot, literally, because such primal life exists only as anterior to that chain. At the beginning of the play, Manfred asks for "Forgetfulness" (I.i.136) in order to loosen the hold of the early Edenic union he once knew, before the advent of language. As long as he feels the pull of this primal "oneness" he will seek to reproduce it in death, another collapse into sameness. Only if he can "forget" the imaginary can he accept life as ordered by society; instead he seeks the Edenic in Astarte. Thus such imaginary union finally destroys the power to create meaning even as the conflagration of desire suggests a death that language holds always in abeyance.

"Death hath nought to do with us" the spirits inform Manfred, just after they also assure him that they answer him "in thine own words" (I.i.163, 159). Language allows its users to create their own realities, or fictions, out of the bricolage that is always constitutive of their worlds. The incantation that curses Manfred "dooms" him to unceasing meaning, so the incantation works on the surface as a major conflict of the dominant narrative, while it serves the poem as its latent wisdom (that language *is* immortality) as well. Manfred is compelled to be his own "proper hell"; "the clankless chain hath bound thee; / O'er thy heart and brain together / Hath the word been pass'd" (I.i.259–61). Thus he delays his suicide ("wherefore do I pause? / . . . / There is a power upon me which withholds" [I.ii.19, 23]) because death occludes difference, an obliteration physically reflected in the mists and clouds rapidly engulfing him on the mountain.[4]

Manfred is aware that his "evil" is not his desire for Astarte, but its consummation. His "embrace was fatal" (II.i.88) because he dared destroy the distinction necessary for meaning, as he murdered or incorporated the object for which he yearned. To this extent, *Manfred* serves as literary pre-text to canto IV of *Childe Harold's Pilgrimage* and to *Don Juan*, both poems in which the final consummation of desire is held untenable.

> If I had never lived, that which I love
> Had still been living; had I never loved,
> That which I love would still be beautiful. (II.ii.193–95)

Manfred acknowledges: "I loved her, and destroy'd her" (II.ii.117).

And yet why fear destruction? Manfred reasons that if "what it is we dread to be" is only "the Grave" (II.iii.179–80) there is no reason to delay death. But the real answer is that Manfred fears death because it will absorb him—even as he absorbed Astarte; it is this fear of an equal recompense that compels him to worry over whether she forgives or condemns him. When the death-dealing power arises and claims Manfred, the mutual gaze they share threatens a wedding of self and other too complete. "Why doth he gaze on thee, and thou on him?" (III.iv.75) the abbot asks the finally shaken Manfred. It is self-annihilation that Manfred confronts, the very collapse of meaning he thought he sought. Contained in his proclamation that "I am prepared for all things, but deny / The power which summons me" (III.iii.82–

---

4. We might invoke here the (often negatively cited) painterly notion of "losing the surface" (Gombrich, e.g., 59), a specter that stalks *Manfred*; and it's not insignificant that artistic renderings of Manfred—such as Ford Madox Brown's *Manfred on the Jungfrau* or Tony Jehannot's engraved illustration of *Manfred* in Amedee Pichot's translation of Byron— emphasize his lonely situation in the Alps (which the poet always insisted was the real inspiration for the poem), almost as if society becomes abstracted into an existential agony commensurate with the emptiness, the Alpine haze, surrounding him.

83) is Manfred's denial of the final claims of a desire pushed to resolution. Astarte now embraces him, even as he suddenly claims the superiority of a life lived in combat and differentiation from others over a death that fells meaning. Manfred insists that in the past he was his "own destroyer" (III.iv.139), and that *he will be hereafter* as well, never becoming the "dupe" of death (III.iv.138).

He therein says no even to a death projected and orchestrated by Astarte, for he finally wants validation exclusive of her. By the end of this drama the anxious underside of Romantic incest is foregrounded as the fear of being overwhelmed by the *suppression* versus the *oppression* of the signifier. *Manfred* increases in interest if we read it as a complex dialectic of desire in which problem and solution comingle, at times indistinguishable from each other.

There is always a murder at the origin of cruelty, of the necessity named cruelty. And first of all, a parricide. The origin of theatre, such as it must be restored, is the hand lifted against the abusive wielder of the logos, against the father, against the God of a stage subjugated to the power of speech and text.

—Derrida, *Writing and Difference*

Published in 1821, though drafted a year earlier, *Marino Faliero* proclaims the infinite regress of meaning through the Law and hence a further valuation of linguistic generation as a source of ontological freedom, a far more "material" solution than that offered in *Manfred* five years before. Furthermore, as a result of its insights, the play incidentally legitimizes the endless random wanderings of Don Juan, Byron's hero who, well under way now for several years, so disturbed Teresa Guiccioli. To the extent that Byron shows himself ready to accept a "natural" or even "legitimate" social hierarchy of authority, *Marino Faliero* reminds us of the Popean cast to this profligate English son. In fact, the play's final wisdom accrues significance precisely as it emerges from an initial willingness toward the Law's authority, for then Byron's Romantic answer seems appropriately hard won. *Marino Faliero* casts a neoclassical fullness of language wherein the Law is valorized against an emptiness that Byron finally locates at the heart of language. One consequence is that the play resolutely if reluctantly exposes authority as always corrupt because of its necessarily stolen nature. Only silence is pure, but silence also obliterates history. Thus the ostensible historical lessons that Byron's study yields hold their greatest importance as they encourage him to celebrate linguistically—guilt-free—humankind's corruption as its very source of immortality, and thereby to assure himself that the "answer" of *Don Juan* is indeed the truth.[5]

Marino Faliero insists upon the inextricability of the political from the personal, of familial desires from those that determine social discourse and destinies.[6] Parricide, not surprisingly, acts as the play's engendering metaphor. Prompted by one bold son's attempts to name himself on the patriarchal throne, filial servants, the "Forty" call upon their joint strength to undercut the patriarch's claims, and to deny his power over the woman. Such a primal scene becomes the central motif of location and dislocation of authority as Byron identifies the lure of the black veil painted over Marino Faliero in the Palace of the Doges: the veil and the Giants' staircase where the doge was "crowned, and discrowned, and decapitated" (preface) seize Byron's imagination and compel his play. The black veil that the guilty sons hope will cover their progenitor suggests as well the gaping tomb of the slain father, or the phallus always hidden behind the veil, with its attendant hope and threat that in locating it one isolates the source of meaning—if only to still its voice. In his claims upon those who shed his blood, however, the father behind the veil refuses to be silent; and so those indebted to him try to black him out.

Steno sins through daring to inscribe his desire for his leader's wife

5. See Philip J. Skerry's structural analysis of the concentric circles that entwine personal and political responsibility for a commentary that supplements my own.

6. Julie Ellison argues for situating Margaret Fuller's overt historical radicalism within (rather than opposed to) "romantic subjectivity": "Some recent readers of Fuller have maintained that romantic subjectivity yields . . . to a more politicized perspective in which socioeconomic categories displace individuals. . . . But the radicalism made possible by this series of associations [Fuller's "identification of mourning with history writing"] operates wholly within romanticism, within the habit of referring political sensation to the interpretive theatre of the observing mind" (xiii). This paradigm identifies exactly the vector of Byronic public/private desire, the strategic implication of one in the other. Criticism serves the poet ill by insisting (old style) on the exclusively autobiographical instruction, or (new wave) by determinedly situating his texts within political allegories.

on that man's throne, for all to see. The obscenity that Angiolina finds easily bearable assumes large proportion to her husband because he understands the challenge being made to an old man whose very age argues against his rightful possession of such a young wife. And Steno has challenged the doge in the most potent way, by offering his word in the place of Faliero's, as both the inscription and its host, the throne, function metonymically for their owners' names. This initiating moment in the drama foregrounds one of Byron's most provocative insights, too often effaced through recent critical attempts to categorize his texts as *either* political or personal: Steno's (textually motivational) sexual misconduct rehearses the ancient Athenian position that sexual acts contained civic significance; in a configuration so different from our own historical dichotomy of private versus public, sex to the Greeks, for instance, was "an aspect of one's participation in the life of the city" (Nussbaum, 572).[7] Byron's poetry after 1816 enlists this reverberative potential of sex in the marketplace to undermine the factitious scruples of those who would claim the purity of distinction, a law that could exist outside of their lived experience as sexual human beings.

Although death at first appears a harsh sentence for Steno's offense, the doge's demand makes better sense as we grasp his own intuition of the connection between the personal vilification and the attenuation of his powers as a leader:

> Was I not the sovereign of the state—
> Insulted on his very throne, and made,
> A mockery to the men who should obey me?
> Was I not injured as a husband? scorn'd
> As man? reviled, degraded, as a prince?
> Was not offence like his a complication
> Of insult and of treason? (I.ii.192–98)

Bertuccio Faliero hints early on at the potential power of the Forty against the state: they are as "secret as the grave to which they doom /

7. The Romantics' interest in the ways in which Greek society configured their social/private domains deserves full, detailed address. As, for example, Marjorie Levinson suggests, albeit in an aside to Wordsworth's particular investment in Greek culture, that "throughout the second-generation canon, the distinctively humane consciousness of the Greeks (their arts, letters, religion) is aligned with their social formations" (*Rethinking Historicism*, 61 n.31).

The guilty" (I.ii.32–33), a proleptic pronouncement on the twisted legalities obtaining by the play's end. Thus the doge's quick transference of anger from Steno ("I have no further wrath against this man" [I.ii.206]) to his "peers" seems a logical displacement onto those who would also mark the old man's death.

Angiolina gains importance when we note her function as vessel of the word. If the name itself is easily impugned, the thought behind the word is guarded in the silence of the woman. The doge's wife retains her serenity at the slander directed against her because to do otherwise reveals a wrongful emphasis on the "name / And not the quality" (II.i.66–67) that the name represents. What becomes increasingly clear, however, is that in the world of men words are all that is available for meaning; quality is a prerogative of the paradoxically empty-though-(ful)filled woman as other. Angiolina is a perfect wife to instigate filial warfare, since she marries a man tethered to her own father by age and friendship, a relationship that thus lends a superficial justice to the sons' claims to appropriate the woman for their generation. The narrative emphasizes the daughterly love that undergirds the conjugal; Marianna asks her friend if she loves the doge, to which the young wife responds:

> I love all noble qualities which merit
> Love, and I loved my father, who first taught me
> To single out what we should love in others,
> And to subdue all tendency to lend
> The best and purest feelings of our nature
> To baser passions. (II.i.93–98)

Although the narrative supports the nobleness of this type of spousal love, the implicit lack of sexual attraction serves the parricidal theme well, as the sons protest the outrage of assigning a woman to a leader whose phallic potency is spent. The woman as marker of the father's power also gains strength here as Angiolina admits her love is for paternal Law, not romance: "My lord," she assures her husband of her motivations for marrying, "I look'd but to my father's wishes" (II.i.342). The doge lauds her, in turn, for her "patriarchal love" (363). Steno thus threatens to castrate the patriarch, for, as Faliero rages, he "stains a lady's and a prince's honour / *Even on the throne of his authori-*

ty" (II.i.228–29). Faliero's outraged description of the illicit writing casts the act as one of dis-semen-ation:

> A wretch like this may leave upon the wall
> The blighting venom of his sweltering heart,
> And this shall spread itself in general poison;
> And woman's innocence, man's honour, pass
> Into a by-word. (II.i.426–30)

Steno dares to claim his phallic power to know and to have the father's wife through the son's own engraven word, a challenge that will force the doge to "Resolve to cleanse this commonwealth with fire," to engender his own flame again (IV.ii.75). Even at his trial, the doge triumphantly maintains that his is the fuller fire; it is Steno's "spark" that fed the doge's "flame" to rebellion (V.i.244).

Important to the legal chaos that ends this play is the suggestion that a fixed, motionless power corrupts as it asserts determination over those it would control. The Forty, for instance, were the doge's "friends / Till they became my subjects" (III.ii.307–8). At the same time, the Forty's own insistence that their friend assume the throne implies the desire to create a totem against which they can vent their own frustrations at lacking a word potent enough to fix time. For there is always the dead Other, the gaping grave that would fix the son with an omnipresent gaze; unassailable, this gaze can be projected onto the anointed leader instead. Faliero rightly proclaims:

> They could not love me, such was not the law;
> They thwarted me, 'twas the state's policy;
> They baffled me, 'twas a patrician's duty;
> They wrong'd me, for such was to right the state. (III.ii.351–54)

At the end, the doge and his betrayers tacitly admit to each other the symbolic roles they play. Faliero contemptuously demands of his council, "Show me the law" (V.i.183) that allows a doge to be tried by his inferiors. He is told, however, that such overwhelming powers of evil as his actions invoke demand that the law be "remodell'd." Just as in earlier times, "The sentence against parricide was left / In pure forgetfulness," so who could have foreseen "sons 'gainst sires, and princes 'gainst their realms?" (V.i.187–88, 192). Faliero's "sin hath made us make a law which will / Become a precedent 'gainst such haught traitors" (V.i.193–94); Faliero as scapegoat, that is, apparently goaded into action by years of subtle abuse, will offer them the chance to veil the father, to cover over the grave. Against Angiolina's plea for mercy, the council insists upon immediate execution, for "His punishment is safety to the state" (V.i.364). Faliero's early intuition that Steno's "stain" would mean that his own "life cannot be long" (II.i.444) is vindicated.

Throughout, the play emphasizes the doge's claims to be Venice's lawful authority, versus those who would wrest that authority from him. When Israel Bertuccio seeks redress, for instance, it is "Of God and of the Doge" (I.ii.329). As the doge himself acts in ways unseemly to his office, however, the covert tension sustaining his position questions the possibility of *any* rightful law. His people may have seated their hero on his throne—"*They made* me so" (I.ii.444), Faliero insists—but at best, even a good doge may be only a function, the scapegoat necessary for the routine sacrifice that a law pretending to renew itself demands. Angiolina recognizes his role as a marker of fixed time:

> all things wear in him
> An aspect of eternity: his thoughts,
> His feelings, passions, good or evil, all
> Have nothing of old age. (II.i.17–20)

Even as he is sentenced to death, the doge adopts a Promethean stance against the mere materiality of an inferior law that deludes itself over having stolen his fire: "our spirits, which shall yet go forth, / And do what our frail clay, thus clogg'd, hath fail'd in!" (IV.ii.310–11). The conflict between the senate's law and their leader's is foregrounded as the doge dares challenge the legal rights of the guard who arrests him in his treason:

> till that warrant has my signature
> It is illegal. . . .
> . . . Hast thou weigh'd well thy life's worth,
> That thus you dare assume a lawless function? (IV.ii.214–17)

The implicit argument over the proper law serves the play's larger emphasis upon the ultimate lawlessness of any community, at least in terms of an unchanging truth that would define all else from its own vantage. Even Angiolina, faithful defender of her lord, recognizes an inevitable corruption at the heart of things, and thus she refuses her assigned role in the parricide:

> Signors,
> I share not in your spoil! From henceforth, know
> I am devoted unto God alone,
> And take my refuge in the cloister. (V.i.540–43)

The competing sons foreclose on the father as they still his "signal [that] / Had thus begun to sound" (IV.ii.266–67), a triumph of the filial law's usurpation of the paternal Law. "All's silent, and all's lost!" (IV.ii.249), the doge recognizes in this exchange of power over the sign. Faliero, previously "named Preserver of the City" (IV.ii.150), confronts his own weakness as he learns of the system that corrupts him against his will. What are we, he asks, "that we must work by crime to punish crime?" (IV.ii.168).

Deeply important to the joyful peace Byron makes with language is his working out in this play of the impossibility of a potent or full word, the lack always instantiated from the start in the father, the *loss* of dis-semen-ation. To declare *honestly* the freedom that comes from subverting language's claims by structuring language through the repetition compulsion, the poet must explore, at least, the possibility of a word that in and of itself delivers complete meaning. Thus the doge is set up as a phallic power that deserves to make fiery pronouncements on life and death. Yet the reference both in the preface and in the poem itself to Faliero's youthful impetuous abuse of the holy father implies the possibility of the hollowness at the heart of the fallen human being. It is, of course, this fracture of the would-be whole self that ensures the need for the repeated word, the unending poem in search of restoring an imagined integrity to the seeker. The next line, the "final" stanza, may locate the Law—but, luckily, it never does.

Consequently, it is Faliero's downfall that he has trusted the senate law to uphold his own higher authority:

> I ask'd no remedy but from the law—
> I sought no vengeance but redress by law—
> I call'd no judges but those named by law—
> As sovereign, I appeal'd unto my subjects,
> The very subjects who had made me sovereign,
> And gave me thus a double right to be so. (I.ii.112–17)

The unhappy truth that Faliero confronts is the impotence, the emptiness always threatening any claim that would authenticate meaning.[8] Thus the doge apostrophizes his ducal cap as signifier of the childish faith with which he previously has worn it: "Thou idle, gilded, and degraded toy, / Let me resume thee as I would a vizor" (I.ii.263–64). Inevitably a properly earned authority is effaced by its subjects, even if they are the source of the original investiture of power. Faliero's Law is vitiated by a textuality that will rewrite him through defensive descendants who omit him from their history, who cover him up with a black veil. If a legitimate leader can take any solace from the family romance writ large in history, it must reside in the perpetually open grave and the continuing signifying power of that grave which accrues to a father dying for his children. "They never fail who die / In a great cause" (II.ii.93–94), Israel Bertuccio tells a co-conspirator:

> still their spirit walks abroad. Though years
> Elapse, and others share as dark a doom,
> They but augment the deep and sweeping thoughts
> Which o'erpower all others, and conduct
> The world at last to freedom. (II.ii.97–101)

Faliero confesses to his own powerful capture by dead fathers: he exclaims to himself to "let the graves gape" and let the dead ancestors "gaze on me!" (III.i.27, 29) as he finds himself entrapped in a corrupt system demanding his participation. Steno's offense, after all, was "generated / By the foul aristocracy" (III.ii.404–5) and thus reflects the battle for recognition between master and slave:

---

8. "The body is bound up [*engage*] in this matter of the phallus—and how—but the phallus, on the contrary, is bound to nothing: it always slips through your fingers" (Lacan, "Desire," 52).

> A slave insults me—I require his punishment
> From his proud master's hands; if he refuse it,
> The offence grows his, and let him answer it. (III.ii.409–11)

In the ever-growing circles of intrigue, wherein one rebellion begets another (equally unlawful), history appears a retelling of an unavoidable theft of paternal fire, which will in turn be illegally appropriated by a new generation. "You overrate my power, which is a pageant," the doge correctly tells the conspirator invoking the leader's strength (I.ii.411). As he conspires with ruffians "leagued to ruin states" (I.ii.582), the unreliability of all law is emphasized: even the father's Law shifts so that it signifies only in relation to historical moments. Ascribing the moral responsibility for his own actions to the senate, the doge insists "it is your history," to which his former subject responds, "Time must reply to that; our sons will judge / Their fathers' judgment, which I now pronounce" (V.i.511, 512–13). The physical execution is, of course, not enough; the Name-of-the-Father must be erased. "Thy name is razed from out [Venice's] records" (V.i.486), Faliero is told, and the "death-black veil / [Will be] [f]lung over these dim words engraved beneath" (V.i.496–97), words inscribing his name and punishment, words to be effaced but never erased by time.

Yet there is wisdom in the sons' pronouncement, as it controverts, unknowingly, the historical impulse to fix moments of truth, or of presence. The veil and the "dim" words imply the slippage of the word beneath the burden of desire it carries.

> Take thou this paper:
> The misty letters vanish from my eyes;
> I cannot fix them (I.ii.52–54)

exclaims Faliero as he tries to read the Forty's decree on Steno. Real history reveals itself as vice, for only in duplicity can the difference necessary to create meaning inhere. Vice signifies and admits its own inability to fix upon the one truth; vice subsists in desire and in language. "Vice must have variety, while virtue / . . . / Drinks life, and light, and glory from her aspect," the doge tells his wife (II.i.396, 398), but this putative elevation of virtue coexists uneasily with the static role assigned to those characters most virtuous. Angiolina's virtue imprisons her in a convent at the play's end, and Bertram, whose compulsion toward mercy finally betrays the doge's plot, reenacts Francis's role in *The White Doe*, as he becomes distinct from the men and assumes the woman's role of ineffective petitioner instead.

Faliero's refusal to answer Angiolina's question about the excess of his reaction suggests his own anger at having his comfortable illusions stripped from him. His anger at Steno results in part from Steno's triggering of the doge's desire to signify, to be more than a historic repetition of his wife's father. He asserts against Angiolina's hope that he will soon be "what you were" that "I will be what I should be, or be nothing" (II.i.452, 53). A woman's place is under the law, as she enacts obedience out of her fixed virtue, but Faliero is willing to play that role only as long as he is the sign against which others create their meaning. His primacy challenged, Faliero eschews the role of silent woman.

If silence, or virtue, is declared an inadequate medium for history, the impossibility of divining truth through the order of things is exposed as a classical myth. Nature may indeed be the realm of virtue and consistency, but the human being in society is false, constituted only by appearance, not truth. It is this knowledge that emerges from the legal confusions of the play, a *Hamlet*-like state of corruption and disarray. Even the structuring trope of concentric circles that Philip J. Skerry points to as dominating the actions suggests the slipperiness of meaning, as the personal signification intrudes into the political and vice versa. Only silence, where the word is not, fixes meaning into a virtuous stasis where history seems immune from time. But the personal and public link hands exactly when the want born out of language—the power to know ourselves not powerful enough—engenders endless circles of displaced desire compelling a cultural life always potentially unraveling at the seams. Silence, as *Cain* will explore through its own family romance, is appropriate only to a preoedipal world, an Eden quite at odds with the real world of fathers and sons who write his-story.

Marino Faliero thus concludes that we possess only the word, a word neither complete nor constant. Faliero wants desperately to believe in a fullness that transcends such an empty tool, and thus he anguishes over his realization that to be doge is still to be only a function marked by its name. "There is no such thing," he rages when recalled to his station as Duke of Venice, "It is a word" (I.ii.99, 100).

Yet it is the power of the word that first incenses the doge when Steno dares inscribe "the grossest insult" (I.ii.123) on the doge's throne. And though Faliero laments being forced to communicate in words that are to him obvious truths ("*must* I tell thee—what thy father / Would have required no words to comprehend?" [I.ii.148–49]), he insists that the poet of the word is worse than the sword: "he who *taints* kills more than he who sheds [blood]" (II.i.245).

His indecision over his stance toward the word, his shifting from its valorization to its denigration as "woman's weapons" (III.ii.153), suggests Faliero's own responsibility for his downfall. He has tried to function as an innocent in a world determined, as he discovers through the engraving of his throne, by an unreliable word. Even as his rebellion ends, truncated by a silenced signal, we understand Faliero's doom to result, in part, from his too-late engagement with the unhallowed chains of an *arbitrary*, not divinely sanctioned, law. Unlike the doge, the senate understands "truth" (V.i.50) to depend upon the deployment of language, and thus the Ten must silence the rebels even as they die: "let their mouths be gagged, even in the act / Of execution" (V.i.101–2). The conclusion of the explicitly political *Marino Faliero*—odd as it may seem, a prolepsis of the metaphysical drama of *Cain*—insists upon the potency of the word as it alone remains to tell, and to rewrite, the story. "Thousands" (V.i.146) of soldiers pursue the rebels who escaped, a pursuit compelled by the subversiveness of language: "we hope / None will escape to utter in strange lands / [Faliero's] libellous tale of treasons 'gainst the senate" (V.i.147–49). The solution Byron presents in *Don Juan*—the open-endedness of desire and language as the subversion of death—suggests itself in this play as the corrupt law seeks above all else to stop the play of signification, to refuse the fragment. The doge promises his subjects that "the future /Will judge . . . / Till then, the truth is in abeyance" (V.i.255–57). But the future inevitably collides with a present that always holds truth "in abeyance," a slippage of time securing therein a guarantee of the word's continued vitality as it reinscribes a new history nonetheless doomed to repeat the same quest for meaning.

Cain, written almost five years after *Manfred* and a year after *Marino Faliero*, explodes the metaphysical anxieties of the earlier play and the parricidal preoccupation of the latter into an ontological triumph:

both life as that which is present to us and immortality as that which confers value are to be located in the *jouissance* of writing. To read *Cain* only as another Romantic attempt to indict an oppressive God is to miss a richer drama.[9] As in *Manfred*, the wisdom of maintaining the word is the subtext Byron weaves even as he inscribes a far more linear plot on the surface—though in this later play the word becomes salvific, so the author's own grouping of it with the history plays is a consistent interpretive move.[10] Contributing to the reader's sense of complexity in both the dramas commonly termed the metaphysical plays, however, is the same latent content that in *Manfred* works against a strong formal coherence, and in *Cain* furthers that end.

Cain expresses to Lucifer the desire that motivates the play's action: "Let me but / Be taught the mystery of my being" (I.i.322). This request neatly points to the dilemma of having lost Eden, that imaginary time when one could ignore the dehiscence at the heart of birth. It is this loss of a primal paradise of identification that saddens Cain. Eve notes the vestiges of the symbiotic ties, and she begs Cain to "let me not see renewed / My misery in thine" (I.i.40–41). The trauma of loss saturates Cain's interpretations, and he chafes at losing paradise "for a fault not mine" (I.i.79). Access to origin is barred, as he gazes upon

> the gates of what [Adam and Eve] call their Paradise
> Guarded by fi'ry-sworded cherubim,
> Which shut them out, and me. (I.i.172–74)

Without his beginnings, he sees "nothing" (I.i.176).

The incest motif of men doubling as husbands and brothers suggests, as Joanna Rapf notes, the innocence of a pre-fallen world (643). "She [Adah] is my sister," Cain tells Lucifer, "Born on the same day of the same womb" (I.i.331). Thus she reflects back to Cain a unified image he lacks in his nonaccess to Eden. Yet, as we have seen in *Manfred*, this incestuous union represents even more importantly the

---

9. Pace Paul Cantor.

10. See Richardson, *Mental Theatre*, 43; for one of the best discussions of *Cain*, see his chapter "Seduction and Repetition in *Cain*" in the same book, though I disagree with his conclusion that "Byron did not view poetry as a socially regenerative force" (83). I hold instead that an implicit call to the *reader* to provide the renovation of interpretation informs both *Cain* and *Marino Faliero*, as well as becoming an underlying structural justification of *Don Juan*.

sameness that *must be lost* as a fallen, linguistic world learns to signify through difference. In a prelapsarian world incest may be paradisal; in postoedipal life it becomes, as in *Manfred*, akin to self-annihilation.[11] The ultimate consummation of self-desire inheres in both incest and Eden; and it is this passion to which Cain refers when he asks of Lucifer either to let him die or to allow him to enter into the intoxicating beauty of the "unimaginable ether," the "aerial universe of endless / Expansion, at which my soul aches to think" (II.i.100, 107–8).

Even as Cain watches his son sleep, he laments the loss of an innocence that kept difference in abeyance. Enoch too will learn he is naked, as he becomes "amerced for sins unknown, / Which were not thine nor mine" (III.i.24–25). Enoch's loss of imaginary self-fullness is the new legacy of grandparents now aware of their indecorous nudity. No child asks for the separation from primal identity, and Cain therefore resents his parents' betrayal into knowledge. The story of Genesis serves as a metaphor of the disenfranchised postoedipal child:

> dream of [Paradise],
> My disinherited boy. 'Tis but a dream;
> For never more thyself, thy sons, nor fathers,
> Shall walk in that forbidden place of joy! (III.i.31–34)

In Adah's plea to end such "melancholy yearnings o'er the past"— "Why wilt thou always mourn for Paradise? / Can we not make another?" (III.i.37–38)—is her own use of an overdetermined sexual bond to reenact the unity that Eden's loss marks: "Where'er thou art, I feel not / The want of this so much regretted Eden" (III.i.39–40). Adah recounts the joys of watching their son awake as he suggests a mirror in which the whole family is reflected:

> For then we are all alike; is't not so, Cain?
> Mother and sire and son, our features are
> Reflected in each other, as they are
> In the clear waters. (III.i.143–46)

But what was lost in Paradise is exactly this sameness, so being cast out from Eden bars any proposed fullness. From now on man and woman

---

11. Rapf helpfully categorizes incest in Byron as self-annihilation versus self-assertion, though her context is quite different from my own.

are doomed to an unending play of signification, as fixed meanings always elude them: such is the double-edged gift of knowledge.

Certainly the sin that Adam and Even committed represents a Promethean theft of divine phallic fire. Even in their punishment—the compulsion to repeat through generation—they retain the divinity they stole, for the Logos as Son of God reenacts the same ontology. The primal and originating potency of the divine word opens the play, as Adam recounts the act of creation by emphasizing God's insistence through "a word"; it is by naming that God makes sense of chaos. None of the worshipers, however, intuits the reflection of divinity that the fall from sameness allows them. Even though the family understands that the world was created by differentiation, Zillah begs God to ensure that the tempting serpent who introduced her parents to knowledge remain an anomaly, the only act of evil. Yet in this family's very ability to recall creation—to tell the story—divinity resonates as the knowledge they have now introjected as their own.

Cain obliquely recognizes his position within a signifying chain, but he laments the cost of his ability to "mean": the loss of his mother. Even though he most often blames Eve for succumbing, he at times implicates his father as the "real," which the serpent merely displaces, and it becomes Adam's phallic claims that both generate the son and bear him into what Lacan would say is unalterable determination: "everything emerges from the structure of the signifier." Cain questions why his

> father could not keep his place in Eden?
> What had *I* done in this? I was unborn;
> I sought not to be born; nor love the state
> To which that birth has brought me. (I.i.66–69)

The fiery swords barring Cain from paradise also serve as the phallus barring him from his mother, as the father's word—Adam, the serpent, God's tree of knowledge itself—becomes the symbol that replaces and therefore kills the mother. Richardson and Muller explain: "the replacement of the mother by a symbol may be considered equivalent to the 'death' of the mother, so that 'the symbol manifests itself first of all as the murder of the thing, and this death constitutes in the subject the eternalization of his desire'" (94).

Cain's curiosity about the serpent's appearance (II.ii) is reminiscent

of the child's precocious sexual interest. He wants very much to see the
serpent who wooed his mother, who imprints the human mark upon
desire as he inscribes the entrance of the symbolic order of knowledge
and the need for the word that saves. But this phallic intrusion bars
Cain from Eden, and thus he sees his mother as a betrayer, perhaps
daring to want the phallus that will forever leave Cain in a state of loss.
The coalescence of origin and death obtains in Cain's confused "fear"
and "longing" as he watches, by the light from the "far-flashing of the
cherubs' swords" (I.i.274), for the appearance of death. Silence will
answer the question articulated throughout this play by the uniniti-
ated: what is death? The reader, however, along with the author, will
accede to a wisdom never acknowledged by the outcasts of *Cain*: the
linguistic imperative to which the serpent tempted our parents overcomes death. The serpent becomes the phallic Other in Lucifer's account:

> The snake was the snake—
> No more; and yet not less than those he tempted,
> In nature being earth also, *more* in *wisdom*,
> Since he could overcome them and foreknew
> The knowledge fatal to their narrow joys.   (I.i.223–227)

Yet the profoundly disquieting if satisfying *circular* use of snake as
metaphor of the Logos to come also informs Lucifer's cagey reference
to the serpent. Activated, ultimately, by this serpent's insistence that
God's children have the right to know themselves divine, the Logos
inhabits the fiery phallus begotten by the Fall.

But from Cain's perspective, all that knowledge begets is a repetition of sorrow: his parents,

> not content with their own sorrow,
> Begot me, thee, and all the few that are
> And all the unnumbered and innumerable
> Multitudes, millions, myriads, which may be,
> To inherit agonies accumulated
> By ages—and *I* must be sire of such things!   (I.i.445–50)

He worries further that taking on the role of father "is merely propaga-
ting death / And multiplying murder" (II.i.70–71), the biological real-

ity allegorized in *Marino Faliero*. The real intelligence of this attitude, however, lies elsewhere. For it is the act of fratricide, exposing for the first time Abel's silence as death, that becomes the instigating act for patricide, the recurrent attempt of the callous son to silence the father and steal the phallic fire for himself. Cain brings silence into the world even as he seeks to put out the fire rising too high on his brother's altar, even as he jealously reclaims his position as firstborn and rightful inheritor of his mother's favor that Abel had appropriated. Cain's aggression toward his brother displaces his hostility from his father to that which shares the father's own blood: the father, after all, is the *real* sword barring Eden.

The slaying of an innocent who stands in—always—for the definitional, binding, paternal Other emphasizes the problem of evil that haunts this play as much as it riddles Christianity.[12] Why does Lucifer exist? *Cain* answers that Lucifer functions as the necessary grounds for meaning; as the principle of différance, of signification. The tree of knowledge is the necessary preface to the tree of life; Cain's parents had to choose a system of meaning before they could know enough to choose life, or voice, over the silence that Abel's murder exposes as death. Lucifer himself recognizes his power to inhere in his distinction; he prefers to be anything but "like" God, because similarity robs him of meaning.

> I have nought in common with him,
> Nor would. I would be aught above, beneath,
> Aught save a sharer or a servant of
> His power. I dwell apart; but I am great. (I.i.305–308)

Lucifer functions as deceiver only in his exclusive emphasis upon the misery that God confers; he is right to point to the "gift" of knowledge itself as coincident with truth. Adah intuits his role as that which sunders unity, creating delusion as well as the lack at the core of

---

12. And the murder also enacts on a semantic level Byron's increasing belief in the grammar of art as words that *are* things: the interplay, that is, between the academic and the real that language negotiates. Bernard Beatty reminds us that the most dramatic movement in *Cain* is, after all, the change from "intellectualized to actual desolation, as from a notion of death to the presence of a dead brother," a notion that "is the point as well as the conclusion of the play. . . . We could put Art's full stop at the point where it all begins" (Beatty and Newey, 7).

existence. "Who art thou that steppest between heart and heart?" she
asks him (I.i.347). When Adah accuses the serpent of lying, Lucifer
corrects her: the tree *was* of knowledge, so that any betrayal was
through the truth, a truth that "in its own essence cannot be / But
good" (I.i.356–57). Without the Lucifer principle, *Cain*'s Miltonic
echo of making one's own heaven of hell or hell of heaven would be
impossible, for Lucifer is the necessary binary opposition that allows
God to exist. He tells Adah, in a sweeping treatise on difference and
meaning:

> Where should I dwell? Where are
> Thy God or Gods, there am I. All things are
> Divided with me; life and death and time,
> Eternity and heav'n and earth and that
> Which is not heav'n nor earth, but peopled with
> Those who once peopled or shall people both—
> These are my realms! So that I do divide
> His, and possess a kingdom which is not
> His. If I were not that which I have said,
> Could I stand here? (I.i.546–55)

What Lucifer forces Cain to confront is his filial desire, the lack
born of opposition. As awesome as is the panorama Lucifer shows
him, Cain nonetheless insists that all is "inferior still to my desires /
And my conceptions" (II.i.82–83). Lucifer's trip to the zone of death
tricks Cain in at least one respect: as Lucifer aligns Cain's desire with
the pursuit of death's shadows, he fails to illumine on earth the very
"things" Cain seeks: words that give Cain and his descendants God-
like power to make their own meaning. Lucifer claims that Cain can
comprehend only the present, not the past (II.ii.131–32), yet the pro-
gression of desire built into language, the process of differentiation to
which Cain is doomed, assigns postoedipal beings precisely to learning
their past, if only in their knowledge of loss.[13]

13. Anthony Wilden's commentary on Lacan's opposition of knowledge to truth is to the
point here. For Lacan, "the adult quest for transcendence . . . lost paradises, lost plenitude . . . can be reduced . . . to the question . . . asked by Oedipus: 'Who (or what) am I?'
The subject, like Oedipus, always knows the answer, but the distinction between knowledge
(*savoir*) and truth repeatedly emphasized by Lacan points up the function of *meconnaissance*
and *reconnaisance* in human life. Truth for the subject is not knowledge but recognition"
(Lacan, *Speech and Language*, 166). We could submit that Cain's struggle is to know himself
divine, to recognize in the putative disinheritance from paradise his own chance to answer
the oedipal question.

Still, Lucifer speaks forthrightly at other seminal moments: "It may be death leads to the highest knowledge," he tells Cain (II.ii.164). Lacan glosses Lucifer well: he explains the "essential affinity of every drive with the zone of death" by invoking the relation of the subject with the Other. This relation can be represented by the "lamella," "the relation between the living subject and that which he loses by having to pass, for his reproduction, through the sexual cycle" (*Four Fundamental Concepts,* 199). Thus coming into life occurs simultaneously with the birth into death through a sexuality bequeathed, through their phallic theft of knowledge, to Adam and Eve. It is this "death" to which Cain's family accedes as it engages in discourse with the Other—the God who exists in knowledge by his Other—so that the tree of knowledge confers death as it confers meaning.

But the "death" introduced by the Fall from Eden, the textuality that will repeat itself through the word, is separate from the silence that Lucifer pushes forward as the "real thing." This collapse into nothing that Cain fears (II.ii.420) also motivated the split between God and Lucifer: they separated in order "to reign" (II.ii.387). As Lucifer tells Cain, "to see / Either of [the two Principles] would be for thee to perish," for both are needed to signify (II.ii.406–7).

The generative wisdom of this play nonetheless escapes Cain, even as its cyclical conclusion—a journey out of the parents' home once again to create a new heaven or hell—opens the text to the reader's own renovation. *Cain* covertly affirms the myth of the fortunate fall, where the Word is offered in place of Eden. One partakes in the immanent God, assuming his immortality as one's word engenders an endless chain of meaning. "Let him reign on, / And multiply himself in misery," Lucifer angrily exclaims of God, "So restless in his wretchedness, must still / Create, and re-create" (I.i.155–56, 162–63). It is this secret, that the tree of knowledge *precedes* the tree of life, that Lucifer elliptically shares with Cain as the latter despairs over his parents' legacy:

> Lucifer.   'Tis your immortal part
> Which speaks within you.
> Cain.   What immortal part?
> This has not been revealed. The tree of life
> Was withheld from us . . .
> . . . .
> And all the fruit [of knowledge] is death.
> Lucifer. They have deceived thee; thou shalt live. (I.i.103–9)

Cain must learn the wisdom of his own intuition that the "thoughts which arise" within him indeed "could master all things" (I.i.177–78). The biblical conjunction of the tree of knowledge and the first "taste" of death retains its traditional emphasis, as the first taste of knowledge implies the division from the Edenic mother/child dyad, where language is not possible. And Cain deeply laments the division in life that the phallic snake instigates. To the extent that *Cain* retells this familiar tale of loss, Byron was right to insist against his flustered critics that his story was, after all, an orthodox one. But Byron's dazzling achievement was to narrate against this conservative motif an opposing triumph, though still orthodox in its theology of the Logos: he posits a realm superior to the imaginary order as he privileges a world of language above Edenic silence.

Lucifer's insight that life and immortality are one suggests Byron's position that just so, the hell or heaven one makes of one's own mind is immortal, exactly as it is a construct of a language that will never cease. We can believe Lucifer when he tells Cain that he does not know death (I.i.289), and we should remember that the dark spirit has already associated Cain's knowledge with his own. Lucifer functions as the negative ground of being, with Cain implicated as a progenitor of Christ, the Logos that will fix immortality in language itself. In this poem, Cain and Christ (the "One") alone make the journey to hell, or at least to the land of the dead, as the two men become incongruously linked through Cain's shedding of the blood of the world's first human sacrifice and Christ's shedding of divine blood that inscribes the redemptive repetition of Cain's act. The Logos saves in the compulsion to repeat, which constitutes textuality as a deferral of death: the Word guarantees Infinity, a salvation hinted at in *Manfred* and asserted throughout the senate's desperation in *Marino Faliero*. In the most succinct explanation of intertextuality that Romanticism has to offer, Cain asks, "What is death?" to which Lucifer answers, "Hath not he who made ye / Said 'tis another life?" (II.ii.35–36). The wisdom of this play exceeds any manifestation by its characters, as the play concludes with implicit optimism: in the unending expulsions from Edens, as even Cain and Adah repeat in their displacement from their parents' home, lies the liberation of the spirit and the word. In the need to repeat is assurance of new life—of the interpretive act itself as life—as well as a reminder of death.

Chapter 9

Paradox Celebrated

Byron was a man of excess, a creature whose own sensuous apprehension of life (engendered from ambivalent positions—a second-rate aristocracy, an almost sister, a plural and early sexuality) instantiates poetically, as we have seen, a subject/object relationship somewhat at odds with the more typical Romantic identity. Romanticism, we all know, was organized in its time and critically reproduced in our own as the problem of marrying self and other. It would probably be too much of a valorization to hold that Byron manages a kind of philosophical good faith in which he is able to objectify the subject, to situate it within a discursive and determining field that both allows access to it qua subject even as its complicity with all it would remark is equally to the fore. But he comes, it seems to me, at least near to this, and thus close to a move beyond the Enlightenment antinomies so limiting in their inevitable, repetitive return. Certainly it is true that we could pose as Byron's major interpretive category too the old, heavily invested terms of inner/outer distinction, private/public, the crux of the post-February marriage disaster, and Byron's new role as social pariah. In dichotomous terms, we could pretend—and I have proceeded at times, in the name of an inexpensive clarity, as if this were the case—that before 1816, Byron articulates a myth of the inner, which, after 1816, becomes outer. We could, in the name of a categorical ease, characterize Byron's movement from a pre-1816 Cartesian self-grounded cogito to a Husserlian intentional consciousness, now aimed outside, always conscious of something other than itself.

But what my arguments have tended toward is the assertion of a philosophically, poetically greater achievement in that Byron preempts this duality, mutually implicating self and other in a contingency so radical as to elide claims to an autonomous subject or object, poet or artifact. This is where he lands in *Don Juan,* the project of *Don Juan,* one might say, aleatory organization of subject and object—but he gets there from radical moments posed in and through those poems that have come before, especially those discussed in this study, wherein he appears to employ the Romantic conundrum of self-origin, even as he ensures its destruction at the same time.

In *Don Juan* especially, Byron comes as close to a specific aesthetic achievement of objectifying the subject (reversing the Romantic tendency to subjectify the object) as we find not only in Romanticism but anywhere in the history of British poetry.[1] Although—and partly as a result of such objectification—*Don Juan* presents the peculiar difficulty that it "is one of the clearest and most accessible of the half-dozen

1. For an argument that shares my concern with dualistic identity formation, see Michasiw (45). At this point, too, I want to pause to emphasize, in addition to the gendered textuality that we will read as subtending Byron's canon as he works out these epistemological inquiries, the very important gendered literary history behind this poem as well, and to offer directions such inquiry could pursue by casting a larger, gendered net upon the question of influences, though such a project is canted on a thematic plane different from that of my argument herein. Jerome McGann, in his essay "'My Brain is Feminine': Byron and the Poetry of Deception," compellingly argues the case of Byron's literary genealogy evolving from Charlotte Dacre and the Della Cruscan school of a poetry of sensibility. By the time of *Don Juan,* McGann suggests, Byron has (admiringly) defined the feminine brain as "mobility," and as a weapon against cant (Rutherford, 42–43). (We might even speculate that his invoking a Horatian, pedestrian muse for *Don Juan* owes something to the bluestocking tradition that routinely cited a "crippled muse" as protectress for the poetry.) I'd like to propose a textual parallel to the way Byron's poem moves, though merely as a speculative accretion to such a gendered taxonomy of mobility, not an assertion of influence over Byron himself. In the third stanza (lines 55–99) of *Beachy Head,* Charlotte Smith's dialectical rhetorical movement operates to set up a position only to undercut it, by reinscribing the negation or affirmation in the subsequent passage by opposition. Thus, for example, she establishes the equation that art is artificial and secondary and then proceeds to valorize the nature to which she opposes it in terms of artifice itself—nature as art. In addition to her arrest of each position and reinscription of it in the next movement, her frequent method of cataloging contributes to the sense of mobility that the poem achieves. These techniques (largely indebted to the romance genre encompassing, for example, *Caleb Williams* and *Frankenstein* as well as Smith's own novels) move toward an ironization that, in both *Beppo* and *Don Juan,* complete the scandal of refusing a stable ontology of subject/object identity and truth. I thank Judith Davis Miller of Sacred Heart University (Connecticut) for sharing with me her provocative explication of *Beachy Head*'s dialectical patterning.

greatest poems in English . . . [and thus it] is extremely difficult to talk about analytically" (McGann, *"Don Juan,"* ix), the poem nonetheless rewards a reading based on its engendering tropes of desire, those formal and thematic motivations that grant a unity to the poem that even enthusiastic critics have too often been reluctant to concede.[2] While in no way intending an exhaustive reading of the epic, I want to suggest the extraordinarily supple, yet philosophically controlled matrix in which *Don Juan* is cast, the terms that make this text speak so much more than its intricate, plotless plotting articulates.[3] Furthermore, it should, in fact, be impossible to talk of this poem without invoking the question of gendered identities, for "woman" (as well as "man") functions here as a nomen nudum that, at every turn, at every digression of the telling of the tale, resists the stabilization that the nomenclature establishes and instead enacts an especially empowering Byronic myth. This slippage of identity, which works toward establishing people (and signification systems) as contingent conduits of meaning, versus meaning itself, exists grammatically at the level of an elaborate syntax alternately paratactic *and* coordinate—metonymy writ large, an active passivity before life—the exemplary conduit of *Don Juan* himself, phallic woman her or himself.[4] In *Don Juan*, time is both historicized and internalized until language can carry the freight of

2. There has been, however, a recent trend to assert such unity; see for example, Bernard Beatty's thoughtful study (*Byron's "Don Juan"*), which at least implicitly, in its teleological reading, argues for a coherence at more than a structural level.

3. Human beings, as Richard Rorty reminds us, "conceive of change not by formulating general theories, but by redescribing their worlds in new words or metaphors"—an insight whose explanatory power embraces the mode, I think, that Byron conceives of for *Don Juan*, as his bold syntactic and semantic movement forces our own realignment of possibilities in the world.

4. Although Allen S. Weiss's *The Aesthetics of Excess* came to my attention too late to be incorporated into the present discussion, it seems to me, at least upon a quick first reading, that part 2, "Sadian Figures," might prove a particularly fecund and appropriately febrile way back into Byron's sex in-the-text, especially as it engages with the idea of sexuality outspeaking language. And Louis Crompton's comprehensive study of Byron's sexuality implicitly reminds us of the extent to which sexuality informs all poetry, that it is inseparable, at least in psychoanalytic terms, from translation into other goals. With Byron's dual sexual identity—as both hetero- and homosexual lover—comes a particularly generative tension for the production of poetry, it would seem. Jerome Christensen's "Setting Byron Straight" cants the homosexuality issue on a class/style plane, provocatively suggesting a more self-consciously constructed sexuality on Byron's part as well as an almost salacious readerly participation in sexing the lord mobile, if nothing else. And for a persuasive and provocative rendering of Byron's pressuring of sexuality against the grain, into functional conduits of identity versus fixed invariables, see Susan J. Wolfson's important essay, "'Their She Condition': Cross-Dressing and the Politics of Gender in *Don Juan*."

244   *Byron*

speaking through a voice other than Kantian antinomies, a voice that recognizes the inevitable lack of self-identity, of the rift covered over by epistemologies that claim grounds for a reconciliation of the Cartesian divorce.[5]

Byronic desire has thus far revealed the impossible pursuit of Romantic freedom from linguistic bondage at the same time that it would locate an ennobling originary authority who could somehow contain both the Law and liberty—the figure Byron hoped to find in the figure of Marino Faliero. Unlike the poetry of Wordsworth or Shelley, both of which perhaps depend upon irresolvable tension for their existence, Byron's "last" unending poem locates his answer in its celebration of language as the very medium that, even as it legitimates meaning, frees desire from the consummation of death. The following self-reflection by Roland Barthes bears comparison with Byron's project of poetic definition:

> He attempts to compose a discourse which is not uttered in the name of the Law and/or of Violence: whose instance might be neither political nor religious nor scientific; which might be in a sense the remainder and the supplement of all such utterances. What shall we call such discourse? *Erotic*, no doubt, for it has to do with pleasure; or even perhaps: *aesthetic*, if we foresee subjecting this old category to a gradual torsion which will alienate it from its regressive, idealist background and bring it closer to the body, to the *drift*.[6]

5. It is such a commonplace of older criticism that Byron was an anachronistic existentialist that we can easily forget, in our eagerness to dislodge now passé critical language, just how significant a claim that becomes when Byron is happily paired with the subtlety of a late Sartre, thinking through, in his *Search for a Method*, the implication of the solitary self intervening in—and being totalized by—the social milieu. Hence I cite the following passage from Sartre's important chapter, "The Progressive-Regressive Method," that indicates the similar ways both Romantic writers conceived of what it means to make sense, to order life through representation: "Man is, for himself and for others, a signifying being, since one can never understand the slightest of his gestures without going beyond the pure present and explaining it by the future. Furthermore, he is a creator of signs to the degree that—always ahead of himself—he employs certain objects to designate other absent or future objects. But both operations are reduced to a pure and simple surpassing. To surpass present conditions toward their later change and to surpass the present object toward an absence are one and the same thing. Man constructs signs because in his very reality he is signifying; and he is signifying because he is a dialectical surpassing of all that is simply given. What we call freedom is the irreducibility of the cultural order to the natural order" (152).

6. I have lifted this quote from its use as chapter epigraph by Naomi Schor, 79; she cites it (no page number) from *Roland Barthes by Roland Barthes*.

Don Juan announces that life imitates art, that reality is modeled upon language, a language that both speaks and is spoken by the desire of the poet. Thus the narrator's role is to shape, through his arrangement of language and signs, all possibilities that "real life" contains; and in so doing, he fulfills the potential of Shelley's *Alastor* poet-framer, an impasse that was a central representational strategy for Shelley. In *Don Juan*, the narrator as Everyman (and here, I think, we see the patriarchal imprint of language—*Don Juan* as poem is oddly gender-free, the narrator male) shows us that in exploiting language, we manipulate life; we make it happen in our own way, in our own time. We can come close to daring to deny, for instance, Lacan's insistence that no one can possess the phallus. *Don Juan*'s poetic language, estranged and formalized as it becomes the fiction of a narrative, embodies desire through the function, or *space*, of Don Juan himself. Juan works as a transparent medium that means first one thing, then another—a signifier for other signifiers—as he defines the organism's (the reader's) need to prolong life until a proper and timely death is assured. In the unsettling, brilliant de-sexualization of the very sexually active hero, the poet suggests a position from which Juan can speak as phallic woman, the one who gets both penis and pen. At the same time, an anachronistic configuring of sexuality itself is played out: the distinction in the sexual relationships has more to do with the activity or passivity of the role played, versus gender.[7] This slippage of the "naturalness" of sexual paradigms is one of the great achievements of *Don Juan*, for Juan's position as conduit of meaning imposes upon the reader the variability and historical dimension of that which the

7. Implied throughout is the ancient Greek configuration of desire in which "what is socially important is to penetrate rather than to be penetrated"; this sexual positioning reflected cultural power (Nussbaum, 572), and further: "Ancient categories of sexual experience differed considerably from our own, and . . . this affected the way desire itself was experienced. The central distinction in sexual morality was the distinction between active and passive roles. The gender of the object . . . is not in itself morally problematic. Boys and women are very often treated interchangeably as objects of desire." David Halperin's exploration of Greek sexuality, the study under review by Nussbaum, strongly asserts the historicity of our modern tendency to categorize people vis-à-vis their sexuality; not merely a question of sexual motility, the Greeks did not *think* through our current categories of sexual organization. Byron's own sexual configurations suggest a similar mental orientation that contrasts sharply with that of the other major Romantic poets, a difference more to the point in our reading of his texts than the sexual profligacy and wantonness with which he is often (wistfully?) charged by his readers.

hero's name would seem to stake out as absolute. Such flux of identity is realized in the act of authorship: the relationship between the power of writing and the power of procreation is vividly realized in this poem, as each dramatic movement inscribed by the narrator begets another libidinal economy that will ensure, in its own turn, the continued erotic overflowing of the male protagonist.[8]

Byron as author aligns himself overtly with the narrator by inscribing identity markers (for example, the invocation of the imprudent mothers who unwittingly promote precocious children [I.110], or the swim across the Hellespont [II.105]) so that we must take seriously the authority of the narrative voice: in the *jouissance* of the text lies the fullest freedom the human being can obtain in this world, as the text opens to an exploitation of the very linguistic medium that contains within itself the alternate threat of a prison house instead. In one sense, *Don Juan* is a giant acclamation, by the would-be liberator of the Greeks, that the way to freedom lies directly in the path of the poet's pen.

Freedom does not reside in the sameness that lives in Shelley's epipsychidion love ideal, which functions for Byron as a similar consummation of desire. We have seen that this self anterior to self, present in Astarte, threatens Manfred with a bliss whose price is too high; and this same ecstasy of sameness, of a self actually locating itself in love of an other, appears in the relationships of Don Juan, whenever Juan invests great feeling: with Haidee, Leila, and Aurora Raby. As so often in Byron's poetry, woman represents Eden in these episodes, where the child's bliss exists *outside* of language, where the child is defined in terms of that imaginary female Other. It is not incidental, then, that this poem, which celebrates the *other* side of Eden, the linguistic fallenness to which the child accedes, predicates itself upon the Don Juan legend. By appropriating Otto Fenichel's analysis to illuminate Byron's psychological subtext, Candace Tate examines the extent to which Byron puts the Don Juan myth to use. In this view, Don Juan sees sexual conquest of women as a means of incorporating that symbol for the mother; yet he also fears, in a way reminiscent of Wordsworth's tension

8. One of the best literary illustrations of the allegorical relationship of writing, procreation, and silence occurs in Heinrich von Kleist's *The Marquise of O*, where Kleist writes from the place of what he conceives of as female sexuality, a female who is always desiring, sexually overabundant, and who cannot help herself: she ends up getting both the pen and child. The man who desires, however, becomes impotent and throws himself on the pity of the woman.

especially, being engulfed by this "reunion" (Tate, 133–34). Hence sexual connection, wherein the man encounters himself through the woman—a "soul" of epipsychidion union—suffocates as it is irrevocably linked with death.

The character of Don Juan serves, then, as a principle of (safe) differentiation opposed to the silence yielded through (dangerous) love of or in a woman.[9] Even in the juxtaposed father/son scenes in the shipwreck (canto II), the relationship of death, desire, and silence is emphasized: "There were two fathers in this ghastly crew" (II.87), and the one who speaks when his son dies is able to see the boy "thrown / Into the deep without a tear or groan." The other father silently holds vigil over his son's death, so deeply bound to the boy that the dying child tries to smile,

> As if to win a part from off the weight
> He saw increasing on his father's heart,
> With the deep deadly thought, that they must part. (II.88)

This father is bound in silence and sameness to the child; thus the son's death vitiates the father's chance to signify: "Then he himself sunk down all dumb and shivering, / And gave no sign of life, save his limbs quivering" (II.90).

These stanzas that align deep, ego-sustaining love with self-annihilation precede by two hundred lines Juan's discovery by Haidee, the silent lover who threatens to fix the play of desire and turn Juan the endless signifier into the silence that the paternal love engendered in the shipwreck scene. The danger is present from the beginning of their encounter, as Haidee and her attendant lift the near-dead Juan into the Imaginary zone of a hidden cave, where Haidee is able "To kindle fire" (II.15). After cataloging her splendors, the narrator alerts us to the real danger in which Juan lies, a danger not ascribed by narrative tone even to the shipwreck: "her eyes / Were black as death" (II.117); and her glance "Tis as the snake late coil'd, who pours his length, / And hurls at once his venom and his strength." The self-reflection that love of Hai-

---

9. But it is quite to the point that Byron is forced, culturally, to inscribe identity in the either/or of male/female; Jane Gallop discusses the limitations of such a "naturally" accepted binary scheme available for sexual coding, as she recounts Roland Barthes's lament that nothing more complex than masculine/feminine exists for linguistic coding (*Thinking*, 111–14). And Byron's gradual un-gendering of Juan is the most radical gift of this poem.

dee will create threatens Juan with the same temptation toward self-annihilation that compelled Manfred to withdraw from Astarte.

Haidee and Juan do not speak a common vocabulary and so they are lexically mute; they attempt to create meaning without the mediation of the word that ensures difference. When Juan sleeps, Haidee, believing that he has called out her name, turns to him, "but she forgot / That at this moment Juan knew it not" (II.135). Unvoiced love traverses the ordinary ways we make sense, as it becomes its own signifying system: "The heart will slip even as the tongue and pen." But while language keeps the play of desire infinite, a system that bypasses mediation threatens the consummation of desire. Thus Haidee's love becomes a totalizing gaze, as she will come to understand her lover only too well without words:

> And then she had recourse to nods, and signs,
>   And smiles, and sparkles of the speaking eye,
> And read (the only book she could) the lines
>   Of his fair face, and found, by sympathy,
> The answer eloquent, where the soul shines
>   And darts in one quick glance a long reply;
> And thus in every look she saw exprest
> A world of words, and things at which she guess'd. (II.162)

The narrative tone becomes suppressed, covertly admonitory as the source of the thoughts described becomes unclear. "It was such pleasure to behold him" (II.173) shifts within the same stanza to a definite narrative intrusion, "But then the thought of parting made her quake," followed by two lines in which both narrator and lover seem merged in prophecy: "He was her own, her ocean-treasure, cast / Like a rich wreck—her first love, and her last." The irreverent narrative interruption six stanzas after the soft verses on love pits the irrelevancy and randomness of language, of narrative that relentlessly pursues the next object, against the tenor of the Haidee section wherein silence threatens to overcome meaning and the poet. "Get very drunk" (II.179) the narrator tells us, as a drunken giddiness disrupts the threat of an overwhelmed signifier. "The coast—I think it was the coast that I / Was just describing" (II.181), he continues, as the play of desire is reestablished and the reader believes that Juan, too, will continue.

But it is the narrator who will sustain Juan's freedom, for Haidee will not escape the annihilation proceeding from this intense love. Before asserting his hero's survival, the narrator insists that we not mistake the severity of the danger:

> they were
> All in all to each other: though their speech
> Was broken words, they *thought* a language there,—
> And all the burning tongues the passions teach
> Found in one sigh the best interpreter
> Of nature's oracle—first love,—that all
> Which Eve has left her daughters since her fall. (II.189)

> Their intense souls, into each other pour'd,
> If souls could die, had perish'd in that passion. (II.191)

"What was said or done / Elsewhere was nothing" to Haidee, for "She had nought to fear, / Hope, care, nor love beyond, her heart beat *here*" (II.202). Yet while Haidee is thus doomed, Juan is saved because the narrator rescues him from the threat of a premature end and reinvigorates him as a signifier who only points to yet another word. The narrator reminds us, at this crucial point where Haidee and Juan threaten to merge into one, that Juan has now quite forgotten Julia. In this digression that foregrounds "inconstancy" and "quicksilver clay" (II.209) as the bane of the speaker's existence, we are assured of continued textuality, for Juan, as narrative function, can be inconstant only until the author wishes Juan's life and the text to die. Juan does escape—absurdly—into the life of a bought lover/slave, so the narrative implies its own autonomous power to rescue; and Haidee, safely ensconced at home in the bosom of those who love her, dies. That she dies bereft of the ability to make sense of things is clear:

> She look'd on many a face with vacant eye,
> On many a token without knowing what;
> She saw them watch her without asking why,
> And reck'd not who around her pillow sat;
> Not speechless, though she spoke not. (IV.63)

To emphasize that Juan himself barely escaped a similar fate, the narrative implies Juan's recognition that the recent real threat to his life was love, not the shipwreck. In a rare narrative moment that sustains the sincerity of the emotion, Juan ranks his separation from Haidee above all other hardships:

> "'Tis not," said Juan, "for my present doom
>   I mourn, but for the past;—I loved a maid:"—
> He paused, and his dark eye grew full of gloom;
>   A single tear upon his eyelash staid
> A moment, and then dropp'd; "but to resume,
>   'Tis not my present lot, as I have said,
> Which I deplore so much; for I have borne
> Hardships which have the hardiest overworn,
>
> On the rough deep. But this last blow—" and here
>   He stopp'd again, and turn'd away his face. (V.18, 19)

Later, on the battlefield, Juan's life will again be similarly at risk when he sees in the orphaned Leila a soulmate:

>   their eyes were fixed
>   Upon each other, with dilated glance,
> In Juan's look, pain, pleasure, hope, fear, mixed
>   With joy to save, and dread of some mischance
> Unto his protégée's; while hers, transfixed
>   With infant terrors, glared as from a trance,
> A pure, transparent, pale, yet radiant face,
> Like to a lighted alabaster vase. (VIII.96)

Although a fellow soldier urges him to leave or resign himself to death, Juan is "immoveable" (VIII.102) until safety is assured his new ward. It is the sense of genuine emotional investment here as well as in the Haidee episode that threatens to complete Juan too fully, to provide a satiety that fixes his play of desire and robs him of his signifying role. Such a threat looms in the British cantos, too, where Juan's interest in Aurora Raby is reminiscent enough of Haidee and Leila to put the reader on guard for a shift in poetic sensibility. Louis Crompton reminds us that Augusta Leigh was gentle and even timid (203); so as the three female characterizations mimic to some degree the nature of Byron's love for his sister, we recall the poet's attraction to a death-dealing epipsychidion love. Such a union both seduces in its intensity and repulses in its totalizing nature. Haidee, Leila, and Aurora are noticeable for their silence, and it is this death to the signifier's omnipotence and alterity that constitutes the most persuasive, serious moments of danger to Don Juan himself, real danger reflected by the narrator's brief respites from ironic tone.

The function of Don Juan is to avoid becoming a reference, a completed text, and instead operate as textuality itself, the process of making meaning. Juan repeatedly escapes the danger of choosing the Freudian wrong casket, of a premature end that confers an inappropriate death. He is instead an organism that will die in its own way, and in its own time. We could do worse than gloss *Don Juan* as the perfect literary precursor to Freud's *Beyond the Pleasure Principle,* an exemplary acting out of the dynamics of narratability in life. "If narrative desire keeps moving us forward, it is because narrative metonymy can never quite speak its name," Peter Brooks asserts (56). Both *Don Juan* the poem and Don Juan its protagonist enact this slippage of language and desire as they recall the inability of an interconnected chain of signifiers ever to pin down the meaning it would utter. Don Juan, in spite of the exotic actions in which he is placed, is himself colorless, a transparent marker of whatever sign the narrator, the poet-legislator, wishes to name. Thus Byron creates the illusion, at least, of the poet controlling language: of writing life through language, yes, but of being himself the first ground for that language and life. Some years ago, Peter Manning cited the oddness of Byron's exclusion from the deconstructionist camp of criticism. Certainly Byron fits in very well with a critical program predicated upon a "tracing of the instabilities of language" (Reviews, 401). As we have seen, however, Byron's often direct engagement with the problem of language frequently merges with the successful illusion he creates of manipulating linguistic instability into an author-controlled text. The subversiveness of *Don Juan*'s form, a repeating fragment that attests to a whole toward which the incomplete organism always drives, may indeed escape a deconstructive criticism unwilling to grant desire the equivalence, at least, of a controlling center.

But desire acts as center in Byron's poem only as it is always *marked,* never stabilized, by Juan: the youth's strange genderlessness allows him to act as a conduit through which countless women can pass. A careful reading of the poem's opening stanza illuminates the narrative ploy: "I want a hero," the narrator announces, an "uncommon want" (I.i) because the public seems top heavy with heroes, albeit ones inevitably unveiled as false. To counter this plethora of factitious heroes, the narrator will take as his protagonist "our ancient friend Don Juan," an extraordinary choice with which to contrast the overblown figures the narrator professes to disdain. But upon reflection, Don Juan is a perfect model: as a legendary predator of women, Juan flits from one lover to another, his very name becoming a sign of promiscuous desire. And, through casting the Byronic Don Juan as a peculiarly unaggressive sexual partner, Byron both thwarts a language that has ostensibly codified a myth and exposes the heart of the legendary myth for other than what it appears: Don Juan's relentless appropriation of women marks an impotence that opposes that annihilating ecstasy of passion wherein self confronts self in the other. Don Juan as Byron's sign becomes language turned in on itself; what appears to signify satiety in fact signifies emptiness in pursuit of satiety instead.

Byron's Don Juan must operate freely, and thus he becomes the very sign of life itself. He is such an innocent that he cannot read signs himself; he only points to other signs, a function that makes him essential to the meaning that others, particularly the reader, make of the history through which he moves. Even when his own emotions change, as at the time of his initial shyness with Julia, he remains unaware of causes: "But as for Juan, he had no more notion / Than he who never saw the sea of ocean" (I.70). Equally important, Juan has no other option; he is not meant to enable conclusions but to function as a disruption of the text. When, for example, Juan has virtuously decried the killing of his father's Spaniel for food, four lines later we find that he "With some remorse received (though first denied) / As a great favour one of the fore-paws" (II.71). And if we miss here the play of signs that effects and effaces in alternate rhythms, we read three stanzas later of something more shocking to the "Muse": Julia's sacred letter to Juan (II.74) becomes the paper for the lots used to determine which survivor's flesh will provide food for the rest. Here writ large is the slippage of the signifier, as the word of love becomes the mark of death instead. An even more flagrant reminder of language's ability to slide from one meaning to another is the naming of Juan in the harem: "Lolah demanded the new damsel's name— / 'Juanna,'—Well, a pretty name enough" (VI.44). Later in this sequence, just as we are promised renewed stability—"'Tis time we should return to plain narration, /

And thus my narrative proceeds" (VI.57)—the confusion of names is highlighted again, as Dudu "Shewed Juan, or Juanna, through and through / This labyrinth of females" (VI.57).

Indeed, Juan's chameleonlike form furthers the theme that things are not as they seem. In the world of this poem, the signifiers do not match neatly to corresponding signifieds; beneath Moslem dress

> Lurked Christianity, who sometimes barters
> Her inward grace for outward show, and makes
> It difficult to shun some strange mistakes. (VII.57)

Truth is less important than perception; Juan pleases the women he and his comrade deposit safely behind the battle lines by his "exaggeration" (VII.75), rather than by speaking to them of reality. Or later, when Juan is in England, the "real" meaning of the, to him, foreign epithet "God damn" escapes him, as he translates it into "God be with you" (XI.12). The conflation of opposite meanings receives validation as the narrator ascribes such a confusion of meaning to the native British tongue. The narrator moves toward the conclusion of canto XII by stressing to the reader the elusiveness of the tale he would tell:

> I will not swear that black is white;
> But I suspect in fact that white is black,
> And the whole matter rests upon eye-sight.
> Ask a blind man, the best judge. You'll attack
> Perhaps this new position—but I'm right;
> Or if I'm wrong, I'll not be ta'en aback:—
> He hath no morn nor night, but all is dark
> Within; and what sees't thou? A dubious spark. (XII.71)

Significantly, we are led to conclude that the triumphs of *Don Juan*'s world do not result from the protagonist's exploits but inhere instead in the narrator's ability to *write* that hero into and out of existence. We can pressure here the earlier critical conundrum that associates Byron's text with the myth of Eden, as well as imbricating it with the wisdom of *Cain:* the Fall from paradise was fortunate, according to this poetics, because it marks the onset of language and desire, the tools that make the poet king. In the four stanzas opening canto X, Newton's revolution, Adam's Fall, and the poetic function converge into one tale. Stanza 1 aligns both Newton's contemplation and Adam's sin with an apple, so stanza 2 begins: "Man fell with apples, and with apples rose." "Rose" because Sir Isaac discovered a mode that "could disclose / Through the then unpaved stars the turnpike road, / A thing to counterbalance human woes." But why this digression? In an extraordinary moment of confession, the narrator attests to his own ambition to continue the reconstruction of history that Adam and Newton have begun:

> And wherefore this exordium?—Why, just now,
>   In taking up this paltry sheet of paper,
> My bosom underwent a glorious glow,
>   And my internal spirit cut a caper:
> And though so much inferior, as I know,
>   To those who, by the dint of glass and vapour,
> Discover stars, and sail in the wind's eye,
> I wish to do as much by Poesy. (X.3)

If a slight embarrassment at his exposed ambition causes the narrator—the Byron of *Childe Harold* at this point—to mock himself a line later ["cut a caper"]—his dominant impulse is clearly to speak from the pen's authority, to assert the role of the writer as purveyor of a new system of signs.

For the poet creates life through words. Still, the claims of this narrator/poet—the Byronic revision of Shelley's poet-framer—are even greater, for he asserts himself as an ontological center as he pretends to determine language itself. Even the dedication and opening stanzas of canto I are meant to distance this writer from those before and around him, just as the flagrant subversion of the traditional Don Juan myth points to his iconoclastic authority. Lillian R. Furst points to the deliberate foregrounding of irony in the narrator's choice of "Don Juan" as a name for his hero, when he asserts that the names of greater men are "not at all adapted to my Rhymes." As Furst notes, the hero's "ill-rhyming name" itself makes the hero subservient to technical consideration of rhyme (the mispronunciation of Don Juan), a subservience that "forcefully and comically underlines the priority of the writing over what is written" (97).

If "Bob Southey" is "representative of all the race" of poets—and poet laureates—the writer of *this* text is obviously something else.

Even in the praise of Milton in the dedication, an element of pity ("those helpless eyes, / And heartless daughters, worn, and pale, and poor" [11]) suggests the narrator's superiority. Perhaps most significant in terms of setting forth his project is the narrator's famous opening line noted above. For this want, or lack, becomes the structural motivation propelling the poem: in a work that at least parodies if not posits the epic, there is no hero, merely a mutable signifier that drives the poem forward *faute de mieux* as it links one arrant meaning to another. Thus desire, or desire in language, *becomes* the "hero," or better still, marks conspicuously the hero's absence as center.

In a compelling revision of the lamentation that drives *Childe Harold*, "Words," not people, "are things" in this text, specifically the writer's word:

> a small drop of ink,
> Falling like dew, upon a thought, produces
> That which makes thousands, perhaps millions, think;
> 'Tis strange, the shortest letter which man uses
> Instead of speech, may form a lasting link
> Of ages; to what straits old Time reduces
> Frail man, when paper—even a rag like this,
> Survives himself, his tomb, and all that's his! (III.88)

The narrator in *Don Juan* allows no traditional distance between art and life: "What though 'tis but a pictured image strike— / That painting is no idol,—'tis too like" (III.103). Indeed, the contempt toward Wordsworth (III.100) stems from his fictionalizing of life; the achievement of *Don Juan*, in contrast, is of reality: "[I]s it not life, is it not *the thing*," Byron gloats to Douglas Kinnaird. Paradoxically, the materiality and prior status of the text stays before us even as the narrator continually reminds the reader of his controlling presence: "Therefore I'll make Don Juan leave the ship soon" (IV.97), he promises, alerting us in his narrative intrusions to his power to complicate the subject/object opposition that a clean separation of artist and artifact establishes.

Language may always already be in place, but it still requires a writer to give it life. To position the writer as anterior to his medium, the narrator calls attention to words qua words, as in the Juan/Juanna slippage and the contradictive meanings apparently inherent in "God damn." In the first canto, the narrator explicitly exposes the working of his craft:

> I only say suppose it—*inter nos*—
> (This should be *entre nous,* for Julia thought
> In French, but then the rhyme would go for nought). (I.84)

The narrator's foregrounding of his own manipulations reinforces the inherent instability of signs. "Poor Donna Julia! starting as from sleep, / (Mind—that I do not say—she had not slept)" (I.140). In such a teasing account both the integrity of the individual and the integrity of the language that bears the individual are questionable. Julia vilifies her husband for his suspicions of infidelity through a vocabulary of lies. "How can you do such things and keep your fame, / Unless this world, and t'other too, be blind?" (I.165) the narrator asks, thus exposing the lack of truth inherent in social discourse through the unreliability of the codes through which human beings speak themselves.

But it is this very dishonesty, bred into the heart of language, that functions as a first principle of life. We have already examined the kind of matched signifiers that produce a perfect union—the zone of death that true relationships yields. The narrator warned us early, in canto I, that in the quiet illuminating moonlight

> There is a dangerous silence in that hour,
>   A stillness, which leaves room for the full soul
> To open all itself, without the power
>   Of calling wholly back its self-control. (I.114)

In the deceit of language, in the teasing and deferring, is the middle text that ensures life. "What is the end of fame? 'tis but to fill / A certain portion of uncertain paper" (I.218). The narrator-poet sustains life through the stammering of signs that keep repeating as they strive to obtain the end of desire, death, as in the same motion they forestall that achievement until exactly the right moment.[10] After four stanzas of metaphysical speculations under the implication of dying as part of

---

10. Peter Manning reads Byron's use of repetition in *Don Juan* as a "free play" of the poem, which "permits him to contemplate his anxieties and not merely remain subject to them" (*Byron and His Fictions,* 178). In contrast to this biographical emphasis, I am interested in the textual commitments this rhetorical structure enacts.

the life cycle, the narrator produces a passage strikingly prescient of the direction Freud's thought would take, as he worked out in the *fort/da* spool game the convergence of human desire, language, and death.

> You know, or don't know, that great Bacon saith,
>> "Fling up a straw, 'twill show the way the wind blows",
> And such a straw, borne on by human breath,
>> Is Poesy, according as the mind glows;
> A paper kite, which flies 'twixt life and death,
>> A shadow which the onward Soul behind throws:
> And mine's a bubble not blown up for praise,
> But just to play with, as an infant plays. (XIV.8)

And if we miss the paradigm of desire in language that the narrator has so masterfully condensed, the next stanza's opening line echoes Milton, so that the fall *into* language as the compensation for the Fall from Eden confronts us: "The world is all before me, or behind" (XIV.9).

There can be no doubt that *Don Juan* is written as a living monument, a poem *always* repeating and insisting upon its own life, and therefore upon the life of its reader. Once again, Lilian Furst notes that "Words [in *Don Juan*] are instilled with whatever meaning suits the moment, evidently on the assumption that the reader will have the agility to go along with these capers. But never is the reader allowed to forget for any length of reading time that a text is here being made before his eyes" (111). In the repetition of the text, Byron staves off the final closure that, paradoxically, is the aim of Freudian repetition. *Don Juan* creates the illusion that it offers the reader endless existence through the *jouissance* of language. *Don Juan*, given Byron's increasing realization of his own textual mastery, could have no end, for the fragmentary is the place of deferral, the home of desire.

As *Don Juan* promises to be interminable, it threatens to be meaningless as well, to lack the retrospective unity that the reader imposes upon a text. By imbuing his poem so strongly with the narrative presence, Byron establishes narration as the "*sjuzet* repeating the *fabula*" (Brooks 97), as a retelling of that which has already happened. Yet at the same time, the inconstant poses and shifting sensibilities of that narrator turn him into a metaphor of the language in place even before the *fabula*, the language that allowed for the very possibility of the *fabula*. In this way, Byron approaches collapsing metaphor and metonym into a nodal point of significance; as one critic notes, "the ontology informing *Don Juan* seems finally to work toward dissolving the dialectic of identity and difference" (Reeves, 456). Such a moment, if achieved, would nonetheless spell death to the poet, so the failure ever to activate fully the collapse in fact generates Byron's text.

Certainly the narrator threatens to continue forever. "I'm sensible redundancy is wrong, / But could not for the muse of me put less in 't," he confesses. And halfway through canto XII, he announces:

> But now I will begin my poem.—'Tis
>   Perhaps a little strange, if not quite new,
> That from the first of Cantos up to this
>   I've not begun what we have to go through.
> These first twelve books are merely flourishes. (XII.54)
> . . . .
> I thought, at setting off, about two dozen
>   Cantos would do; but at Apollo's pleading,
> If that my Pegasus should not be foundered,
>   I think to canter gently through a hundred. (XII.55)

The text functions as foreplay that keeps in abeyance the climax:[11]

> Oh, reader! if that thou canst read,—and know,
>   'Tis not enough to spell, or even to read,
> To constitute a reader; there must go
>   Virtues of which both you and I have need.
> Firstly, begin with the beginning—(though
>   That clause is hard); and secondly, proceed:
> Thirdly, commence not with the end—or, sinning
> In this sort, end at least with the beginning. (XIII.73)

Thus *Don Juan* triumphantly creates itself out of the very context of Byronic desire that we have seen undergirds Byron's other texts. That is, this poem finally locates authority that seems, to its author, licit in

---

11. Certainly *Don Juan* is an exemplary "text of bliss," as Roland Barthes sets forth such a liberation: "The text that imposes as state of loss; the text that discomforts (perhaps to the point of a certain boredom), unsettles the reader's historical, cultural, psychological assumptions, the consistency of his tastes, values, memories, brings to a crisis his relation with language" (*Pleasure of the Text*, 14).

its truthfulness: its self-admission that it can only lie. Determined to make his heaven in this world, Byron celebrates the word as it perpetuates desire through the constant deferral and reconsummation of language, in what may be one of the boldest psychic defenses poetry records. Language's inability to mean fully bestows upon the poet the never-ending mandate to write. In effect, Byron turns the Wordsworthian/Shelleyan tensions and despair into the very means of subverting and thereby conquering the Law they contest.

In one sense, then, the jubilant aim of *Don Juan* is to abolish the pretense of an ontology that deflects from the truth of desire. Instead, meaning inevitably becomes entwined with the real human act of dying, and so in Byron's *jouissance* of free play—his celebration of a certain type of meaninglessness—he outruns death, outplays those systematic schema he deplored. Unlike Wordsworth and especially Shelley, who wanted to embrace death and remain alive, Byron seeks rather to defy it and live. Combining Roman Jakobson's location of the metonymic axis in prose fiction with Lacan's equation of metonymy and desire enables us to understand *Don Juan* as the quintessential narrative statement—iconoclastic as it is—of the Romantic project that would situate the subject and object of epistemological inquiry in the slippery constellation of desire, death, and language. Far as it was from Shelley's own style and typical subject, *Don Juan* nonetheless prompted Shelley's recognition of the poem's brilliance, and indeed, both poets shared a kindred instinct toward liberation from an effete law that kept properly in their place those who yearned for more: there is no resting place in Byron's epic. *Don Juan* serves as a paradigm of the temporal nature of narration: the sequence of transformations in Byron's poem "engages and suspends time, in a single movement; it permits discourse to acquire a meaning without this meaning becoming pure information; in a word, it makes narrative possible and yields us its very definition" (Todorov, 233).

In the confusions and unclear futures that inhabit this poem, then, we have a very model of the movement of desire. In the process, we finally assuage the frustration of poets who would escape the confines of language: turn that language upon itself, in an act that paradoxically ensures its never-ending lack, its inability to effect a closure that closes out the poet; this poem will *always* need a writer and a reader both. To the extent that the fragment approaches the status of genre during the Romantic period, it is at least partially because it keeps Romantic desire from ever being fully spoken.

Yet if *Don Juan*—as the logical culmination of the Byronic quest for (non)meaning—reveals a compulsion to repeat that mocks origin and end, it also creates the conditions for constant iteration of the Other, wherein we learn the language we inhabit. Desire is desire of the Other; but Byron's greatest poem celebrates the myth of our ability in language, as textual beings, to create the Other in our own image, rather than the (Lacanian) other way around.[12] It is, in the end, only another myth—more cheerful than that of Wordsworth or Shelley— another strategy to confront the emptiness in desire; but its bravado makes it particularly appealing, and may in fact help explain Byron's popularity with the reading public. Jerome McGann rightly points to a reliance upon self-generated myths that sustained Romantic poetry (*Romantic Ideology*, 131). But it is Byron alone who self-consciously promoted the illusion of a "solution." The "idea that poetry, or even consciousness, can set one free of the ruins of history and culture is the grand illusion of every Romantic poet," McGann claims (*Romantic Ideology* 137). At the same time, we nonetheless must entertain se- riously Shelley's opposite conclusion that only death could free the poet of history and culture; and we must confront the position that Wordsworth staked out *from the beginning* that only language—history and culture—could allow for the grounds of a lifelong poetry, al- though some came to see it as (and Wordsworth feared it would be) a *lifeless* poetry. Byron, however, while acquiescing to the structural power of language, at the same time creates—and revels in—the out- rageous illusion that through his profligate dissemination of the potent word, it is the poet who spends his desire, and not a language—or culture—against his will.

Just as Freud recognized, the analytic reader who stands open be- fore the poet's text is awed by the power of artistic intuition, of those poetic insights that seemingly precede the very tools later deemed

---

12. Wilden maintains that the informing desire of the traditional *Don Juan* myth be- comes a "pathological quest for the self in the other" (Lacan, *Speech and Language*, 165), so that the very choice of "hero" seems a summation at points of what the Romantic canon explored in more serious tones elsewhere.

necessary for their discovery. "Art, as the power to invent, is paradigmatic of man's capacity to take existence itself into his mind and rewrite it according to the images of desire," claims Tilottama Rajan
(*Dark Interpreter,* 13). We might qualify her wisdom by claiming that
desire instead (under)writes both existence and art, and poetry thus
becomes a priori far less an idealizing linguistic form than Rajan's
statement suggests. Freud, who taught Lacan to love—to believe in—
literature, thought hard about poetry and desire. In "The Theme of the
Three Caskets," for instance, he discusses how the profound effect of
texts such as *King Lear* exceeds what would appear to be the easily
located formal and thematic pleasures. He credits this excess yield to
the poet, whose capacious imagination and intuition inscribe full psychological myths and mental processes not consciously available to the
average person. Freud believes that in the poet's mind, "a reduction to
the original idea of the myth [that in daily life we distort] is going on,
so that we once more perceive the original meaning containing all the
power to move us that had been weakened by the distortion of the
myth" (77). Thus, in contrast to the estrangement, for example, that
the Russian Formalists would claim as the particular power of great
art, Freud would assert the familiarization, the sense in profound art of
the coming home of the psyche whose daily medium is otherwise
intrigue and deceit. Through art, Freud wanted to claim, we know
ourselves for the first time. And through their vigorous engagement
with language, the Romantic poets created a paradigm of that mythological self-knowledge, recognizing that in the tension between being
spoken into selfhood and speaking the word into being instead, they
could give vision to the birth of human desire, or to what makes us
human. Out of the inherent paradox in language, its inability to satisfy
the very yearning to which it gives rise, develops the psychological and
linguistic matrix for a Romantic poetry that articulates the enduring
potency of a discourse of desire.

Works Consulted

Aarsleff, Hans. *From Locke to Saussure: Essays on the Study of Language and Intellectual History*. Minneapolis: University of Minnesota Press, 1982.

Adorno, Theodor W. "Lyric Poetry and Society." *Telos* 20 (1974): 56–71.

———. *Negative Dialectics*. New York: Seabury Press, 1973.

Alexander, Meena. *Women in Romanticism: Mary Wollstonecraft, Dorothy Wordsworth, and Mary Shelley*. Totowa, N.J.: Barnes and Noble, 1989.

Althusser, Louis, "Freud and Lacan." *New Left Review* 55 (1968): 48–65.

Ault, Donald. *Narrative Unbound: Revisioning Blake's "The Four Zoas."* Barrytown, N.Y.: Station Hill Press, 1987.

Bahti, Timothy, "Wordsworth's Rhetorical Theft." In Reed, 86–124.

Barrell, John. *Poetry, Language, and Politics*. Manchester: Manchester University Press, 1988.

Barthes, Roland. *The Pleasure of the Text*. Trans. Richard Miller. New York: Hill and Wang, 1975.

———. *Sade, Fourier, Loyola*. Trans. Richard Miller. New York: Hill and Wang, 1976.

Bataille, Georges. *Death and Sensuality: A Study of Eroticism and the Taboo*. Ed. Robert Kastenbaum. Salem, N.H.: Ayer, 1977.

Bateson, F. W. *Wordsworth: A Re-Interpretation*. London: Longman's, 1954.

Beatty, Bernard. *Byron's "Don Juan."* Totowa, N.J.: Barnes and Noble, 1985.

———, and Vincent Newey, eds. *Byron and the Limits of Fiction*. Totowa, N.J.: Barnes and Noble, 1988.

Benjamin, Jessica. *The Bonds of Love: Psychoanalysis, Feminism, and the Problem of Domination*. New York: Pantheon, 1988.

Bersani, Leo. *Baudelaire and Freud*. Berkeley: University of California Press, 1977.

Bewell, Alan J. "Wordworth's Primal Scene: Retrospective Tales of Idiots, Wild Children, and Savages." *ELH* 50 (1983): 321–46.

Blank, G. K. "Wordsworth's Style of Poetic Problems." *Wordsworth Circle* 16 (1985): 40–43.

Bloom, Harold. *The Anxiety of Influence: A Theory of Poetry*. London: Oxford University Press, 1973.

——. *A Map of Misreading*. London: Oxford University Press, 1975.

——. *Poetry and Repression: Revisionism from Blake to Stevens*. New Haven: Yale University Press, 1976.

——. *The Visionary Company: A Reading of English Romantic Poetry*. Garden City, N.Y.: Doubleday, 1963.

Bone, Drummond J. "*Beppo:* The Liberation of Fiction." In Beatty and Newey, 97–125.

Brenkman, John. "The Other and the One: Psychoanalysis, Reading, the Symposium." In Felman, *Literature and Psychoanalysis*, 396–456.

Brennan, Teresa. "Impasse in Psychoanalysis and Feminism." In *Between Feminism and Psychoanalysis*, ed. T. Brennan, 45–65. London: Routledge, 1989.

Brewer, William D. "Questions without Answers: The Conversational Style of 'Julian and Maddalo.'" *Keats-Shelley Journal* 38 (1989): 127–144.

Brisman, Leslie. *Milton's Poetry of Choice and Its Romantic Heirs*. Ithaca: Cornell University Press, 1973.

——. "Mysterious Tongue: Shelley and the Language of Christianity." *Texas Studies in Language and Literature* 23 (1981): 389–417.

——. *Romantic Origins*. Ithaca: Cornell University Press, 1978.

Brisman, Susan Hawk. "'Unsaying His High Language': The Problem of Voice in *Prometheus Unbound*." *Studies in Romanticism* 16 (1977): 51–86.

Brooks, Peter. *Reading for the Plot: Design and Invention in Narrative*. New York: Knopf, 1984.

Brown, Marshall. Review essay, *Keats-Shelley Journal* 37 (1988): 166–69.

Bruns, Gerald L. *Modern Poetry and the Idea of Language: A Critical and Historical Study*. New Haven: Yale University Press, 1974.

Bush, Douglas. *Mythology and the Romantic Tradition in English Poetry*. Cambridge: Harvard University Press, 1969.

Byron, George Gordon Baron. *Byron's Letters and Journals*. 12 vols. Ed. Leslie A. Marchand. Cambridge: Harvard University Press, 1973–82.

——. *Lord Byron's "Cain": Twelve Essays and a Text with Variants and Annotations*. Ed. T. G. Steffan. Austin: University of Texas Press, 1968.

——. *Lord Byron: The Complete Poetical Works*. 5 vols. Ed. Jerome J. McGann. Oxford: Clarendon Press, 1980–.

Caldwell, Richard S. "'The Sensitive Plant' as Original Fantasy." *Studies in Romanticism* 15 (1976): 221–52.

Cameron, Kenneth Neill. *Shelley: The Golden Years*. Cambridge: Harvard University Press, 1974.

——. *The Young Shelley: Genesis of a Radical*. New York: Macmillan, 1950.

Cantor, Paul A. "Byron's *Cain:* A Romantic Version of the Fall." *Kenyon Review*, n.s. 2.2 (1980): 50–71.

Chandler, James. *Wordsworth's Second Nature: A Study of the Poetry and Politics*. Chicago: University of Chicago Press, 1984.

Christensen, Jerome. "*Marino Faliero* and the Fault of Byron's Satire." *Studies in Romanticism* 24 (1985): 313–33.
——. "Setting Byron Straight: Class, Sexuality, and the Poet." In Scarry, 125–59.
——. "Wordsworth's Misery, Coleridge's Woe: Reading 'The Thorn.'" *Papers on Language and Literature* 16 (1980): 268–86.
Claridge, Laura. "Pope's Rape of Excess." *Perspectives on Pornography: Sexuality in Film and Literature.* Ed. Gary Day and Clive Bloom. London: Macmillan, 1988.
Claridge, Laura, and Elizabeth Langland, eds. *Out of Bounds: Male Writers and Gender(ed) Criticism.* Amherst: University of Massachusetts Press, 1990.
Cooke, Michael G. *Acts of Inclusion: Studies Bearing on an Elementary Theory of Romanticism.* New Haven: Yale University Press, 1979.
Cooke, Michael G., and Alan Bewell, eds. "*The Borderers:* A Forum." Special issue of *Studies in Romanticism* 27 (Fall 1988).
Cosgrove, Brian. *Wordsworth and the Poetry of Self-Sufficiency: A Study of the Poetic Development, 1796–1814.* Salzburg: Instituit für Anglistik and Amerikanistik, 1982.
——. "Wordsworth's Moonlight-Poetry and the Sense of the 'Uncanny.'" *Ariel* 13 (1982): 19–32.
Crompton, Louis. *Byron and Greek Love: Homophobia in 19th-Century England.* Berkeley: University of California Press, 1985.
Cronin, Richard. *Shelley's Poetic Thoughts.* New York: St. Martin's, 1981.
Culler, Jonathan. *On Deconstruction: Theory and Criticism after Structuralism.* Ithaca: Cornell University Press, 1976.
——. *Structuralist Poetics: Structuralism, Linguistics, and the Study of Literature.* Ithaca: Cornell University Press, 1976.
Curran, Stuart. *Shelley's Annus Mirabilis: The Maturing of an Epic Vision.* San Marino, Calif.: Huntington Library, 1975.
Davis, Robert Con, ed. *The Fictional Father: Lacanian Readings of the Text.* Amherst: University of Massachusetts Press, 1981.
——. *Lacan and Narration: The Psychoanalytic Difference in Narrative Theory.* Baltimore: Johns Hopkins University Press, 1983.
——. "Lacan, Poe, and Narrative Repression." In Davis, *Lacan and Narration,* 983–1005.
Dawson, P. M. *The Unacknowledged Legislator: Shelley and Politics.* Oxford: Oxford University Press, 1980.
DeJean, Joan. *Fictions of Sappho, 1546–1937.* Chicago: University of Chicago Press, 1989.
De Man, Paul. *The Rhetoric of Romanticism.* New York: Columbia University Press, 1984.
Derrida, Jacques. *Psyche: Inventions de l'autre.* Paris: Galilée, 1987.
——. *Writing and Difference.* Trans. Alan Bass. Chicago: University of Chicago Press, 1978.
Eagleton, Terry. *Criticism and Ideology.* London: NLB, 1978.
——. *The Ideology of the Aesthetic.* Oxford: Basil Blackwell, 1990.

———. *The Rape of Clarissa: Writing, Sexuality, and Class-Struggle in Richardson*. Minneapolis: University of Minnesota Press, 1982.

Eaves, Morris. Review of John Barrell, "The Political Theory of Painting from Reynolds to Hazlitt: 'The Body of the Public.'" *Studies in Romanticism* 27 (1988): 429–42.

Ellison, Julie. *Delicate Subjects: Romanticism, Gender, and the Ethics of Understanding*. Ithaca: Cornell University Press, 1990.

Felman, Shoshana. "Beyond Oedipus: The Specimen Story of Psychoanalysis." In Davis, *Lacan and Narration*, 1021–53.

———. *Jacques Lacan and the Adventure of Insight: Psychoanalysis in Contemporary Culture*. Cambridge: Harvard University Press, 1987.

———, ed. *Literature and Psychoanalysis: The Question of Reading—Otherwise*. Baltimore: Johns Hopkins University Press, 1982.

Ferguson, Frances. "Coleridge on Language and Delusion." *Genre* 11 (1978): 191–207.

———. "Shelley's 'Mont Blanc.'" In Reed, 202–14.

———. *Wordsworth: Language as Counter-Spirit*. New Haven: Yale University Press, 1977.

Foot, Michael. *Politics of Paradise*. New York: Harper and Row, 1989.

Foucault, Michel. *The History of Sexuality*. Trans. Robert Hurley, Vol. 1. New York: Pantheon, 1978.

Freud, Sigmund. *Character and Culture*. Ed. Phillip Rieff. New York: Macmillan, 1976. (*CC*)

———. *The Standard Edition of the Complete Psychological Works of Sigmund Freud*. Trans. and ed. James Strachey et al. 24 vols. London: Hogarth, 1953–74. (*SE*)

———. "The Acquisition of Power over Fire." In *CC*, 294–300.

———. "The Antithetical Sense of Primal Words." In *CC*, 44–50.

———. *Beyond the Pleasure Principle*. In *SE* 18: 7–64.

———. *Civilization and Its Discontents*. In *SE* 21: 64–145.

———. "The Economic Problem in Masochism." In *SE* 19: 157–70.

———. "The Theme of the Three Caskets." In *CC*, 67–79.

———. *Three Essays on the Theory of Sexuality*. Trans. and ed. James Strachey. New York: Basic Books, 1962.

———. "The Uncanny," In *SE* 17: 219–52.

Friedman, Michael H. *The Making of a Tory Humanist: William Wordsworth and the Idea of Community*. New York: Columbia University Press, 1979.

Fry, Paul H. "The Absent Dead: Wordsworth, Byron, and the Epitaph." *Studies in Romanticism* 17 (1978): 413–33.

———. "Made Men: A Review Article on Recent Shelley and Keats Studies." *Texas Studies in Language and Literature* 21 (1979): 433–54.

———. *The Poet's Calling in the English Ode*. New Haven: Yale University Press, 1980.

———. *The Reach of Criticism: Method and Perception in Literary Theory*. New Haven: Yale University Press, 1983.

Furst, Lilian R. *Fictions of Romantic Irony*. Cambridge: Harvard University Press, 1984.

Gallop, Jane. *The Daughter's Seduction: Feminism and Psychoanalysis*. Ithaca: Cornell University Press, 1982.

——. *Thinking through the Body*. New York: Columbia University Press, 1988.

Galperin, William H. *Revision and Authority in Wordsworth: The Interpretation of a Career*. Philadelphia: University of Pennsylvania Press, 1989.

George, Diana Hume. *Blake and Freud*. Ithaca: Cornell University Press, 1980.

Gleckner, Robert. *Byron and the Ruins of Paradise*. Westport, Conn.: Greenwood, 1980.

Gombrich, E. H. "The Evidence of Images." In *Interpretation: Theory and Practice*, ed. Charles S. Singleton, 35–104. Baltimore: Johns Hopkins University Press, 1969.

Goodman, Alice. "Wordsworth and the Sucking Babe." *Essays in Criticism* 33 (1983): 108–25.

Halperin, David M. *One Hundred Years of Homosexuality and Other Essays on Greek Love*. New York: Routledge, 1989.

Hartman, Geoffrey H. *Beyond Formalism: Literary Essays, 1958–1970*. New Haven: Yale University Press, 1970.

——. "The Poetics of Prophecy." In *High Romantic Argument: Essays for M. H. Abrams*, ed. Lawrence Lipking, 15–40. Ithaca: Cornell University Press, 1981.

——. "Psychoanalysis: The French Connection." In Kurtzweil and Phillips, 353–62.

——. "A Touching Compulsion: Wordsworth and the Problem of Literary Representation." *Georgia Review* 31 (1977): 345–61.

——. *Wordsworth's Poetry, 1787–1814*. New Haven: Yale University Press, 1977.

Heffernan, James A. W. "The Presence of the Absent Mother in Wordsworth's *Prelude*." *Studies in Romanticism* 27 (1988): 253–72.

Heidegger, Martin. *Being and Time*. Trans. John Macquarrie and Edward Robinson. New York: Harper. 1962.

Hoagwood, Terence Allan. *Skepticism and Ideology: Shelley's Political Prose and Its Philosophical Context from Bacon to Marx*. Iowa City: University of Iowa Press, 1988.

Hodgson, John A. "Poems of the Imagination, Allegories of the Imagination: Wordsworth's Preface of 1815 and the Redundancy of Imaginative Poetry," *Studies in Romanticism* 27 (1988): 273–88.

——. "Wordsworth Teaching: 'To Joanna.'" *Wordsworth Circle* 9 (1978): 362–64.

Hogle, Jerrold E. "Shelley's Poetics: The Power as Metaphor." *Keats-Shelley Journal* 31 (1982): 159–97.

——. *Shelley's Process: Radical Transference and the Development of His Major Works*. New York: Oxford University Press, 1988.

Homans, Margaret. *Bearing the Word: Language and Female Experience in Nineteenth-Century Women's Writing*. Chicago: University of Chicago Press, 1986.

Hughes, D. J. "Coherence and Collapse in Shelley, with Particular Reference to *Epipsychidion*." *ELH* 28 (1961): 260–83.

Jacobs, Carol. *Uncontainable Romanticism: Shelley, Brontë, Kleist*. Baltimore: Johns Hopkins University Press, 1989.

Jacobus, Mary. *Reading Woman: Essays in Feminist Criticism.* New York: Columbia University Press, 1986.

——. *Romanticism, Writing, and Sexual Difference: Essays on "The Prelude."* Oxford: Oxford University Press, 1989.

——. *Tradition and Experiment in Wordsworth's "Lyrical Ballads" (1798).* Oxford: Clarendon Press, 1976.

Jameson, Fredric. "Imaginary and Symbolic in Lacan." In *The Ideologies of Theory: Essays 1971–1986.* Vol 1. Minneapolis: University of Minnesota Press, 1988.

——. *The Political Unconscious: Narrative as a Socially Symbolic Act.* Ithaca: Cornell University Press, 1981.

——. *Sartre: The Origins of a Style.* New Haven: Yale University Press, 1961.

Janowitz, Anne. "Coleridge's 1816 Volume: Fragment as Rubric." *Studies in Romanticism* 24 (1985): 21–39.

——. *England's Ruins: Poetic Purpose and the National Landscape.* Oxford: Basil Blackwell, 1990.

Johnson, Barbara. "The Frame of Reference: Poe, Lacan, Derrida." In Felman, *Literature and Psychoanalysis,* 457–505.

Johnston, Kenneth. *Wordsworth and "The Recluse."* New Haven: Yale University Press, 1984.

Keach, William. *Shelley's Style.* New York: Methuen, 1984.

Kelsall, Malcolm. *Byron's Politics.* Totowa, N.J.: Barnes and Noble, 1987.

Kerrigan, William. *The Sacred Complex: On the Psychogenesis of "Paradise Lose."* Cambridge: Harvard University Press, 1983.

Kirchoff, Frederick. "Shelley's *Alastor:* The Poet Who Refuses to Write Language." *Keats-Shelley Journal* 32 (1983): 108–22.

Knight, Richard Payne, and Thomas Wright. *Sexual Symbolism: A History of Phallic Worship.* New York: Julian Press, 1957.

Knoepflmacher, U. C. "Projection and the Female Other: Romanticism, Browning, and the Victorian Dramatic Monologue." In Claridge and Langland, *Out of Bounds.*

Kofman, Sarah. *The Enigma of Woman: Women in Freud's Writings.* Trans. Catherine Porter. Ithaca: Cornell University Press, 1985.

Kristeva, Julia. *Desire in Language: A Semiotic Approach to Literature and Art.* Ed. Leon Roudiez. Trans. Alice Jardine and Thomas Gora. New York: Columbia University Press. 1980.

——. "The Father, Love, and Banishment." In Kurtzweil and Phillips, 389–99.

Kurtz, Benjamin P. *Pursuit of Death: A Study of Shelley's Poetry.* Saint Clair Shores, Mich.: Scholarly Press, 1971.

Kurtzweil, Edith, and William Phillips, ed. *Literature and Psychoanalysis.* New York: Columbia University Press, 1983.

Lacan, Jacques. "Desire and the Interpretation of Desire in Hamlet." *Yale French Studies* 55/56 (1977): 11–52.

——. *Ecrits: A Selection.* Trans. Alan Sheridan. New York: Norton, 1977.

——. *Feminine Sexuality.* Ed. Juliet Mitchell and Jacqueline Rose. Trans. Jacqueline Rose. New York: Norton, 1982.

——. *The Four Fundamental Concepts of Psychoanalysis.* Ed. Jacques-Alain Miller. Trans. Alan Sheridan. New York: Norton, 1981.

———. *Speech and Language in Psychoanalysis*. Trans. and ed. Anthony Wilden. Baltimore: Johns Hopkins University Press, 1981.

Langbauer, Laurie. "An Early Romance: Motherhood and Women's Writings in Mary Wollstonecraft's Novels." In Mellor, 208–19.

Laplanche, Jean. *Life and Death in Psychoanalysis*. Trans. Jeffrey Mehlman. Baltimore: Johns Hopkins University Press, 1976.

Le Doeuff, Michele. "Women and Philosophy." *Radical Philosophy* 17 (1977): 2–11.

Lentricchia, Frank. "The Resentments of Robert Frost." In Claridge and Langland, *Out of Bounds*, 268–89.

Levinson, Marjorie. *Keats's Life of Allegory: The Origins of a Style*. Oxford: Basil Blackwell, 1988.

———. *The Romantic Fragment Poem: A Critique of a Form*. Chapel Hill: University of North Carolina Press, 1986.

———. *Wordsworth's Great Period Poems: Four Essays*. Cambridge: Cambridge University Press, 1986.

———. ed. *Rethinking Historicism: Critical Readings in Romantic History*. Oxford: Basil Blackwell, 1989.

Lindenberger, Herbert. *On Wordsworth's "Prelude."* Princeton: Princeton University Press, 1963.

Liu, Alan. "The Power of Formalism: The New Historiciam." *ELH* 56 (1989): 721–72.

———. *Wordsworth: The Sense of History*. Stanford: Stanford University Press, 1989.

Lovell, Ernest J., ed. *His Very Self and Voice: Collected Conversations of Lord Byron*. New York: Macmillan, 1954.

McFarland, Thomas. *Romanticism and the Forms of Ruin: Wordsworth, Coleridge, and the Modalities of Fragment*. Princeton: Princeton University Press, 1981.

McGann, Jerome J., *"Don Juan" in Context*. Chicago: University of Chicago Press, 1976.

———. *Fiery Dust: Byron's Poetic Development*. Chicago: University of Chicago Press, 1968.

———. "The Meaning of the Ancient Mariner." *Critical Inquiry* 8 (1981): 35–67.

———. "'My Brain Is Feminine': Byron and the Poetry of Deception." In *Byron: Augustan and Romantic*, ed. Andrew Rutherford, 26–51. London: Macmillan, 1990.

———. *The Romantic Ideology: A Critical Investigation*. Chicago: University of Chicago Press, 1983.

McWhir, Anne. "The Light and the Knife: Ab/Using Language in *The Cenci*." *Keats-Shelley Journal* 38 (1989): 144–161.

Manning, Peter J. *Byron and His Fictions*. Detroit: Wayne State University Press, 1978.

———. "*Don Juan* and Byron's Imperceptiveness to the English Word." *Studies in Romanticism* 18 (1979): 207–33.

———. Review of *Byron: A Poet before His Public*, by Philip W. Martin, and *English Romantic Hellenism, 1700–1984*, by Timothy Webb. *Studies in Romanticism* 23 (1984): 401–9.

Marchand, Leslie A., ed. *Byron's Letters and Journals*. 12 vols. Cambridge: Harvard University Press, 1975.

Mellor, Anne K. *Mary Shelley: Her Life, Her Fiction, Her Monsters*. New York: Methuen, 1988.

———. ed. *Romanticism and Feminism*. Bloomington: Indiana University Press, 1988.

Michasiw, Kim Ian. "The Social Other: *Don Juan* and the Genesis of the Self." *Mosaic* 22 (1989): 29–48.

Milosz, Czeslaw. "The Nobel Lecture, 1980." *New York Review of Books* 28 (1981): 11–15.

Morse, David. *Romanticism: A Structural Analysis*. Totowa, N.J.: Barnes and Noble, 1982.

Nussbaum, Martha. "The Bondage and Freedom of Eros." *Times Literary Supplement* 4 (1990): 571–73.

Ong, Walter J. *Fighting for Life: Contest, Sexuality, and Consciousness*. Ithaca: Cornell University Press, 1981.

Onorato, Richard J. *The Character of the Poet: Wordsworth in "The Prelude."* Princeton: Princeton University Press, 1971.

Parker, Reeve. "'Oh Could You Hear His Voice!': Wordsworth, Coleridge, and Ventriloquism." In Reed, 125–43.

———. "Reading Wordsworth's Power: Narrative and Usurpation in *The Borderers*." *ELH* 54 (1987): 299–332.

Paulson, Ronald. *Representations of Revolution (1789–1820)*. New Haven: Yale University Press, 1983.

Perkins, David, ed. *English Romantic Writers*. New York: Harcourt, 1967.

Peterfreund, Stuart. "Shelley, Monboddo, Vico, and the Language of Poetry." *Style* 15 (1981) 382–400.

Pierce, John B. "'Mont Blanc' and *Prometheus Unbound:* Shelley's Use of the Rhetoric of Silence." *Keats-Shelley Journal* 38 (1989): 103–26.

Privateer, Paul. *Romantic Voices: Ideology and Identity in Early Nineteenth-Century British Poetry*. Athens: University of Georgia Press, 1991.

Rajan, Balachandra. *The Form of the Unfinished: English Poetics from Spenser to Pound*. Princeton: Princeton University Press, 1985.

Rajan, Tilottama. *Dark Interpreter: The Discourse of Romanticism*. Ithaca: Cornell University Press, 1980.

———. Introduction to special issue on Nietzsche. *Studies in Romanticism* 29 (1990): 3–8.

———. "Romantic Studies after Paul de Man." *Studies in Romanticism* 24 (1985): 451–74.

———. *The Supplement of Reading: Figures of Understanding in Romantic Theory and Practice*. Ithaca: Cornell University Press, 1990.

———. "Wollstonecraft and Godwin: Reading the Secrets of the Political Novel." *Studies in Romanticism* 27 (1988): 221–52.

Randel, Fred V. "Frankenstein, Feminism, and the Intertextuality of Mountains." *Studies in Romanticism* 23 (1984): 515–32.

Rank, Otto. "Life and Creation." In Kurtzweil and Phillips, 39–54.

Rapaport, Herman. "Staging Mont Blanc." In *Displacement: Derrida and After,* ed. Mark Krumpnick, 59–73. Bloomington: Indiana University Press, 1983.

Rapf, Joanna E. "The Byronic Heroine: Incest and the Creative Process." *Studies in English Literature* 21 (1981): 637–45.

Reed, Arden, ed. *Romanticism and Language.* Ithaca: Cornell University Press, 1984.

Reeves, Charles Eric. "Continual Seduction: The Reading of *Don Juan.*" *Studies in Romanticism* 17 (1978): 453–63.

Reiman, Donald H. *Shelley's "The Triumph of Life": A Critical Study.* Rpt. New York: Octagon, 1979.

Richardson, Alan. *A Mental Theatre: Poetic Drama and Consciousness in the Romantic Age.* University Park: Pennsylvania State University Press, 1988.

——. "Romanticism and the Colonization of the Feminine." In Mellor, 13–25.

Richardson, William, and John Muller. *Lacan Interpreted: A Reader's Guide to Selected Texts.* New York: International University Press, 1981.

Ridenour, George M. "*Don Juan* and the Romantics." *Studies in Romanticism* 16 (1977): 563–71.

——. *The Style of "Don Juan."* New Haven: Yale University Press, 1960.

Rieger, James. *The Mutiny Within: The Heresies of Percy Bysshe Shelley.* New York: Braziller, 1967.

Ross, Marlon B. *The Contours of Masculine Desire: Romanticism and the Rise of Women's Poetry.* Oxford: Oxford University Press, 1989.

——. "Naturalizing Gender: Woman's Place in Wordsworth's Ideological Landscape." *ELH* 52 (1986): 391–409.

——. "Troping Masculine Power in the Crisis of Poetic Identity." In Mellor, 26–51.

Rougemont, Denis de. *Love in the Western World.* Trans. Montgomery Belgion. Princeton: Princeton University Press, 1983.

Rousseau, Jean-Jacques. *The First and Second Discourses.* Ed. Roger D. Masters. Trans. Roger D. Masters and Judith R. Masters. New York: St. Martin's, 1964.

Said, Edward. *The World, the Text, and the Critic.* Cambridge: Harvard University Press, 1983.

Sartre, Jean-Paul. *Search for a Method.* Trans. Hazel E. Barnes. New York: Knopf, 1963.

Scarry, Elaine, ed. *Literature and the Body: Essays on Populations and Persons.* Baltimore: Johns Hopkins University Press, 1988.

Schapiro, Barbara A. *The Romantic Mother: Narcissistic Patterns in Poetry.* Baltimore: Johns Hopkins University Press, 1983.

Schleiffer, Ronald. "The Space and Dialogue of Desire: Lacan, Greimas, and Narrative Temporality." In Davis, *Lacan and Narration,* 871–90.

Schneidermann, Stuart, *Jacques Lacan: Death of an Intellectual Hero.* Cambridge: Harvard University Press, 1983.

——, ed. and trans. *Returning to Freud: Clinical Psychoanalysis in the School of Lacan.* New Haven: Yale University Press, 1980.

Schor, Naomi. *Reading in Detail: Aesthetics and the Feminine.* New York: Methuen, 1987.

Scrivener, Michael Henry. *Radical Shelley: The Philosophical Anarchism and Utopian Thought of Percy Bysshe Shelley.* Princeton: Princeton University Press, 1982.

Shelley, Percy Bysshe. *The Letters of Percy Bysshe Shelley.* Ed. Frederick L. Jones. 2 vols. Oxford: Clarendon Press, 1964.

———. *Shelley's Poetry and Prose.* Ed. Donald H. Reiman and Sharon B. Powers. New York: Norton, 1977.

Silverman, Kaja. "History, Figuration, and Female Subjectivity in *Tess of the d'Urbervilles.*" *Novel* 18 (1984): 5–28.

———. *The Subject of Semiotics.* New York: Oxford University Press, 1983.

Simpson, David. "Criticism, Politics, and Style in Wordsworth's Poetry." *Critical Inquiry* 11 (1984): 52–81.

———. *Wordworth and the Figurings of the Real.* Atlantic Highlands, N.J.: Humanities Press, 1982.

———. *Wordsworth's Historical Imagination.* New York: Methuen, 1987.

Skerry, Philip J. "Concentric Structures in *Marino Faliero.*" *Keats-Shelley Journal* 32 (1983): 81–107.

Smith, Joseph H., and William Kerrigan, eds. *Interpreting Lacan.* Psychiatry and the Humanities 6. New Haven: Yale University Press, 1983.

Smith, Roberta. "Bill Jensen: Roughing It on 57th Street." *New York Times* (17 March 1991): H35.

Sperry, Stuart M. *Shelley's Major Verse: The Narrative and Dramatic Poetry.* Cambridge: Harvard University Press, 1988.

———. "Towards a Definition of Romantic Irony in English Literature." In *Romantic and Modern Revaluations of Literary Tradition.* Ed. George Bornstein, 3–28. Pittsburgh: University of Pittsburgh Press, 1977.

Spivak, Gayatri C. "Sex and History in 'The Prelude' (1805): Books IX to XII." In *In Other Worlds: Essays in Cultural Politics,* 46–76. New York: Methuen, 1987.

Steiner, George. *Language and Silence: Essays on Language, Literature, and the Inhuman.* New York: Atheneum, 1967.

Storch, R. F. "Wordsworth's *The Borderers:* The Poet as Anthropologist." *ELH* 36 (1969): 340–60.

Tate, Candace. "Byron's *Don Juan:* Myth as Psychodrama." *Keats-Shelley Journal* 29 (1980): 131–50.

Thorslev, Peter L., Jr. *Romantic Contraries: Freedom versus Destiny.* New Haven: Yale University Press, 1984.

Todorov, Tzvetan. *The Politics of Prose.* Trans. Richard Howard. Ithaca: Cornell University Press, 1977.

Van Ghent, Dorothy. *Keats: Myth of the Hero.* Rev. and ed. Jeffrey Cane Robinson. Princeton: Princeton University Press, 1983.

Vasallo, Peter. *Byron: The Italian Literary Influence.* New York: St. Martin's, 1984.

Vendler, Helen. *The Odes of John Keats.* Cambridge: Harvard University Press, 1983.

Waldoff, Leon, "The Father-Son Conflict in *Prometheus Unbound*: The Psychology of a Vision," *Psychoanalytic Review* 62 (1975): 79–96.

———. *Keats and the Silent Work of Imagination.* Urbana: University of Illinois Press, 1985.

Walker, Constance Hunter. "Bards of Passion: Enlightenment Psychology in English Romantic Poetry." Ph.D. diss., University of Pennsylvania, 1982.

Wasserman, Earl R. *The Subtler Language: Critical Readings of Neoclassic and Romantic Poems.* Baltimore: Johns Hopkins University Press, 1959.

Watkins, Daniel P. *Social Relations in Byron's Eastern Tales.* Rutherford, N.J.: Fairleigh Dickinson University Press, 1987.

Watts, Ann Chalmers. "Pearl, Inexpressibility, and Poems of Human Loss." *PMLA* 99 (1984): 26–40.

Webster, Sarah McKim. "Circumscription and the Female in the Early Romantics." *Philological Quarterly* 61 (1982): 51–68.

Weiskel, Thomas. *The Romantic Sublime: Studies in the Structure and Psychology of Transcendence.* Baltimore: Johns Hopkins University Press, 1976.

Weiss, Allen S. *The Aesthetics of Excess.* Albany: State University of New York Press, 1989.

White, Newman Ivey. *Portrait of Shelley.* New York: Knopf, 1945.

Winkler, Karen J. "A Controversial Philosopher States His Case on Politics, Poetry, and Moral Principle." *Chronicle of Higher Education,* 3 May 1989, A7–9.

Wolfson, Susan J. *The Questioning Presence: Wordsworth, Keats, and the Interrogative Mode in Romantic Poetry.* Ithaca: Cornell University Press, 1986.

——. "'Their She Condition': Cross-Dressing and the Politics of Gender in *Don Juan.*" *ELH* 54 (1987): 585–617.

Woodring, Carl. *Politics in English Romantic Poetry.* Cambridge: Harvard University Press, 1970.

Wordsworth, William. *The Borderers.* Ed. Robert Osborn. Ithaca: Cornell University Press, 1982.

——. *The Letters of William and Dorothy Wordsworth.* Ed. Ernest de Selincourt and Mary Moorman. 2d ed. Vol. 2. Oxford: Clarendon, 1969.

——. *Peter Bell.* Ed. John E. Jordan. Ithaca: Cornell University Press, 1985.

——. *The Poetical Works of William Wordsworth.* Ed. Ernest de Selincourt and Helen Darbishire. 5 vols. Oxford: Clarendon, 1940–49.

——. *The Prelude: 1799, 1805, 1850.* Ed. Jonathan Wordsworth et al. New York: Norton, 1979.

——. *The Prose Works of William Wordsworth.* Ed. W. J. B. Owen and Jane Worthington Smyser. 3 vols. Oxford: Clarendon, 1974.

——. *The Salisbury Plain Poems.* Ed. Stephen Gill. Ithaca: Cornell University Press, 1974.

——. *The White Doe of Rylstone.* Ed. Alice Pattee Comparetti. Ithaca: Cornell University Press, 1940.

——. *The White Doe of Rylstone.* Ed. Kristine Dugas. Ithaca: Cornell University Press, 1988.

Worton, Michael. "Speech and Silence in *The Cenci.*" In *Essays on Shelley,* ed. Miriam Allott, 105–24. Totowa, N.J.: Barnes and Noble, 1982.

Young, Robert. "The Eye and Progress of His Song: A Lacanian Reading of *The Prelude,*" *Oxford Literary Review* 3 (1979): 78–98.

Index

Library of Congress Cataloging-in-Publication Data

Claridge, Laura P.
    Romantic potentcy : the paradox of desire / Laura Claridge.
      p.   cm.
    Includes bibliographical references and index.
    ISBN 0-8014-2696-0 (cloth : alk. paper). — ISBN 0-8014-8016-7
(pbk : alk. paper)
    1. English poetry—19th century—History and criticism.
    2. Wordsworth, William, 1770–1850—Criticism and interpretation.
    3. Shelley, Percy Bysshe, 1792–1822—Criticism and interpretation.
    4. Byron, George Gordon Byron, Baron, 1788–1824—Criticism and
interpretation.   5. Romanticism—Great Britain.   6. Desire in
literature.   I. Title.
PR590.C54   1992
821'.709145—dc20   91-55556